Good to Great

Good to Great

Coaching Athletes through Sport Psychology

Mark H. Anshel, Ph.D.

 PRESS

Copyright © 2019 by Mark H. Anshel. All rights reserved. No part of this publication may be reprinted, reproduced, transmitted, or utilized in any form or by any electronic, mechanical, or other means, now known or hereafter invented, including photocopying, microfilming, and recording, or in any information retrieval system without the written permission of Cognella, Inc.

First published in the United States of America in 2019 by Cognella, Inc.

Trademark Notice: Product or corporate names may be trademarks or registered trademarks, and are used only for identification and explanation without intent to infringe.

Cover image: Copyright © 2016 iStockphoto LP/triloks.

Printed in the United States of America

ISBN: 978-1-5165-2517-1 (pbk) / 978-1-5165-9254-8 (eb) / 978-1-5165-9255-5 (em)

www.cognella.com   800-200-3908

Contents

ACKNOWLEDGEMENTS   IX

INTRODUCTION   XI

1	MOTIVATION: THE COACH'S ROLE	1
2	COACHING STYLES	39
3	GREAT COACHES ARE GREAT TEACHERS	69
4	THE PSYCHOLOGY OF SUCCESSFUL ATHLETES	117
5	USING MENTAL SKILLS TO REGULATE THOUGHTS AND EMOTIONS	127
6	COACHING FOR THE COMPETITION	167
7	COACHING THE INJURED ATHLETE	185

8	BUILDING TEAM COHESION	207
9	COACH COMMUNICATION BEYOND ATHLETIC PERFORMANCE	233
10	COACHING YOUTH SPORTS	249
11	COACHING WITH DIVERSITY IN MIND	283

EPILOGUE	305
APPENDIX A	321
APPENDIX B	329
APPENDIX C	333
APPENDIX D	335
REFERENCES	339
ABOUT THE AUTHOR	347

This book is dedicated to the memory of my parents, Bernard and Rochelle Anshel, who supported me through the years to make a difference in the lives of others. They provided me with opportunities to learn from my mistakes, to grow and mature as a person and student, and to overcome adversity in my quest to establish a professional career in the expanding field of sport and exercise science. My parents, together with selected teachers, coaches, family members and peers, helped me to establish the proper set of values, and to live my life consistent with those values (e.g., learning, family, health, faith, performance excellence).

Finally, my experiences as a former competitive athlete, combined with the expanding knowledge of sport (coaching) psychology, provided me with the incentive to write this "hands on" book, particularly in reference to developing a more sophisticated approach to effective sport leadership behaviors.
My sincere thanks to all. —MHA

Acknowledgements

Thank you to Alisa Muñoz, Kaela Martin, Casey Hands, Emely Villavicencio, Natalie Piccotti, Tiffany Mok, Dani Skeen, and everyone else at Cognella for their support in the development and publication of this book.

Introduction

The purpose of this book is to provide coaches and anyone else who works closely with athletes and sports teams, insight into an area of research that is relatively unknown and underused as part of the repertoire of skills, techniques, and interventions that may be used to enhance sports performance. The focus of this book is *sport psychology*, and after reading this, you will feel prepared to apply sports psychology principles and practices to enhance the "mental game" of your athletes as part of the sport experience.

What Is Sports Psychology?

The terms, "sport psychology" or "sport psychologist" often conjure the idea of a person who requires clinical treatment. Perhaps you imagine athletes who need counseling because they are experiencing a hardship or a mental disorder that requires professional intervention; or they have a deficiency in some psychological process, such as lacking mental toughness, confidence, or low self-esteem that interferes with their athletic performance. Presumably, the psychologist in this context helps athletes address the thoughts and emotions that are hurting their performance.

While this may be the context some of the time, the reality is that there are many more applications for sport psychology and more than one role the sport psychologist can have.

A common claim by sports participants and commentators is that "success in sport is 90% mental." That's simply untrue; there is no research to support that. Ultimately, nothing replaces the development of sport skills and successful performance outcomes through proper physical training and instruction to help each athlete reach—or attempt to reach—his or her optimal athletic potential.

What is true, however, is this: If two athletes have similar skills in a given sport, one athlete will be more successful than the other in sport competition 90% of the time due to a mental advantage. Successful athletes bring a full set of mental skills that allow them to anticipate success, concentrate on the task at hand, transfer skills and strategies developed in practice settings into competition, and overcome adversity. Sport psychology is about understanding and properly executing the "mental game." Sport psychology is concerned with understanding the factors that help explain how to reach and consistently maintain optimal performance, to strive to achieve one's best.

To help athletes and teams understand the role and value of sport psychology in the context of competitive sport, one must ask this question: "Are you performing at your very best and is there no room for improvement?" Not surprisingly, no one will answer this question affirmatively. The follow-up question then is, "Okay, so you are telling me that there is a gap between your current skill level and the level at which you are capable of performing—what we call your performance capacity. Is that right? You can improve, correct?" They will nod in agreement.

The field of sport psychology is all about playing that mental game and reducing the gap between the athlete's current level of performance and what he or she is capable of doing. Top athletes bring to every competition a full arsenal of mental skills and strategies they know will make a difference between winning and losing, between success and failure, and sometimes those outcomes are a matter of a single incident. It is one situation, the execution of one skill—or sometimes a matter of a few inches—that separates athletes who regularly and consistently reach their capacity and those who don't. Understanding the mental game often helps athletes overcome the widely held myth that sport psychology is for athletes who are mentally weak. Just the opposite is true; sport psychology is for athletes who are secure enough to use every tool within their reach to perform consistently at the highest level.

Sport psychology is multidisciplinary and consists of two fields of study and practice, psychology and sport science. It is derived from, and therefore includes, many of the traditional disciplines of psychology, such as social psychology (the study of group behavior and environmental/situational factors that affect a person's emotions and actions); developmental psychology (changes in cognition and behavior with age); cognitive psychology (the link between thoughts, emotions, and performance); educational psychology (factors that influence learning and remembering sport skills and strategies); clinical psychology (examining personal issues that require professional guidance, sometimes called psychopathology, to overcome barriers to optimal performance); psychology of sport injury (called rehabilitation psychology in general psychology); and others. Among these subdisciplines of psychology, exercise psychology is the only area that is not a traditional subfield in psychology, though it is linked closely to health psychology.

Psychology concepts such as attention, anxiety, motivation, group dynamics, leadership, communication skills, and aggression are just a few examples of areas commonly studied in general psychology that have been studied and applied by sport psychology researchers and practitioners.

The sport science domain may also be referred to as kinesiology, exercise science, human movement, health, or physical education. Similar to psychology, sports science is interested in emotion regulation, effective leadership, motivation, and communication skills. Unique to sport science, however, are sport pedagogy (i.e., teaching sport skills), sports injury rehabilitation, exercise psychology, and psychophysiology (i.e., understanding the physiological processes that explain and predict performance). Using the combined frameworks of psychology and sport science allows researchers, educators, and effective coaches to describe, explain, and predict behavior in the sports context.

What has become increasingly clear to educators, researchers, and sports professionals is that the field of sport psychology is a science based on scientific research published in journals after passing sophisticated reviews (critiques) by scholars. This science has become so respected today that sport psychology specialists are now an integral part of preparing elite athletes. For example, there is a major presence of sports psychologists in training programs for the Olympic Games; sport psychologists often accompany Olympic teams to provide on-site mental preparation and crisis management. The behavior that sports psychology seeks to understand and improve is affected by two primary sources: the athlete and the team leader (i.e., the coach).

This book is about providing state-of-the-art information to sports participants, particularly coaches, about the psychological factors that will move athletes from "good" to "great" in sport competition. Change can be uncomfortable for some, but a great leader welcomes new insights and adapts accordingly. The coach who is neglecting to incorporate the mental game into his or her team preparation, or who is leaning solely on antiquated training methods (e.g., using harsh language or abusive strategies), is employing just a fraction of athletes' performance potential. This book will provide several highly useable topics of an arsenal of mental skills derived from sport psychology that can make a huge difference in how we perceive and experience competitive sport.

For the sake of simplicity, I will be referring to the coach, the athlete, and the team throughout the book. The coach is intended to mean the team leader; however, the concepts and strategies that are discussed can also be adopted by others who work directly with athletes and/or teams such as trainers, managers, physical therapists, sport psychologists, educators, or parents (with younger athletes).

The Athlete

If we define sport psychology as a field of study and practice in which concepts from general psychology and sport science are applied within the context of competitive sport, then sport psychology must begin with the athlete. It is the competitor who most benefits from the proper use of mental skills and serves as the primary focus of research and consultation. When athletes are unable to maintain concentration for the duration of a competition, or cannot control their emotions following a stressful event (e.g., making an error, receiving a penalty), the sport psychologist or the well-informed coach will teach mental skills to the athlete to overcome these obstacles. Sometimes sport psychologists work with athletes (and coaches) in a clinical setting in an attempt to locate and overcome sources of the athlete's thoughts or emotions that are inhibiting favorable performance. Examples include failing to meet performance expectations in pressure conditions (i.e., choking) or treating athletes for depression, anxiety, stress, poor coping skills, or some other mental condition.

The competitive athlete is at the heart of traditional sport psychology. The person who is key in helping athletes achieve and perform at their best is their coach.

The Coach

American author Henry Miller once wrote, "The real leader has no need to lead—he (or she) is content to point the way." And so it is with effective coaches in sport. The coach is the team leader. Given the player's talent and the coach's knowledge of sport skills and strategies, the team leader's primary goal is to develop the physical and mental skills of athletes so that they, individually and as a team, can achieve consistent success. Success may not always be defined as winning; success may also be defined as performance improvement and even participation satisfaction. A coach may be successful (i.e., a good won-loss record), but not effective (i.e., athletes who are not fulfilled or have not enjoyed competing on their team). Sport psychology addresses the ways in which coaches can be effective in terms of successful game outcomes. How coaches define success will largely depend on the level at which they are coaching. For example, while concern about the athletes' enjoyment of the sport experience is irrelevant to coaches of organized, more advanced competition (i.e., high school and beyond), sport enjoyment is particularly important in youth sport. If child athletes do not find the experience of competitive sport pleasant, they are likely to quit. Building the child's intrinsic motivation (discussed later) helps to prevent quitting and promotes sport satisfaction. Sport psychology offers a vast array of strategies that will help ensure that child athletes have enjoyed their experience and have contributed to the team.

The successful management of a team is a complex and sophisticated skill. The ability to make everyone in the group feel that he or she contributes to team success, and promoting desirable behaviors (e.g., developing team cohesion and quality player leadership, showing team loyalty, maintaining motivation and team member satisfaction) while inhibiting inappropriate behaviors, is a challenge for any coach. Sport psychology provides a way to reach these desirable outcomes.

chapter one

Motivation

The Coach's Role

There is a reason that the topic of motivation is the first chapter of this book. Motivation is the foundation of high quality athletic performance and a requirement for purposeful and successful behavior; motivation is required when striving for optimal performance. Without motivation there is no commitment to train and to prepare for competition—and be successful at it. Low motivation often explains upsets in sport; poor motivation is often one reason that an athlete or team failed to beat an opponent who—supposedly—had inferior skills and should have lost. The so-called "inferior" team who outplays their "superior" opponent likely had strong and well-defined motivation that carried them to victory. Unless the athlete is motivated to learn skills and strategies and to perform at a high level on a consistent basis, often under stressful or high-pressure conditions, and to engage in meaningful and intense practice conditions, the coach's ability to expect skilled athletic performance to occur regularly will be restricted.

This chapter will teach you—the coach—about (a) the different types of motivation that have direct implications for competitive sport, (b) common coaching practices that actually impede motivation, and (c) progressive coaching techniques that will help you motivate your athlete or team and everyone involved in their success. First, however, it is important to define and understand motivation.

The concept of motivation should be defined before designing strategies that improve the motivation levels of all sports participants, especially athletes, but other team members as well. Defining the various types of motivation allow coaches and sport psychologists to be "on the same page" in understanding, developing, and carrying out mental and behavioral skills.

Before we define motivation and address ways to effectively motivate athletes, let's briefly examine common *ineffective* ways coaches motivate athletes. The following strategies and examples are often viewed as "traditional"; however, they are anathema to sports psychology research.

Intimidation. During team tryouts, the coach tells the participants, "Most of you aren't good enough to make this team. You're going to have to go out there and show me you deserve to play for me." Or an athlete makes an error and the coach threatens, often in the presence of team members, to dismiss the athlete from the team unless the player can "get it together" and perform at a higher/better level.

Threats. The coach grabs (i.e., forcefully holds) an athlete who has just made an error and, eyeball to eyeball, makes a physical threat if the competitor doesn't "do it right next time."

Criticism. "What a stupid play. That's the worst performance I've ever seen. If you can't do better than that, then you can sit on the bench or leave this team."

Criticism with sarcasm. "Hey, rubber hands, try using a basket to catch the ball," or "My grandmother can pass the ball better than that."

Guilt. "I'm really surprised at you guys. I can't believe what I'm seeing. You should be ashamed of yourselves. You call yourselves athletes?"

Physical abuse. In my discussions with sports coaches in different countries, I learned that physical punishment (e.g., face slapping, punching) is often used to "motivate" athletes to improve performance in selected countries. As one coach from an Asian sports team informed me, "In our country, the coach becomes the athlete's father and may offer physical reprimands *after* performance errors."

Exercise as punishment. The coach requires the athletes to run ten 40-yard sprints in 90-degree heat after the regular practice session. Or, athletes are awakened at 5 a.m. for a 5-mile run as punishment for being late for practice the previous day or losing the previous game. Or, the coach deprives the athletes of water (for whatever reason), which often deteriorates performance at best and at worst is life-threatening.

In these examples, the coach is attempting to induce short-term, even immediate, changes in the athlete's behavior. But at what cost? A verbally or physically abusive coach assumes that the athlete will respond favorably to harsh treatment and/or humiliating comments—and some athletes will perform better initially. However, what novice or unsuccessful coaches do not realize is that desirable changes in behavior that occur in response to harsh negative treatment have only short-term effects, if any. In fact, motivating athletes by aversive means often has long-term negative effects on athletic performance; for example, when exercise is used as punishment, athletes may begin to develop negative attitudes toward physical training in general, which ultimately hinders motivation. This is suggested as a reason why over 70% of college athletes do not exercise regularly and usually lead sedentary lives after they leave sport. In the next section, we define motivation and how to harness an athlete's motivation positively, effectively, and over the long term.

Motivation

The term "motivation" is derived from the Latin word *movere*, meaning "to move." Motivation provides the energy and direction to initiate and maintain the athlete's thoughts, emotions, and behavior. More formally, motivation is the tendency for the direction and selectivity of behavior to be controlled by its consequences, and for behavior to persist until a goal is achieved.

The direction of motivation refers to the purpose and the desired actions of the activity that will lead to the desired outcome. An athlete is energized to engage in a purposeful and meaningful task. When an athlete is motivated, physical training, learning and practicing sport skills, and the overall aim to perform at optimal levels becomes focused; their behavior has a purpose, a defined focus, and a destination.

Deciding which task(s) to perform is selectivity of behavior. No one can—nor should—be motivated by everything all the time. Being in a state of constant motivation can lead to mental and physical fatigue and, eventually, disengagement and burnout. The coach should be able to communicate to their athletes what they expect from them and to prepare them thoroughly so that they may fulfill that expectation in both experience and perception. With the exception of meeting biological needs (e.g., hunger, thirst, sleep), motivation is rarely an "automatic" (i.e., sub-conscious) process. Instead, sport motivation requires conscious thought and planning.

Mentoring Athletes

Athletes often need assistance in areas that will improve the likelihood of success, happiness, higher quality of life, and of course, sport performance. For example, many athletic departments in higher education provide athletes with instruction on time management and study skills, participating in media interviews, and acknowledging the importance of representing the team and the school with integrity, maturity, and making the right choices. Some athletes, similar to students, in general, do not obtain desirable grades because they have not been trained to manage the time constraints placed on them. Relatively few athletes have developed proper study skills (Lanning, 1982). These problems may inhibit concentration, academic standing, and even interfere with the athlete's concentration and sport performance. Coaches should mentor athletes about and provide resources for achieving success in academics, in sport, and maintaining a healthy lifestyle. Coaches should be empathetic about the daily pressures and time constraints with which athletes are confronted, yet at the same time, provide mentoring strategies on how to plan and manage time and establish and meet deadlines. This is especially important given the physical, emotional, mental, and time demands on athletes.

Usually, people in management or administrative positions need to structure the mentoring process. Here is a brief example of how one head coach of a university women's basketball team mentors each athlete:

> The coach evenly divides the team of 12 players into three groups. Then he and two (female) assistant coaches meet privately with each athlete several times before, during, and after the season. They rotate these subgroups on three occasions during the season so that each coach eventually meets with all the players. They discuss performance goals; exchange views about the player's role on the team; offer feedback on athletic performance, academic performance, and potential concerns in these areas; and engage in verbal exchanges on personal and social topics (e.g., relationships, goals, and family matters). The players also have the opportunity to offer their views about the team, relationships with teammates, and coaching behaviors and decisions. All information is respected, open for discussion, and held confidential. The players are convinced that they are respected by the coaching staff and that they are perceived as students and adults in addition to their athletic roles and responsibilities.

Tips for Mentors

Here are some coaching guidelines offered by Chappell (1984), Sullivan (1993), and Yukelson (2010).

1. Make personal contact with every athlete on the team—starters and substitutes. This includes establishing an open-door policy.
2. If the head coach is unwilling or unable to establish rapport with an athlete, make sure that at least one other member of the staff (even the coach's spouse) can. The important thing is that all performers need someone with whom they can speak privately and confidentially.
3. Talk regularly with support staff (e.g., athletic trainers, medical personnel, a sport psychologist or other consultants, academic and mental health counselors, family members) about the needs of each athlete. Their impressions can help to support or dispel the head coach's perceptions, although at the same time, you'll have to respect the athlete's confidential relationship with each support staff member.
4. Be genuine. Even children are aware of insincerity. Be yourself and respond honestly—the athletes will respect this and will give you, their coach, more trust and credibility. Respect the athlete's willingness to seek help from specialists; it's a sign of emotional strength, not weakness.
5. Be supportive and strive at all times to build the players' self-esteem and self-confidence. A positive self-image improves performance and other aspects of the players' lives. Criticisms related to skills and specific performances are necessary but can be done constructively, at the proper time and place.
6. Encourage the athlete's outside interests and a balanced preparation for life beyond the sport experience. Coaches must communicate to the players that sport is only one facet of life, albeit an important one. There are some coaches, for example, who discourage athletes from having reading material (even

studying for school) on away trips, thinking (presumably) that the reading material is a distraction to their game mental preparation. Just the opposite is true. In addition to working toward higher grades, reading reduces thoughts that produce anxiety, self-doubt, and low confidence. Reading is a source of recovery from the pressures of competition and should be encouraged, not discouraged.

7. Do not treat all athletes alike. The psychological needs, past experiences, and personal characteristics of each athlete differ. For instance, not all players respond to the same approach; some need—even expect—a stricter approach than others, while others are more sensitive and require a less intense communication style. Experts in industrial/organizational psychology suggest that managers think about treating others not so much the way they would want to be treated but, rather, the way they feel that their subordinates would want, or need, to be treated. The same principle goes for coaches.

8. When it comes to team rules, however, all athletes should be treated alike. The starter should receive the same reaction for breaking a rule as the substitute. Inconsistency will affect the coach's credibility with other team members.

9. Sometimes the individual's best interests should be put above the team's best interests (though many coaches would find this suggestion controversial). Examples include not playing an injured athlete, allowing an athlete to practice less to study (especially at non-elite levels), or taking the pressure off a key player in the big game because of extraordinarily high stress. This approach may appear to reduce the team's chances of winning the next competition, but it will more likely pay off in the long run. Perhaps a player who stays qualified academically or stays healthy and well adjusted will ultimately be of greater benefit to the team.

10. Be aware of the way in which athletes relate to one another. Discourage cruel, nonsupportive behavior. The coach sets the

example; to allow (or model) such behavior is to condone it, and team member satisfaction will suffer.
11. Try to meet each athlete's parents or other family members. They can serve as excellent sources of support in the attempt to enhance the player's attitude and performance if they are convinced that the coach's priority is their athlete/child's well-being.
12. Finally, remember your responsibility as the team adult leader and supervisor. Sometimes this means setting rules and limits on player behavior. It also means that you do not need to justify every policy and action. Sometimes coaches need to help athletes overcome peer pressure to do the "wrong thing." Group (team) members feel more secure when they know their leader (coach) is in control. Coaches should demonstrate their knowledge, concern, and leadership by doing what they think is in the athletes' best interests, without abusing the athlete's integrity and self-esteem.

Personal vs. Situational Motivation

Where exactly does motivation come from? What factors contribute to a person's motivation? Why do some athletes have the drive to study the playbook and receive feedback constructively from their coach, while others ignore their coach's instruction and feedback, maybe even becoming defensive and blocking out or ignoring their coach's criticism? What gives some athletes the motivation to prepare many hours for competition, while others devote minimal time for game preparation?

Sport psychologists have concluded that sport motivation is based on the combination of two factors: (a) the athlete's personal characteristics and (b) the conditions, or situations, in which behavior occurs; in other words, the context.

Personal Factors

Our behavior is often guided by a set of characteristics that are stable, permanent, and developed from childhood through adulthood called personality traits. Examples are need achievement, self-esteem, perfectionism, trait anxiety, and coping style. Other characteristics we possess fluctuate from time to time and are less stable and permanent. These are called orientations or states. Examples are goal orientation, confidence, competitiveness, and mental toughness. The combination of an athlete's traits and their orientations play a powerful role in explaining and predicting an athlete's behaviors. These states also describe how athletes will be influenced by different types of situations. What motivates one athlete may not motivate another partly due to their personal characteristics.

This section should be of particular interest to sports coaches because athletes are more likely to become motivated to reach their ideal performance state when they are intrinsically motivated. Most athletes compete in sports for the pleasure and enjoyment they receive. These positive feelings keep athletes interested in improving their performance and enjoying their sport experiences. Thoughts of quitting, giving less effort, or feeling dissatisfied rarely enter the mind of the intrinsically motivated athlete. This section is devoted to reviewing the ways in which sports coaches may increase and maintain the athlete's intrinsic motivation (IM).

Intrinsic and Extrinsic Motivation

Explaining IM begins with a brief overview of cognitive evaluation theory, first developed by Professor Edward Deci (1975). IM is usually defined as "doing an activity for its own sake, for the satisfactions inherent in the activity" (Ryan & Deci, 2007, p. 2). In fact, Ryan and Deci contend that IM has a dual meaning: On one hand, IM concerns a person's innate tendency to act, rather than being externally initiated and directed. On the other hand, IM refers to the fact that the rewards accrued from an activity are inherent in the activity rather than being important to reducing biological drives (e.g., sleeping, eating, drinking). Engaging in an activity, not just the outcomes from that activity, creates its own rewards. For example, an athlete who finds the act of "playing catch" with a baseball without reliance on the outcome from the catching activity (e.g., improving throwing accuracy or speed, building endurance in the throwing arm, focusing one's attention on an enjoyable task rather than doing something less enjoyable) is intrinsically motivated to play catch. Engaging in or persisting in an activity due to some external reason (e.g., money, recognition, and award) in the absence of pleasure and satisfaction reflects extrinsic motivation (EM).

Increased dependence on achieving EM may explain why so many younger athletes drop out of their sports program; they tend to be motivated to play sports by attempting to achieve outcomes, such as a performance statistics or winning. Often, these outcomes either take many weeks to achieve or are rarely experienced because other teams play at a higher level. The experience of sport competition, alone, is rarely pleasurable to the novice athlete because we are a culture that recognizes and celebrates positive outcomes (e.g., winning, high skills) rather than good effort or improvement.

Competence Motivation Theory

Competence motivation theory (CMT) has strong implications in sport. The theory posits that humans have an intrinsic need to deal effectively with their environment. Behavior is selected, directed, and persists based on the person's need for competence starting in childhood. We habitually attempt to master our surroundings, and when we're successful, we feel pleasure. Children, in particular, are motivated by mastery, curiosity, challenge, and play to satisfy their urge toward competence (discussed later). Their rewards for achieving competence are feelings of internal pleasure, based on its fun, enjoyment, and personal satisfaction.

Individuals are motivated by, and attempt to exhibit, mastery of sport skills in achievement situations, such as sport competition or any condition that requires an evaluation of competence. If they are successful, their experiences result in pleasant emotions and heightened self-confidence. In turn, these feelings will lead to continued incentive to engage in competitive sport. Individuals high in perceptions of competence and self-control in the sport environment will exert more effort, persist longer at tasks in achievement situations, and experience more positive feelings than individuals lower in perceived competence and self-control. Competence motivation increases if athletes engage in sport activities that promote feelings of satisfaction, achievement, and enjoyment.

Athletes also need to feel successful (i.e., competent) by their affiliation with meeting individual and team goals. Often, these outcomes are more likely when coaches help athletes overcome barriers and put their problems in the right (accurate) perspective. Failure is inevitable in sport, but handling failure in a constructive way provides athletes with the coach's reassurance that they have the competence to learn from mistakes and keep working toward a more successful future.

Competence motivation can be improved if competitors feel good about the level of success they feel as sports competitors, especially if the game outcome was successful. Effort and improvement should be emphasized rather than—or at least in addition to—winning or losing. In addition, athletes should be taught to formulate accurate perceptions of their ability. Does the athlete possess the necessary fundamental skills to succeed? What must he or she continue to work on to create a more desirable outcome? Parents and coaches should do everything possible to persuade young athletes to think positive thoughts about their future involvement in sport. This is why learning new skills and having an opportunity to perform them are so important in maintaining motivation.

At the same time, always having a (false, or inaccurate) excuse for failing is not productive. If the demands of a sport are too great for the performer, perhaps more time for instruction and practice is needed before the individual is placed in a pressure-filled competitive situation. I have seen many athletes quit their team due to failing to properly and accurately perform fundamental sport skills. This is why instruction during practice sessions is so important to the athlete's motivation and long-term commitment to sport involvement.

Situational Factors

Each of us has a personality that informs or explains our motivations and behaviors. An individual's personality traits are constant; however, certain situations or environmental conditions can facilitate or pronounce certain personality traits while repressing others.

For example, an athlete who is more susceptible to feeling anxious does not necessarily go through their day-to-day life feeling anxious (i.e., nervous, worried, threatened). However, their tendency toward anxiety may very well affect them negatively in high-pressure sport situations, such as coming to bat with the bases loaded, or running the football on "fourth and one." This would be in opposition to an athlete who does not tend to feel anxious; these athletes will generally perform well in high-pressure roles or situations, such as baseball relief pitchers, quarterbacks, and tennis players.

Increasing an athlete's internal (intrinsic) motivation to participate in sport is far more valuable over the long term, as opposed to relying on short-term incentives that are based on external sources. Viewing motivation through a situational lens suggests that athletes will be more likely to thrive within a supportive environment. They will be motivated to perform a certain skill or to meet a particular goal if the circumstances improve their confidence, attentional focus, and other desirable psychological states. You begin to see very quickly that these two sources of motivation—personal and situational—are closely linked and work together to promote long-term desirable outcomes.

How Personal and Situational Motivation Interact

As indicated earlier, there are primarily two sources of motivation: personal and situational. Personal motivation and situational motivation are mutually exclusive processes, but they interact with each other. Personal sources, consisting of personality traits (e.g., self-esteem, confidence, competitive, anxiety) and behavioral tendencies (e.g., developing routines, setting goals, engaging in vigorous training, using cognitive strategies), combine with situational factors (e.g., athlete thrives on a competitive environment, proper use of coping strategies, performs successfully under high-pressure situations) to produce optimal motivation. For example, some athletes can feel highly motivated to prepare properly for the competitive event even when they know they are not starting and may not even be called on to participate. The combination of high competitiveness, a personal source of motivation, and a competitive environment, a situational source of motivation, interact to produce a high motivational state. The same process can work in reverse, however. Athletes may also feel unmotivated to prepare to compete because they do not anticipate entering the competition. This is especially the case with younger, less-skilled athletes, but can also occur with older athletes whose role on the team has not been well defined or is viewed as unimportant toward team success.

To build IM, the first question parents should ask their child athlete after they've competed in a sports competition is not "Who won?" but rather, "Did you have a good time?" If the response is "no," parents should try to find out the reasons and help their child resolve the issue by encouraging him or her to reappraise the experience in a more favorable light; a parent might say, for instance, "Winning is more fun than losing, but if you gave it your best, I'm still proud of you," or "Even if you lost, did you learn something from the game?" Creating the right motivational climate includes communicating to athletes that one criterion of success is improvement, even in the practice setting, as opposed to relying on performance outcome as the only means to improve IM.

Information Function

Researchers call it "perceived ability," and it is a very powerful factor in IM theory. It has been well known for many years that having positive feelings about our sport skills, or at least about our ability to learn and improve skills over time for better performance—competence—is a basic human need. Hence, it is not surprising that almost central to IM is the perception of high ability. Most of us, especially athletes who usually have high confidence about their skill level, will rarely continue to engage in a task that they are not performing well, at least based on their own perception. For example, one goal of every coach, parent, and teammate should be to offer encouraging remarks to the athlete regardless of the actual outcome. Positive feedback should and can reflect performance effort and improvement, as well as reflecting actual performance outcomes, if warranted. Feedback can increase IM if it serves to reinforce the performer's feelings of competence, that is, to provide athletes with useful information. If the coach compliments the athlete about performing a skill or strategy, or exhibits some other form of desirable behavior (e.g., providing verbal support from the bench or helping a teammate warm up before the competition), the athlete's feelings of competence will likely rise. A similar increase in IM can also follow negative feedback if it is accompanied by a positive message (e.g., "You still have to improve the speed of your throw, Carla, but I see nice improvement"). Repeated negative feedback, however, can reduce IM if the message reflects the athlete's reduced perceived competence. In addition, the amount of pleasure received from the activity is markedly reduced, perhaps even leading to dropping out from further participation under extreme conditions.

Another form of feedback, described earlier, is receiving an award (e.g., a trophy, certificate, or any other form of tangible reward) for participating. Awards can either reduce or increase IM depending on how athletes perceive the message. Awards are intrinsic motivators if athletes perceive them as representing their success (e.g., improved performance, contributions to the team, winning). The award, then, has positive information value, which reflects high perceived competence and achievement. However, if athletes engage in sport primarily to receive an award, rather than for the fun, pleasure, and perceived competence sport brings, and if they expect and even depend on receiving the award as one reason for engaging in sport, then the award is an extrinsic, not an intrinsic, motivator.

The best suggestion for using the information function to increase IM is to keep the message positive. This means either (a) give token rewards, such as certificates or a small trophy to everyone on the team (for different reasons, such as "best fielder," "best hustler," "best supportive team member," and so on), or (b) offer verbal recognition to all players for their effort but give special rewards to no single individual. The objective here is to avoid making rewards the reason to participate, and instead to make rewards a reflection of success. As Duda (1993) concluded, "[I]ndividuals are less likely to perform up to their potential and maintain their involvement in achievement activities when they do not feel competent" (p. 426). Therefore, it is very important that coaches and parents do everything they can to help athletes avoid feelings of low ability and to search for and recognize any form of desirable behavior exhibited by the participant.

Need for Achievement Motivation

Personality studies (which we'll discuss later) have revealed that a primary characteristic of successful athletes is their high need to achieve. This need is commonly referred to as the need for achievement motivation (N-ach). Success is based on the athlete's perception that optimal effort will lead to achieving a desirable outcome and meet the athlete's goals. Athletes with a high need to achieve tend to strongly believe that success is possible, even likely. This is one reason high-need achievers prefer challenging rather than easy activities in which to participate. Athletes will feel great satisfaction when they conclude that their high effort resulted in overcoming difficult challenges and experiencing success. This is why coaches should provide positive verbal feedback to athletes after they experience success and should associate successful performance with putting in the time and effort needed to be consistently successful.

How two athletes define success may differ though; what is success for one person may be failure for another person, especially if so-called "performance failure" occurred in crucial situations that altered the competition's outcome. The context or situational factors can alter the definition of success. For example, some athletes may not try very hard during a competition if they entered it believing that their opponent is superior and their chance at winning was slim. According to achievement motivation theory, these athletes, who are likely low-need achievers, will not necessarily interpret losing as failure because they didn't even try. Blame for losing is usually attributed to low effort, not due to the athlete's poor ability or lack of skills. On the other hand, high-need achievers give extra effort in these conditions because for them it is this optimal level of effort that contributes to their definition of success, not only performance outcome.

Goal Orientation: A Part of Achievement Motivation

Goal orientation refers to the extent to which an athlete is motivated by setting and then meeting goals and the *types* of goals they prefer to set. Goal orientation in a sport context reflects two thought processes of athletes: achievement goals (e.g., "What do I need to do to feel I have accomplished something meaningful and challenging?") and their perceived ability ("Do I have the skills needed to meet this goal?"). The answer to these two questions will affect self-evaluations of demonstrated ability.

Therefore, an athlete with high goal orientation will (a) set a challenging, yet realistic and achievable goal (e.g., "I will make 75% of my free throws"); (b) feel a moderate to high degree of certainty about meeting this goal based on his or her high perceived ability (e.g., "I have the confidence to make most of the free throw shots"); and (c) will select and persist at a task with optimal effort until this goal is achieved (e.g., "I will practice an extra hour each day on free throw shots"). Because goal orientation (GO) is a disposition (i.e., situation), not a personality trait (i.e., permanent and across situations), GO can be more apparent in some situations than in others; it can be learned, and it is affected by previous experiences that result in perceived success or failure. This means that GO can become stronger or weaker for a given time period, for a specific task or goal, or within a given context (e.g., sport, academic, work, or social settings).

How NOT to Motivate Athletes

Sometimes a coach will contend that sending athletes with negative, even threatening, messages has high motivational value. Can athletes benefit—feel more motivated—if threatened with expulsion from the starting line-up or being dismissed from the team? Certainly athletes will tend to increase their effort if the coach threatens expulsion from the team or some other unpleasant consequence, such as performing highly intense exercise. Negative reinforcement (e.g., short-term threats and punishments such as withholding positive messages or experiences) does have motivational effects. It is also true that sometimes this type of treatment from an authority figure is desired, even needed, to increase the athlete's incentive to change his or her behavior or attitude.

However, reliance on negative motivational techniques has two shortcomings. First, usually it has only short-term, not long-term, effects because the athlete's behavior changes only until the source of threat is removed (e.g., not being allowed to participate with the team until the athlete completes a predetermined exercise regimen). After the threat is removed (performing the exercises), the incentive to persist in this activity (either when the coach is not monitoring the exercise session, during the off-season to stay in shape, or after one's sport career has concluded) is minimal.

The second shortcoming is that threating another person affects situational (extrinsic), not personal (intrinsic), motivation as an incentive to improve motivation and to change behavior. That is, the reason for the activity is based on achieving some external reward (e.g., recognition, participating on the team, not being punished). Intrinsic rewards related to pleasure and satisfaction derived from performing the activity are rare. Only if the athlete views exercise and keeping in top physical condition as beneficial to his or her athletic performance, or an extrinsic motivator, such as studying the playbook, learning to use new mental skills, or extensive practice time and effort results in successful performance outcomes, will some intrinsic value be derived. Thus, many of these so-called "motivational techniques" generate only short-term incentives for athletes. In the long run, however, the influence of these techniques may actually wane or have the opposite (undesirable) effect.

Ultimately, motivation in sport is dependent on the balance between athletes' personal feelings and attitudes associated with their sports performance (personal sources of motivation) and the external factors that affect athletes (situational sources of motivation), with coaches' leadership and the goals they set forth being key influencers. Coaches' comments to players that are abusive, disrespectful, and humiliating have very short-term "value" in changing player behavior.

Here is a list of myths that do *not* improve player motivation or have a short-term effect. It is important to keep in mind that some of these "false motivators" may be more effective with certain athletes—older and more skilled versus younger and less skilled, for instance—than others. In general, however, coaches should rethink using the following:

Exercise for punishment. "Okay, Jones, that will cost you four laps for being late to practice." "If you guys had won on Saturday, practice would have been over. But you didn't, so we're running an extra 10 laps." Many athletes (and physical education students) are very familiar with perhaps the most common form of punishment used by coaches and physical education teachers—physical exercise. Whether it's push-ups, sprinting, pull-ups, or jogging, exercise has been used by coaches and physical education teachers for years as a tool to punish and control the behavior of students and athletes. Here are three reasons why this approach should be avoided:

First, exercise for punishment will likely contribute toward the athlete's life-long sedentary lifestyle. When athletes' sports career has ended, they are not likely to want to remain physically active, in part due to overtraining and negative attitudes toward exercise. Exercise becomes associated with unpleasant feelings and experiences.

Second, the student or athlete may be suffering from a physical injury, disease, or other condition that would be made worse from vigorous physical activity.

Finally, according to a position statement by the National Association for Sport and Physical Education (NASPE, 2010), "Administering or withholding physical activity as a form of punishment and/or behavior management is an inappropriate practice" and "coaches should never use physical activity or peer pressure as a means of disciplining athlete behavior" (p. 17). Exercise, when used for disciplinary purposes, they claim, is a form of corporal punishment and is illegal in 29 states.

The pregame talk. Age, skill level, the type of sport, the competition's environment (e.g., high vs. low pressure, highly competitive vs. recreational, level of game importance), are factors that influence the content and emotional intensity of the pre-game talk.

The purpose and content of the pregame talk, however, is of less importance than most leaders think, especially at the professional level. Of more importance to the athlete's motivation and emotional status is the level of mental readiness and arousal elicited by the message. For the most part, game preparation, including the "mental game," occurs at practice. The pregame talk should be simple, brief, and make a point. Long lectures or messages that are riddled with guilt (e.g., "If we don't beat our opponents we should be ashamed"), threat (e.g., "Beat these guys or we practice tomorrow at 6 a.m."), or condescension (e.g., "If you can't beat our opponents you have no business being on this team") should be avoided.

Being critical of opponents. Occasionally, coaches will try to motivate the team by criticizing their opponents (e.g., "They are not a very good team") or discounting the opponent's skills ("They can't hit breaking balls"; "They can't match our pitching"). For several reasons, most players are uncomfortable hearing the coach's derogatory remarks about opponents unless they have a specific weakness that can be detected and countered.

1. The remark might not hold true in the approaching event since the opponent may prove far better than the coach has indicated.
2. If the opponent is poorly skilled and the coach's team still loses, the athletes will feel more humiliated than if they lost to a more skilled opponent. If the coach's team wins, the players may attribute the victory to an easy task or unskilled opponent rather than to their own high ability or high effort, which is not very reinforcing. Athletes may want to think that their success was due to their own skilled performance, their high degree of preparation and training, and effort, not because the opponent was weak. Past performance might not be a good predictor of future outcomes for this opponent.
3. It's unrealistic to think that an opponent has "weaknesses" but no strengths. Every competitor is capable of winning, and every athlete wants to know the strength of that capability.
4. Finally, athletes typically have a great deal of empathy and mutual respect toward one another, even toward opponents. Some athletes believe that criticizing another sports

competitor is unethical and disrespectful toward the spirit of sport competition.

Treating team players differently. Athletes become incensed when the coach is not consistent in his or her interactions with all team members. Over my career, I interviewed a few former (retired) highly successful professional athletes and addressed what single trait stands out in their minds about the best coaching they've experienced. They all agreed that the ability to treat everyone with the same respect and maturity was among the most important qualities in a good coach. They said that showing favoritism and inconsistency among team players did more to demotivate and upset players than anything else. These findings lend insights into the thoughts and experiences of very successful competitors on the issue of treatment toward team members.

"If they don't complain, they're happy." Coaches often assume that a "quiet" (non-complaining) player is a contented player. Not necessarily! Unhappy athletes may be consumed by their own unpleasant thoughts. Instead of focusing on the actions and tendencies of opponents, while remembering their own skills and strategies, dissatisfied players are thinking about issues that interfere with preparing for and participating in the competition. Negative attitudes also poison the team's climate and, consequently, could reduce team cohesion.

"What do athletes know, anyway?" No one can argue with the claim that most coaches have a sound knowledge base about the technical aspects of their sport. By the time individuals become the head coach of a team, they tend to feel "in control." Great coaches monitor and communicate constructively with their athletes during practices and games. Is there a reason why a certain play didn't work? Does the other team have a certain weakness or tendency that we can use to our advantage? Do we have certain weaknesses that we need to work on immediately? Was the official correct in calling that penalty? Why not ask the players for at least some of the answers? A combination of player input and coach receptivity to their messages will promote team cohesion and coach-player relationships.

Finally, do not punish athletes for winning because they did not perform perfectly. For example, I observed a high school baseball team running laps in the outfield after their team *won* the game. I asked one player later why they ran after the game and he told me, "The coach said we should have played better." And we wonder why so many athletes despise physical activity when their playing days are over.

Demonstrate power selectively. Coaches who motivate athletes successfully are usually perceived as secure, knowledgeable, intelligent, intuitive, and sensitive. They excel in a disposition called self-awareness. They know how to share their power so that all members of the team (including players and assistants) have a sense of ownership and responsibility for team activities and outcomes. Coaches, indeed, all individuals in the position of power, have to be careful not to abuse that power. It should be used selectively and consistently, not constantly.

For example, the assistant coach of a university baseball team was well liked by the players. Soon after being promoted to head coach on the same team, however, he became uncharacteristically aggressive, demanding, and hostile toward the players. He threatened to dismiss any player who committed even the slightest infraction. Conditioning exercises were grueling. In fact, he told the team of his intention to "weed out the weak links" on the team. This coach greatly disappointed his players soon after his promotion. They became increasingly depressed, unmotivated, and began to lose interest in the team's performance. His player loyalty shrunk to near zero. The team's low morale was accompanied by a poor win-loss record. Sadly, this individual resigned after only one season under pressure.

Should athletes fear their coach? While all coaches want to be respected by their athletes, some coaches—depending on the sport and the athlete's skill level and age—also want their athletes to fear them. These coaches want to gain their athletes' attention to important information and to heighten the athlete's level of physical and mental arousal. Often, fearing a coach is in response to the coach's fiery speeches, threats, harsh criticism, and insults. But is this outcome always desirable? Is it in the coaches'—and athletes'—best interest to be feared?

Anxiety, which increases if athletes fear their coach, will diminish attentional focusing and the speed and accuracy of processing information and will compromise optimal effort. They will become preoccupied with pleasing the coach rather than enhancing team communication and encouraging a relaxed team climate.

Improving Personal Motivation

How can the coach build IM? In two ways: increasing the athlete's feeling of personal control and building the athlete's perceived competence (i.e., maintaining a flow of positive information). IM increases when athletes feel in control—*controllability*—of their sport-related decisions (e.g., the coach allows the quarterback to call one or more plays; a baseball pitcher convinces the manager that he or she remains capable of staying in the game and achieving a successful outcome). Another component of IM is called the *informational aspect*—positive (i.e., praise/compliments) or negative. (i.e., criticisms/negative information feedback). Positive (not negative) feedback about the quality of the athlete's performance results in higher IM. As we will review in the communication chapter, even negative (constructive) information feedback can be given with compassion and support. Building on either of these two dimensions—the controlling aspect and the informational aspect—improve IM.

Thus, the cognitive/mental approach to motivation involves making choices about goal-directed behaviors aimed at successful outcomes. These choices increase pleasure and enjoyment and form the main reasons individuals decide to engage in competitive sport. IM is central to promoting sport participation and forms the foundation of maintaining involvement—preventing athletes from dropping out either mentally (i.e., giving low effort) or physically (i.e., quitting the team).

Motivating the Athlete

An indicated earlier, an individual who participates in an activity for its enjoyment and without an external reward is said to be intrinsically motivated (IM). Extrinsic motivation (EM), on the other hand, is the desire to perform an activity due to the anticipation of some external reward, such as money, recognition, meeting a challenging goal, or winning a trophy. IM is highly desirable in sport because it forms the individual's motives for participating in sport over the long term. An excellent example of an intrinsically motivated person was the renowned scientist Albert Einstein, who said, "I am happy because I want nothing from anyone. I do not care for money. Decorations, titles, or distinctions mean nothing to me. I do not crave praise. The only thing that gives me pleasure, apart from my work, my violin, and my sailboat, is the appreciation of my fellow workers."

Shifting from EM to IM. What happens to the athlete's IM when he or she is offered extrinsic rewards? Why, for instance, do children participate in playground games for fun and then, when placed in a competitive sport situation, monitor the score and consider winning and losing important? Why do kids play sports "to have fun," yet drop out of competitive sport at alarming rates—over 70% by some published accounts? And why is receiving a trophy so important if having fun is the main reason most children engage in sport competition in the first place?

EM may override IM when the source of control is no longer within the person, that is, the performer engages in an activity for some external purpose (e.g., approval of "significant" others, recognition, financial gain) rather than for the activity's inherent enjoyment. This occurs quite frequently in professional sports, at least in the United States, when athletes perform at a very high level over a season and indicate to management that they deserve a higher salary. While athletes' original motive to compete in sports was likely intrinsic, no doubt a combination of factors, such as high performance quality and comparing their current salary with the salary of other athletes of similar status and skill, it may result in replacing intrinsic with extrinsic sources of motivation. Other common forms of EM include awards (e.g., trophies, ribbons, prizes), parental or peer pressure, recognition in the media, approval, and other forms of information that recognize success.

The effects of a sports program that relies on a selective reward system, whereby some athletes receive tangible rewards (e.g., trophies, tickets to events) and others do not are even more potentially damaging to IM. Does this mean that trophies should never be used? Not at all. Rewards may be used in a positive and supportive way to convey information to athletes about their competence. For example, athletes can receive an award for their effort (e.g., "Most Motivated" or "Best Effort"), improvement (e.g., "Most Improved"), support of other teammates (e.g., "Best Team Player"), leadership (e.g., "Mr. [Ms.] Leadership"), skill ("Strongest Arm"), and so on. In each of these examples, the recipient should feel rewarded for accomplishing a task, meeting a goal, or demonstrating competence. The trophy serves to reinforce this recognition. Or, all team members can receive the same award, such as a "Good Job Award" or "Achievement Award."

The overjustification hypothesis. Coaches and parents have the (bad) habit of assuming that athletes, especially youth sports participants, possess a high need for trophies and other external awards to derive satisfaction from sport. In fact, adults may do more harm than good in the area of offering rewards to athletes when none are needed.

In a benchmark study on this topic, psychologists Lepper, Green, and Nesbitt (1973) examined the effects of rewards on children's IM. Specifically, they wanted to determine the effect of giving children a reward when they performed an activity they already enjoyed on changes in their IM. Their research question was whether the introduction of external rewards, such as trophies, can significantly reduce IM or increase EM. Will removing the fun component in competitive sport reduce IM and increase EM among children? Yes, it can! They found that adding external rewards as an incentive to engage in an activity the children were already enjoying without the reward actually reduced their IM about the enjoyable activity.

Children often play sport because it's fun. When an external reward (e.g., a trophy, financial compensation, other awards or prizes) is introduced into the situation, however, the athlete's incentive to play shifts from fun to obtaining a trophy or winning the championship; the trophy represents an "overjustification" for playing sport. Fun was the primary justification to play; now comes the strong influence of a trophy, which now becomes the new source of motivation to compete. The result is a reduction in fun—and IM. This is why external rewards can do more harm than good when it comes to building IM. Recognition and approval can successfully replace rewards if used often and consistently over time, as indicated by the information function of this theory. If external rewards are inherent in a sports organization, coaches and parents need to be sure that the sport experience was also enjoyable and that skilled performance was improved during the season.

Trophies can improve IM and not "overjustify" sports participation if the purpose of these rewards is to provide information about the player's (improved) competence. An example would be to receive an award for performing at an extraordinary level. Thus, rewards can serve the valuable role of building the competitor's perceived competence—serving an information function.

Positive Information Improves IM

Feelings of competence and self-determination are other factors in the extent to which extrinsic rewards can affect IM. Deci (1975), in support of White's (1959) competence motivation theory, contends that people are attracted to activities in which they feel successful (i.e., in which they experience perceived competence). Performers who have high perceived ability will likely be intrinsically motivated. Rewards can have the same favorable effect on IM if they increase the athlete's feelings of competence and self-worth. In this way, rewards can foster IM if they provide all participants with some recognition for demonstrating success, be it improvement in performance, high effort, or showing competent skill execution.

Perceived control/self-determination (SD) improves IM. Self-determination reflects an athlete's degree of perceived control in his or her actions and decisions. Sample issues of SD include "Am I playing the position that I selected to play?" "Is the coach allowing me to call the shots during the game?" (in most team sports), and "Will the coach keep me in the game to finish the inning?" (in baseball).

High SD enhances IM. For instance, a team member who does not feel that he or she contributes to the team's success will feel less SD and, therefore, will be less intrinsically motivated in contrast to feelings of high contribution. Coaches can foster players' feelings of SD and personal responsibility for outcomes by consulting players for suggestions about selected team policies, codes of player behavior, and game strategies and plans. Examples include asking team members to take turns leading warm-up exercises or voting for team captain(s). Central to promoting self-determination (SD) and IM is encouraging "full engagement" by athletes and preventing feelings of alienation. The athlete's perceptions of excessive externally based control and feelings of helplessness foster alienation and markedly reduce or extinguish IM.

Motivating the Team

Most sports consist of teams; teams are groups that require different strategies to enhance motivation, as opposed to individual athletes and various sport types. Former Oakland Raiders (U.S.) football coach John Madden said in an interview, "I only had three rules for my players: Be on time, pay attention, and play like heck when I tell you to." Madden had a profound influence on his teams because his demands were realistic, focused on game-related tasks, and sincere. He had tremendous player loyalty and credibility. Thus, the challenge for any coach is to determine each athlete's goals—what he or she realistically wants from competing—and to convince the athlete of what he or she must do to reach them.

The ability of a coach to affect the behaviors, feelings, and attitudes of their team members begins with the coach–athlete relationship. Some of the most important ingredients of this relationship include the following:

- Communicating openly and honestly
- Teaching skills and strategies
- Rewarding players with praise, recognition, and encouragement
- Dwelling on strengths, while recognizing areas for further improvement
- Appearing organized and in control
- Inserting occasional times for fun, humor, and relaxation
- Developing mutual respect between coach and athlete
- Knowing when to take a break and when to give the athletes a day off, a concept called *active recovery*
- Developing leadership skills among players
- Making sure that all athletes are experiencing high team satisfaction and that there are no isolates or anyone being harassed by other team members, such as assistant coaches, athletic trainers, and spectators.
- Supporting the athletes after errors and losses as well as on making good plays and winning
- Setting limits (restrictions and appropriate punishments) on inappropriate player behavior fairly and consistently for all team members

- Not embarrassing, intimidating, or criticizing the character of an athlete

Some effective techniques for motivating athletes to reach their potential, that is, the "do's" of coaching success, include the following:

Get to know each athlete; build a relationship. Knowing each team member starts with learning and using each athlete's first name. This promotes trust, importance, and respect between coach and athlete. Players become less intimidated by the authority figure. The nonverbal message is "the coach knows, recognizes, and respects me."

The next step is developing a relationship with the athlete that goes beyond the sport venue. This does not include socializing with the players—players are typically uncomfortable spending "free time" with their coach—but rather, attempt to listen to the players' feelings on team-related issues, while being open to discussing topics unrelated to the team (e.g., academic experiences, movies, current events), and showing a genuine concern for the athlete as a person, not only as a sports participant.

Plan it out. Influencing the thoughts and actions of others doesn't usually happen by itself. Effective coaches anticipate the future needs of team members and then develop routines that are intended to enhance player motivation. Examples include structuring a practice session to improve team morale, using a particular strategy during the competition based on player recommendations, using confidence-building statements, inviting guest speakers to address the team on a relevant topic, particularly if the visitor is well known in that sport, taking a break from the daily grind of practice, changing the content of practice sessions, giving players the opportunity to receive recognition by fans or the media, attending off-campus events that promote the team or the school (e.g., a children's hospital), and attending to injured athletes to let all team members know that no one is forgotten and that everyone is appreciated for his or her contribution.

Agree on future goals and actions. American philosopher Eric Hoffer said, "The only way to predict the future is to have power to shape the future." The coach's ability to create and plan for athletes' future aspirations is dictated by his or her ability to convince players of two things: (a) the worthiness of these aspirations, and (b) the athletes' ability to act on and to achieve them. To move in the same direction, coaches and players must share—and communicate—the same vision.

Develop skills. There is no greater motivator in sport than success. But success does not happen accidentally. It requires constant effort and determination. If coaches expect athletes to learn skills, improve their performance, maintain motivation, engage in proper physical training, and eventually succeed, they must teach skills and strategies as a central component of their job.

Everybody needs recognition. The need for prestige, status, dominance, attention, importance, appreciation, and recognition are firmly based in human nature; they form the foundation of motivation. These needs may even be greater in higher skilled athletes than in nonathletes. An occasional pat on the back, literally and figuratively, gives the athletes deserved recognition and a reason for continuing their efforts.

Discipline is not a four-letter word. Some athletes test the coach's ability and willingness to carry out team policies and disciplinary measures. Testing is the individual's way of making sure that the adult guardian (e.g., the parent, coach, or teacher), cares about him or her. To paraphrase psychiatrist, Haim Ginott (1965), athletes often feel more secure when they know the borders of permissible action. In fact, athletes suffer from increased anxiety when the coach allows behavior that the athlete knows should not be tolerated. These words reflect the fundamentals of human behavior. The coach who sets limits and responds quickly and appropriately when "tested" communicates sincerity, consistency, and credibility.

Perceptions are reality. As an old adage says, "An ounce of image is worth a pound of performance." Athletes' perception of their role on the team, the interpretation of a coach's actions and statements, and other personally held views are reflections of their version of "the truth" through their eyes. For example, an athlete may attribute a lack of playing time to a poor relationship with the coach. "The coach just doesn't like me," he or she might complain. If an athlete feels that the coach "does not like me," it's this perception that the coach must react to rather than how the coach really feels—which may or may not be accurate. This is especially important if the athlete's perception is wrong. Coaches must deal with reality as their players interpret it.

Consistency and sensitivity are signs of strength. Coaches, male and female, should exhibit similar behaviors and attitudes whether interacting with male or female participants. From shedding tears to disclosing personal feelings, to showing aggression, these should be perceived as normal types of expression for athletes of both genders. Motivation is also an emotion that is virtually blind to gender differences. Female athletes are often as "mentally tough" as their male counterparts. In addition, studies indicate that athletes of both sexes share similar psychological characteristics. Therefore, male and female coaches should treat athletes of both genders in a similar manner, while being sensitive to individual differences irrespective of the athletes' gender.

The Science of Goal Setting

Goal setting serves the primary purposes of improving the athlete's level of motivation, focusing the performer's effort on particular outcomes, and providing a means to monitor progress or success. Not only do most quality competitors tend to set goals, but they also use correct guidelines for doing so. Elite athletes correctly set higher, more challenging, and more realistic goals than their less skilled counterparts. Elite competitors do not tend to sell themselves short; they "dream big." Coaches need to assist their athletes to set proper goals. Here are some guidelines for coaches to perform this important task:

1. Schedule a goal-setting meeting with each individual athlete. Make it a team function so that individuals do not feel self-conscious that the coach singles them out as "needing" a goal-setting meeting.
2. Conduct your session in an area that is private, free of noise, and cannot be observed or be heard by others. This is a very personal process.
3. Write down the goals that coach and athlete have decided to generate and monitor.
4. Set goals in absolute (observable) terms.
5. Goals should be short term (e.g., each day, week, or month) and long term (e.g., typically a full season).
6. Set goals jointly, with coaches and athletes agreeing on the final set of goals, which form expectations for future performance.
7. Every goal should include two basic components: *direction* and *amount* (quantitative). Direction means focusing one's behavior. Amount or quantitative indicates a minimal standard of performance that is anticipated and desired. Thus, goals should primarily to motivate the athlete to take direct action, focus their attention, increase effort and intensity, and encourage new strategies to solve problems and foster persistence, especially after experiencing failure.
8. Check in with each athlete, let's say by mid-season, to determine if the athletes are making progress toward meeting each goal. It is also wise to find out if the goal—set pre-season—is creating more trouble than it's worth. In other words, coaches need to monitor the athlete's progress toward meeting each goal and, perhaps, concluding that the goal is creating anxiety and stress. Some athletes do not find goal setting very motivating. Instead, goals can create pressure, distract the athlete, and impede performance. Goal setting may not be valuable for some athletes, and coaches should give players a chance to opt out of the goal-setting program (without rancor or negative feelings).
9. Goals may be applied both in practice and during competition for improving self-confidence.

10. Goals should reflect performance (e.g., making 75% of my free throws) rather than (or in addition to) outcome (e.g., winning the championship). Performance goals represent better control of the effort needed to meet the goal. And performance goals are measurable. Outcome goals are more focused on "yes-no" outcomes. Examples of *good* performance goals are as follows: (a) "I will relax and feel confident before the swim meet"; (b) "I will make contact with over 50% of the pitches thrown." Examples of *poor* performance goals are as follows: (a) "We will win the game"; (b) "I will be a starter on the team." Neither of these poor goals is under the player's control and, therefore, will more likely undermine motivation and focused effort.
11. An advantage of performance-based goals is that they are observable and measurable. How would a competitor know if a goal was attained, that is, if performance was successful, unless the executed movements could be seen or measured? In this way, meeting goals becomes motivating to the performer and forms the basis to define future goals.
12. Be realistic. If one purpose of a goal is to provide incentive, then it has to be within the athlete's perceived reach. Otherwise the performer will tend to view the goal as not meaningful. The result may lead to reduced effort, feelings of helplessness, and the need to discard the goal altogether. One way to be sure a goal is realistic is to base it on past experience. The athlete's recent history of performance should indicate what he or she will be able to do in the near future.
13. Negotiate. One of my former students was a collegiate swimmer who became despondent after her coach told her to swim at a speed that, in the swimmer's view, was totally unrealistic. She became so depressed and upset about this unattainable goal that she could not continue to give a 100% effort during practice. If her coach would have negotiated the goal based on past performance with input from the performer, the goal-setting strategy would have had its intended benefits. Within a year this swimmer quit further competition.

14. Athletes should be involved in the setting of future performance goals and expectations. This is called joint goal setting. Players must be able to identify with each goal and feel committed to attaining it.
15. Make goals challenging. Top athletes enjoy—even need—a challenge to reach their potential. The suggestion that goals should be realistic and negotiated between player and coach does not mean that they should be easy to attain. On the contrary, goals that are viewed by the performer as too easy do not increase motivation.
16. Make goals specific to the type and demands of the task. Challenging goals are even more effective when they are specific. Asking athletes to improve their performance speed by 5 seconds, a particularly difficult goal in all-out tasks such as swimming or track and field, is more effective than "do your best" or "try to improve" types of goals.
17. Ensure goal "ownership." The concept of setting goals based on previous performance appears to form a rational basis for determining reasonable, yet challenging expectations about future performance. There is a note of caution about focusing on the exclusive use of performance outcome to determine success or failure. As noted earlier, effort and improvement are other determinants of success, in addition to the end result. Goals also have value when they reflect performance in practice settings or mastery of subskills and learning, rather than exclusively on competition outcomes. Goals are motivating when athletes have input into their development. The athlete will then feel accountable for meeting the goal. Goals that are set by outside sources, such as coaches and parents, may not have the same incentive value because the competitor may not endorse, or "own," the goal.
18. Make goals short term and long term. Elite athletes know at what level they want their performance to be on both a long-term (several weeks or months away) and short-term (today, tomorrow, or next week's performance) basis. The short-term

goal serves the purposes of providing immediate incentive to perform at optimal levels and, predictably, to experience early success. It is important for athletes to feel that their efforts will soon lead to the achievement of some desirable outcome or that success was due to such effort. Short-term goals allow us to meet these needs.

Examples of short-term goals used by top competitors include running or swimming at a particular speed, lifting a particular weight in power lifting or weight training, making a given number of tackles, or scoring a predetermined number of points.

Long-term goals allow a competitor to evaluate the quality of his or her performance when compared with (a) goals that were established or outcomes that occurred before the season or last season, and (b) the performance of opponents. Ideally, a series of short-term goals should lead to a realistic, yet challenging long-term performance goal. Here's an example:

Long-term goal: I will bat .300 at the end of this baseball season. Series of short-term goals: (a) I will practice my batting 30 minutes at each practice at least 3 days a week; (b) I will make solid bat contact with at least 50% of the pitched balls.

Team Goals

Many coaches and athletes do not tend to establish team goals that are specific, measurable, and both short and long term. Consequently, often goals do not have their intended favorable result on team performance. Team goal setting can serve to improve performance in targeted indices. For instance, if one goal of a basketball team is to increase field goal shooting percentage, it is likely that the motivation, effort, teammate support, and practice time devoted to this aspect of the game will increase, and that performance in this area will improve. Sometimes pursuing individual goals detracts from team goals.

If, for instance, a player's goal is to maintain a basketball game average of 15 points, the player might be less willing to make the effort to play defense, or more likely to take the shot rather than pass to an "open" teammate. Group goal setting appears to be optimally effective when the tasks are highly interdependent. Sports, such as basketball, field hockey, ice hockey, and soccer are examples. In such cases, group goals are likely to enhance player cooperation and communication as opposed to individual goal setting.

Individual and team goals may be compatible and mutually beneficial. Remaining with the basketball example, individual goals could be set for different team members that improve the chance of meeting the team's goal (e.g., the number of shots taken, number of rebounds, and time of ball possession). Different individual goals might include points scored for the team's best shooter, number of assists for the team's playmaker, number of offensive and defensive rebounds for the team's forwards and center, and so on.

There are some disadvantages to team goal setting. First, some team goals are effective under practice conditions as well as in actual competition. Researchers have found that when there was greater clarity of team goals and when the players believed that the goal could be achieved (i.e., realistic goal setting), it produced higher team member satisfaction (i.e., realistic goal setting). In addition, teams that possessed better task and social cohesion felt greater satisfaction with the team's goals. The players' participation in team goal setting is related to improved task and social team cohesion, that is, a sense of comradery, mutual respect, and fondness among team members. It is important, then, for coaches to allow team members to have a primary role in setting challenging, yet realistic, performance-based goals to obtain the optimal benefits of team goal setting.

In summary, goal setting is generally more effective in producing high-quality performance—for the short term and long term—if the goal-setting strategy follows these guidelines. At the same time, not every athlete wishes to set goals. After all, when you set a goal, even if using the correct techniques, it does create the opportunity for failure (i.e., not achieving the goal). Goals, therefore, do add pressure to the competitive environment. In addition, setting goals can reduce intrinsic motivation in which the athlete is more consumed with meeting the goal than enjoying the sport experience. Finally, a disposition called *goal orientation* indicates individual differences among athletes on the extent to which goals are motivational and challenging. Athletes who score higher on the goal orientation questionnaire are more likely to prefer goals as an incentive to achieve their best.

Motivating the Nonstarter

Making the starters happy and keeping them motivated is easy compared to having the same effect on the nonstarters. The process begins with using proper titles that do not belittle their team role and respect the integrity of each position. "Nonstarter," which is highly accurate and appropriate, is far superior to "benchwarmer," "second string," and "substitute/sub." The psychological challenges that beset the nonstarter include frustration, alienation, futility, and a loss of self-confidence due to their nonparticipation. Ultimately, the coach's primary task is to help every team member feel that he or she is an important and valued team contributor. The extent to which a group of athletes identifies with the team depends on the coach's ability to define and communicate each person's role in the group. Group identity also reflects the athlete's perception of his or her role as an important contributor to team success. Motivation will be a natural outcome of this process.

How can coaches motivate athletes who have limited playing time? This is where coaching really is a science. First (and foremost), as indicated earlier, coaches should avoid labeling anyone a "substitute" or "benchwarmer." These athletes are nonstarters, and they are only one injury away from being a starter. Every athlete should feel that he or she is contributing to the team's welfare. This means that starters should not have more privileges than nonstarters, even though the coach may put more time into preparing the starting team.

A second important suggestion is to provide nonstarters with opportunities to learn and demonstrate skills, particularly under practice conditions that simulate actual competition. Inserting nonstarters into the competition whenever possible will allow them to demonstrate their skills and gain valuable experience under actual competitive conditions. This strategy also allows coaches to provide the nonstarter with instruction and feedback. Finally, as indicated earlier, the nonstarter is only one injury away from entering the competition. No one should feel that he or she is "wasting time" practicing for the competition, a frequent complaint of nonstarters. Such opportunities should include a liberal dose of positive verbal and nonverbal cues that indicate admiration, respect, and trust in the nonstarter's ability.

Finally, it's important to remember that sometimes we perform at our best when it's fun. Undoubtedly, coaches want their team to win, but it's dangerous to produce a team climate that is continuously submerged in a sea of hard work, seriousness, and time-consuming preparation. In human motivation, more is not always better. Having fun and allowing down (personal) time for the players to engage in activities unrelated to the team or the approaching competition is important. I have observed college coaches (wrongly) criticize their athletes when the athletes are "caught" reading class notes and studying for an exam on road trips. Occasional team humor, if at the appropriate time and proper content, can create a pleasant experience, reduce stress and anxiety, and promote IM. Don't forget to keep it fun out there.

chapter two

Coaching Styles

A leader is a person who directs and coordinates activities of an organized group toward meeting and achieving specific goals. Effective sport leadership is of paramount importance in helping athletes achieve excellence in sport. Can high quality coaching skills really make a difference between teams that consistently win versus frequently lose? Absolutely. The content of this chapter will show how using the proper coaching style under the "right" conditions can bring out the athlete's and the team's best performance and result in the athlete's optimal satisfaction.

Sport leadership is both an art and a science. It's an art in reflecting a coach's ability to build solid communication skills with others, to earn the respect of all team members, and to be self-aware about the need to maintain proper ethics, integrity, honesty, and professionalism. Sports coaching is a science as demonstrated by providing athletes with proper instruction for building sport skills, by attending to the athletes' needs for maintaining motivation and optimal effort, incorporating the contributions of all team members, and by staying up to date on the scientific literature in the sport and exercise sciences. What few people realize is that there is a difference between *successful* and *effective* coaching. This chapter will describe and compare four primary styles of sport leadership, the pros and cons of each, and the optimal conditions under which each style should be applied.

Successful Versus Effective Leadership

We rarely distinguish between successful and effective coaching. One leadership style is clearly preferred over the other and, therefore, both are worth exploring. Successful coaching concerns experiencing desirable outcomes (e.g., desirable team performance, coach-generated strategies that lead to performance success) that meet the coach's needs. Effective coaching, on the other hand, not only includes meeting the coach's needs, but also considers the needs of group members—the athletes.

Cribben (1981) distinguishes successful and effective leaders in the corporate sector, a comparison that has direct implications for sports coaches. A *successful* coach is a person whose teams win far more games than they lose; outcome is the essential feature of success. An *effective* coach, on the other hand, not only has a winning record, but in addition to winning, the coach is also concerned with, and achieves, a high level of team member satisfaction.

Leadership may be categorized into three types, each of which have implications for coaching competitive sport. These are attempted leadership, successful leadership, and effective leadership. Attempted leadership is any effort the group leader (coach) makes to influence (others). Using a particular leadership style under the wrong conditions and situations may result in leadership failure: attempted but not successful nor effective.

Successful leadership is the ability to get others to perform as the team leader—the coach—intended. Leadership is successful when the coach's needs are satisfied (e.g., achieving optimal performance; winning); the needs of other team members, however, are ignored.

Effective leadership results in the combination of athletes performing at optimal levels and in accordance with the coach's expectations and they feel that their—the athletes'—needs are satisfied. According to Cribben (1981), "[O]ne can be successful through coercion, dominance, threats, manipulation, fear, trickery, or persuasion. It is equally clear that successful leadership yields only short-term results. Thus, success has to do only with getting the job done, whereas effectiveness adds the concept of satisfaction on the part of those who do the job" (p. 35). Effective leaders must be recognized as having the most influence on the behavior of group (team) members. But a leader who is not capable of altering the behaviors and attitudes of group members, that is, who has no or very little influence, is not effective in the position.

Competitive sport is "results driven," that is, success is defined by the number of wins, or victories, while ignoring, or at least being unconcerned with, athlete satisfaction, from local to international levels. It is not surprising that most coaches, and indeed, sports fans and sport administrators, are also consumed with winning—the desirable end product of sport. Sensitivity to the athletes' needs may not be viewed as an important ingredient of team member satisfaction. Thus, success has to do with getting the job done—winning or performance success—whereas leadership effectiveness adds the component of satisfaction on the part of those who do the job—the athletes. This is a very important distinction.

In the sport leadership literature, successful coaching is about consistently achieving a desirable outcome. Examples include the team winning repeatedly and certain players performing very admirably, playing their position well, scoring many points or goals, playing good defense by inhibiting the opponent's performance, reaching or surpassing predetermined performance goals, and includes the team being ranked high in league standings and exhibiting vast improvement from the year before, as well as the coach or team achieving an award that recognizes the team's performance success.

Successful coaches, although usually open to input from others—assistant coaches, players, medical staff—still consider winning a priority, no matter what it takes. Sometimes, for example, an athlete may feel compelled to meet his or her coach's expectations by entering the competition, even at the cost of the player's health and well-being. For example, sometimes athletes are "encouraged" to remain in the game even though they have been injured. This happens when a possible concussion was sustained, particularly by the starting quarterback. Getting hit by a pitch in baseball or tackling in football—giving or receiving –or struck by the puck in ice hockey are other examples. And, yet, the coach may ignore the player's apparent discomfort or "encourage" or "urge" the injured player to remain in the game.

Effective coaching is consistent with coaching behavior that voluntarily changes or attempts to change a "'bad" habit. Effective coaches adapt to challenging situations by recognizing their strengths and limitations. Sometimes they'll attend workshops or seminars and read professional literature in an attempt to improve their skills or change a particular approach or habit that impedes effective communication. Or, the coach might consult with specialists such as sport psychology/mental skills consultants, educators for improving teaching skills, athletic trainers, and even researchers (e.g., university faculty members or other experts who have a particular area of expertise that needs to be explored).

Effective coaches are sensitive to the needs of all team members whose contribution to the team or organization is valued, required, and solicited. Athletes' individual needs, unique personality, skill level, expectations, and relationships with others require the coach to approach and interact with each athlete differently, yet consistently.

The results of multiple studies indicate that effective leaders are approachable, not threatening or intimidating to their athletes, knowledgeable, and demonstrate high quality teaching. In general, good leaders are excellent communicators—which is understandable if they are going to transfer their knowledge to team members and gain the loyalty of their players. In turn, the players feel that they can risk communicating most thoughts to the team leader without retribution or ill feelings. In this atmosphere of trust, the coach can listen and respond to the needs of each athlete. This is particularly important if the coach wants players to perform without thoughts and feelings that interfere with performance preparation and participation.

In one typical situation, the coach may receive information that a player is struggling in class; the student athlete's grades are low, and his or her future in this course looks ominous. The counseling coach would immediately seek to meet with the athlete's teacher/professor to discuss the concern about academic status and immediately generate a strategy to remediate the problem. The coach would then meet with the athlete to (a) decide jointly on selected strategies to overcome the poor classroom performance, (b) set specific, realistic goals for academic improvement (e.g., improving class attendance, submitting assignments by the due date, meeting with a tutor) and (c) agree on regular meeting times to track progress.

Some coaches contend that their relationship with athletes extends beyond leadership "on the field or court" and includes a personal bond and friendship with team members. Can a coach ever really be an athlete's "friend?" Should coaches and athletes relate to one another as though they are in the same peer group, have similar interests, and share the same circle of friends? The answer is a simple no, at least during the time of an athlete's participation on the coach's team. Athletes want to admire and respect their coaches. The athlete views the older, more experienced coach in a very different light than a teammate or friend. The player's expectations of the coach's behaviors and attitudes differ from those of the player's peers. Athletes tend to be uncomfortable with the coach who tries to be "good friends" with the players and wants to socialize (e.g., meals, alcohol, "hanging out") with them. An occasional team social event is different, but athletes must not feel forced to attend.

An element of friendship, however, is often included as one component of any healthy player-coach relationship. It's called *mentoring*. Mentoring, unlike friendship, "occurs when a coach willingly invests time in the personal development of the athlete, when a trusting relationship evolves, when needs and interests are fulfilled, and when imitation of behavior takes place" (Bloom, 2002, p. 441). The mentoring process is an integral component of learning to coach in sport. It's an ongoing process that teaches athletes, many of whom become coaches, leadership styles, strategies, and philosophy. The positive outcomes from mentoring are a primary reason why coaches should be available to interact with athletes in a meaningful way, even away from the sport arena. Thus, a relationship built on trust, honesty, disclosure of feelings, support, and, to a degree, nurturance can be constructive.

To summarize, successful coaches may have a strong team record, winning many more games than losing games. The coaches' needs must be met first before the athletes' needs are considered. Here are other examples.

Effective coaches do not ignore nonstarters. Nonstarters receive instruction and information feedback as do starting players, and nonstarters—who are one injury away from starting—enter the game and receive coach feedback as often as possible. While the starting players deserve the coach's primary attention and time, effective coaches groom nonstarters as likely participants and give them a chance to learn and grow.

Coaches want to gain each athletes' trust, respect, and admiration. This is far more likely to occur if the coach is actively involved in the development of each team member—starter and nonstarter, healthy and injured. Sometimes the effective coach assumes a parental role with a given athlete.

One role that effective (but not necessarily successful) coaches bring to their team is that of a "parent." A good example of the parental role that coaches bring to their relationships with athletes is how some players view their current or former coaches.

Most high quality coaches provide their athletes with stability, a sense of purpose, a vision about what they want to achieve, a mission about how to achieve their goals, values about what is important to each player (i.e., about what each competitor feels passionate), opportunities to help players establish their respective role on the team (the role of leader, for example), respect for each player, and instilling a sense of team and individual integrity (i.e., being true to yourself, true to your standards and ideals, and keeping promises).

Still, respected team leaders also set limits on their players' actions. Good coaches want team leaders who deliver in the clutch. Respected players with leadership potential have to be highly skilled team members in order to have the respect of teammates and coaches. Instead of feeling humiliated or angry, highly skilled team members inspire and challenge themselves to keep improving all aspects of their game. Effective coaches maintain a parental role in their coaching practice. Great coaches are beloved by their players.

There is considerable use of psychology in sport leadership. Separating leadership into categories of successful and effective is important for understanding the process of behavior change in sport. Leadership has been defined as the ability to get others to behave as the manager intends them to behave (Zaleznik, 1977). The job may be completed, and the coach's needs may be satisfied; however, the players' needs for instruction, communication, trust—and more—are ignored. Perhaps the coach spends most of his or her time with the starters while ignoring substitutes. In effective leadership, the athletes perform in accordance with the coach's intentions and, at the same time, find their own needs satisfied.

As Cribben (1981) points out, "Success has to do only with getting the job done, whereas effectiveness adds the concept of satisfaction on the part of those who do the job" (p. 35). In this way, the positive feelings of subordinates usually contribute to long-term benefits such as team loyalty, teammate and coach support, and enjoyment of participation, an important component of intrinsic motivation. For instance, team captains might feel better about their role—and would be more helpful to the team—if the coach gave them a sense of importance and direction.

In particular, they can be given responsibility for leading a team meeting or gathering information from team members on an issue that the coach is requesting player input. In addition, resolving conflicts in the privacy of a coach's office rather than in the presence of teammates certainly contributes to team and coach loyalty. The message is "the coach respects me."

Successful (but Ineffective) Leaders

Leaders of groups, such as sports coaches, may be successful, but not necessarily effective. Teams led by "successful" coaches may win competitions more often than not, and they may even like or respect their coach. However, these leaders might intimidate, offend, disrespect, or hurt the feelings of selected team members, thereby limiting the achievement of each player's potential.

I recall quite vividly the actions of a well-known and respected (NCAA Division 1) football coach who heatedly berated his (football) quarterback on national (U.S.) television when the player did not execute a particular strategy by running out of bounds, thereby stopping the clock when the game was almost over and victory was at hand. The player, who was strongly admonished by the coach in front of television cameras, was humiliated. Consequently, the player transferred to a different university soon after the season had ended.

Effective Leaders

It might be said about effective coaches, such as the late college basketball coach, John Wooden, is that they receive excessive admiration and respect from their players because (a) they have a genuine concern for people, (b) they are excellent teachers, which translates into their players' improved sport performance, (c) they reveal their knowledge and intelligence in sport by demonstrating a "take charge" attitude at practices and competitions, and (d) they communicate their knowledge with extraordinary effectiveness. They respect others and, in turn, get it back several times over. Phoniness and intimidation are not part of the profile. Relationships are based on a long-term commitment to the program and the desire to reach team and individual goals.

Horn (1992) reviewed literature in examining the factors that most contribute to team leadership effectiveness and was asked to identify which decision style and personal characteristics they preferred in coaches. Horn found that a coach's behavioral tendencies would be more effective in some situations and sports than others. In addition, certain traits of effective leaders were relatively consistent and generalizable to most athletes, sport situations, and sport types. Examples include high frequency of rewarding behavior, social support, and fairness in decision making style (i.e., using input from athletes when it is warranted and beneficial). It's particularly important to recognize that effective coaching should include a humanistic (i.e., sensitivity to players' needs) component, not only a "take charge," autocratic leadership style so often practiced by coaches.

Several researchers have asked coaches with highly respectable winning records representing various sports at the high school and collegiate levels their "secret formula" for winning. The results were that none of these coaches intimidated, ignored, deceived, or embarrassed an athlete to evoke some desirable mental state or to enhance physical performance. For example, one former head football coach reinforced the importance of honesty and being "genuine" with athletes. The coach praised the use of nonverbal cues in effective communication, such as thumps up, a sign for "A-Okay," or a pat on the back. It appears that high quality coaches use integrity as a primary approach to leadership. They demonstrate mutual respect to their athletes.

How should we interpret the actions of coaches with consistent winning records and, yet, have been known for their hot tempers and aggressive leadership styles? These coaches have maintained high winning percentages year after year, yet do not fit the description of "effective" leadership. Perhaps this is because they were able to recruit elite athletes who, like most top performers, could mentally overcome a more assertive, even abusive, communication style from their coach. However, it is quite likely that these coaches interacted with the players in a more mild and sensitive manner outside of the competitive arena. For example, to build trust, some coaches get to know their players on a more personal basis by having "after practice" social events between games (e.g., meals, attending community or religious social events, occasionally structuring social time when the team is on the road). Therefore, with the building of trust with more social contact with which to share thoughts, the players may not take the occasional verbal assault personally. Often, the print media might report an interview with an athlete who claims that he "lets the coach blow off some steam," so the athlete does not take his coach's temper personally. Some coaches even inform their athletes that they—the coach—get emotional so "let it pass" and eventually they'll be fine.

Most effective coaches use a variety of coaching styles at one time or another, sometimes in rapid succession. As indicated earlier, some styles are more appropriate in certain situations than others. This is why identifying the characteristics of at least some of these styles, describing their advantages and disadvantages, and determining the times at which each would be most appropriate are useful exercises. These leadership styles are authoritative (also called autocratic), behavioristic, humanistic, and democratic.

Authoritarian Coaching

The authoritarian (also referred to as authoritative or autocratic) leader is characterized as achievement oriented and projects an image of being in control and making all the decisions. Authoritarian coaches have strong decision making skills and have great confidence in their ability to make the right decisions—and win. In all probability, authoritarian types were exposed to similar models in one of their former coaches. "If it was good enough for me, it's good enough for my players" is their motto. Many athletes perceive the coach's role as an authority figure and, thus, expect authoritarian behaviors. Authoritarians believe that athletes seek dominance from the coach.

Why do many aggressive coaches maintain player loyalty? Well-known head basketball coach, Bobby Knight, was able to win more games than any other NCAA basketball coach in history during his career and maintain the loyalty and respect of most of his players. Coach Knight also had one of the highest player graduation rates in the United States. And, yet, he maintained a very controversial authoritative communication style (according to print media reports). What many basketball fans and even sports journalists did not know is that Coach Knight was very dedicated to his players, making sure they went to class, maintained high academic standards, carried out their responsibilities on and off the court, met the standards to graduate, and even assured the player's parents—during recruiting and throughout the player's team participation—that he, Coach Knight, would make sure they were in good, safe hands.

An analysis of descriptions of Bob Knight's behavioral patterns, as reported in the book, *Season on the Brink*, (Feinstein, 1986), coach Knight's relationships with his players, his communication style, and features of his personality clearly reveals why some players could not cope well with his level of intensity, expectations, dedication, and commitment to playing Division 1 college basketball in the United States. Eventually, many players who could not embrace his intensity would quit the team. Yet, others flourished and competed at levels that reached, perhaps went beyond, their potential. In addition, virtually all the players who remained with his team graduated, a relatively rare outcome on college sports teams.

Perhaps understanding the methods of any authoritarian coach whose teams consistently win is to understand the concept of a balanced coaching style. Balance means that there are times for expecting strict adherence in carrying out team strategy, demonstrating full commitment and concentration in playing up to one's capability, taking responsibility for your performance, and never giving up.

Yet, many of these authoritarian coaches tend to have winning teams because their players realize that their coach cares about them as people, as students, and as their parents' sons and daughters. In addition, their parents have entrusted this coach with helping their child athlete succeed in sport, in school, and in life. The authoritarian coach need not necessarily behave in a belligerent manner. They can, in fact, show great sensitivity toward team members.

Advantages of an authoritarian coaching style are as follows:

1. *The athletes feel secure.* The insecure athlete may feel more protected with a strong, assertive leader, one who makes virtually all the decisions with high confidence.
2. *Aggression can be redirected.* Theoretically, an authoritative approach may heighten aggression in the athlete (if more aggression is desired), perhaps by increasing his or her frustration or arousal level. The intended result of this strategy is to translate these intense feelings into heightened (what is called "displaced") aggression. Ostensibly, the athlete's aggression level is redirected toward an opponent. One limitation of this technique is that many sport performers require relatively low levels of additional arousal and aggression, making increased aggression counterproductive. Arousal can be too high, which hinders rather than improves emotional control and performance outcomes. Further, not all individuals react to frustration in the same manner; some persons pout or withdraw. Others do not enjoy such treatment, become unhappy, demotivated, and may even quit the team.
3. *The coach's needs are met.* An authoritative style can be an expression of the coach's assertive personality. As a result, the coach is more effective.

4. *The authoritarian coach is viewed as efficient and decisive.* Nothing is more expeditious than a one-person system of decision making. If coaches take responsibility for all decisions, then they also take responsibility for the outcomes. One objective of effective coaching is to determine when and with whom this style is best suited.
5. *Autocratic leadership is necessary for making quick decisions.* Autocratic leadership is quick; a single decision maker is expedient when there is little time for consultation or gaining a consensus among players and other coaches.

Disadvantages of an authoritarian coaching style are as follows:

6. *The need for input from others.* A single decision maker fails to take into account the experience and expertise of other team members, especially assistant coaches. Players may also feel they have feedback that coaches need to hear based on the player's game experience. If an athlete can run much faster than his or her opponent, then coaches need to have this information on which to base future game strategies.
7. *The appearance of arrogance.* Autocrats may come across as "know-it-alls" or "arrogant" in feeling that they always know what is best for team success. Often they do—but not always.
8. *Feeling ignored and disrespected.* It is important for athletes to take "ownership" of performance outcomes. If the football quarterback feels certain that the team can score from the one yard line on fourth down but the coach calls for a field goal without consulting the players, don't expect athletes to feel respected or take ownership of that decision.
9. *Explaining the causes of success and failure.* "We lost/won because . . ." is a common phrase following the competition. Autocratic coaching should include making accurate explanations for why the team won or lost, played according to expectations, or fell flat.

Taken together, authoritarian sport leadership is very common and even expected in certain sports. But if coaches want to have the loyalty of their players, perhaps "less is more"; that is, less demonstration of power and control sometimes plays a greater role in effective coaching than demonstrating who's in charge at all times.

Behavioristic Coaching

Coaches who pat a player on the back after he or she makes a good play or who expresses negative emotion, such as anger, after a disappointing performance are practicing a style of leadership called *behaviorism*, or behavioristic coaching. This approach is based on the contention that human behavior is shaped or reinforced by its consequences. Coaches use behavioral techniques all the time but do not realize it. This style is not unlike returning to a favorite restaurant because you have previously had a positive dining experience at that location.

Reaching a goal or receiving a reward is dependent (contingent) on performing certain desirable behaviors. For example, an athlete who clearly gives a 100% effort during some task may be rewarded by the coach's words, "Nice going, Susan. Way to hustle. "Keep giving me 100%." Ignoring the athlete who consistently performs poorly, or who behaves in an inappropriate manner is another example. This process is called *contingency management* in which desirable responses from the coach are contingent on expected, desirable performance. The desire to receive positive recognition, an integral part of human nature, is well understood by the coaching profession as a tool to influence athlete motivation.

A behavioristic approach in group leadership, including sport, can be a sophisticated science if conducted properly. Rather than merely giving orders and directing the behaviors of subordinates, which reflect autocratic leadership, the behaviorist sets up conditions in the environment that either cause certain behaviors that have a desirable outcome or reinforce certain behaviors that can increase or decrease the probability of similar behaviors occurring in the future.

Here's an example of a behavioristic strategy to improve group cohesion:

A soccer team coach noticed that many of the players were forming groups among team members, called subgroups or cliques, after practices and games. If a player was not part of a subgroup that player was ignored. Playing status—starters and nonstarters—was not an issue in forming these groups. The coach was concerned that this grouping would reduce group (team) cohesion and lessen the intensity to support all team members. Team member satisfaction was at risk. The coach used behavioral coaching in planning two programs, one on the field and one off the field, designed to weaken the subgroups and bring the team closer together.

The objective of the on-field strategy was to have the different cliques work together in practice drills. Three practices were planned. The coach did the following:

1. Observed who was interacting as a subgroup and wrote down the names of those players
2. Developed a new list of practice groups that included athletes who were and were not represented in each subgroup, including members of different racial and ethnic backgrounds, positions, and starting status (starters and nonstarters)
3. Created drills that mandated interacting with each other. The athletes had to depend on one another during the practice interaction. Each subgroup was assigned a different practice drill. The objective was to get players who normally did not congregate to interact around a common goal and work together to meet that goal
4. The coach offered verbal (e.g., "Excellent pass") and nonverbal (e.g., smile, thumbs up, pat on the back) congratulatory cues after several—but not all—successful performance. Effective feedback to players, whether positive or negative,

> consists of intermittent, or consistent, reinforcement rather than constant (i.e., continuous) reinforcement.
>
> Due partly to this drill, players began to feel more comfortable with one another. In fact, they learned and used one another's first names. Further, the players helped one another to reach the desired outcomes. This carried over into games, where they supported teammates after errors or striking out, as well as after making great plays and getting hits. The team grew closer. Team harmony improved dramatically.

The aversive approach to behaviorism has a few potentially serious drawbacks.

Disadvantages of a behavioristic coaching style are as follows:

1. *The downside of punishment.* The fact that immediate changes in behavior are evident does not necessarily mean that future behaviors will be affected. Researchers have known for many years that punishment has an immediate effect on performance but that often its impact fails to carry over to future situations. The athlete is less inclined to attempt skills that do not virtually ensure successful outcomes. This is not desirable because good sport performers are risk takers.
2. *Coaches need time to plan and carry out the plan using the proper behavioral strategy to reach the objective.* Setting up the right conditions, applying the specific strategy, and allowing the process of behavior change to evolve do not appear right away, at least not usually. Coaches need to have a detailed action plan and then step away and let the plan evolve and a change in behavior/performance to occur.
3. *Improper use of the behavioristic coaching style.* The behavioristic approach in coaching can be used inappropriately. Incorrect uses of behaviorism in coaching are related to punishment and threatening statements. Threatening statements

such as "If you can't do 'such and such,' you'll sit on the bench" are supposed to increase the athlete's motivation and, perhaps, aggression or arousal. In fact, they may, but usually for a short time. Often, however, such statements have the opposite effect. Exposure to threats may result in withdrawal and diminished incentive, especially among younger or less-skilled performers.

As Martin and Hrycaiko (1983) assert, punishment and negative statements may "cause tension and anxiety in the punished individual, which can interfere with desirable athletic performance" (p. 42). In addition, athletes may feel insulted, embarrassed, or angry at the source of this input—usually the coach. This undesirable form of behaviorism is called *aversive stimulation*. The proper use of behaviorism in coaching entails respecting and being sensitive to the athlete's needs, which forms the foundation of the next leadership style, humanism.

Humanistic Coaching

According to Sage (1980), "The goal of school sports . . . for the humanist is the production of increasing uniqueness and independence, and this cannot be achieved in an autocratic atmosphere in which the team is built around an omniscient authority figure where all decisions are made by the coach while players are relegated to passive followers of orders" (p. 224). Humanism explains behavior in terms of the relationship between the individual (coach) and the environment (team). It implies the coach's desire to understand the athlete's emotional and psychological make-up and how these factors affect the player's sport performance. The thrust of this style is to treat each player in the way that the coach feels the player would like to be (and needs to be) treated (i.e., with respect, sensitivity, and fairness). According to Sage, the humanistic coach starts with the basic premise that the sport is for the players, not the coaches, at least for nonelite, younger, less-skilled competitors.

Mike Davis, former Indiana University head basketball coach, had to teach his players to be more independent when he took over a team that was formerly coached by a highly authoritative and demanding individual. As described by *New York Times* sports columnist, George Vecsey, "Davis did it by listening and sometimes even doing what they wanted. For example, if the players wanted to go right home after a game instead of going to a planned team event, Davis requested that they ask his permission" (p. 3). Nothing was out of the question. This is an example of humanistic coaching.

Mechikoff and Kozar (1983) describe the frequent use of humanistic strategies by former Western Illinois University head cross-country and track coach Dick Abbot. He was very concerned about his athletes as students and citizens as well as athletes. He tried to communicate with his athletes not just on the track, but between classes, visiting them at the residence, etc. He sought the help of other athletes in giving psychological and emotional help and guidance to the athlete. One of the most important techniques he had was his attempt to listen to athletes and allow them opportunities to vent their feelings. He feels the simple process of having someone care and providing them the opportunity to vent their concerns perhaps reduced some feelings of anxiety and tension and thus allowed them to perform well.

The humanistic coach cares about meeting the competitor's needs as well as achieving the outcome. In fact, the former should benefit the latter. Caring about the athlete's feelings and attempting to establish warm, trusting relationships with players should result in heightened loyalty, greater physical effort, and higher self-esteem.

Humanism may also be extended to how the head coach interacts with coaching assistants. Head coaches have an obligation to solicit the input of assistants when making many team-related decisions. The sharing of authority and decision making gives assistant coaches a sense of meaningfulness and responsibility on the team. This aspect of humanism is referred to as the *participative approach*. In this way, the head coach uses the capabilities, experience, and knowledge of each assistant and maintains "the congruence between [team] goals and the assistant's personal aspirations" (Magnotta 1986, p. 18). Thus, an important objective of humanistic coaching is to disprove a statement from the late baseball manager, Leo Durocher, "nice guys finish last."

In addition to these behavioral traits, the humanist is approachable. Players can confide in a humanistic coach and disclose their feelings to him or her. No question from a player is regarded as "stupid." The humanist understands that inquiries from athletes are desirable; they show interest and curiosity. Because this coach invests in the growth and learning of his or her players, typical responses from performers such as making mistakes, not remembering information, asking questions, and even having trouble making friends on the team are dealt with in a constructive and positive manner.

Humanism is the "fundamental concern for the person . . . having a measure of autonomy, choice, and self-determination" (Sage 1980, p. 219). Humanistic coaches try to allow players the freedom to experiment, to take risks, to make decisions, and to learn from their decisions. The objective is personal growth.

Another aspect of enhancing personal growth in humanistic coaching is encouraging athletes to "think at a higher level," to develop a sense of sophistication, creativity, maturity, and intelligence. For example, athletes tend to form closely knit peer groups that demand conformity to certain rules. Team members who do not conform are isolated rather than respected for their individuality, especially in the preadolescent and adolescent age groups. The humanistic coach, observing team members isolating or even scapegoating another teammate, would bring the parties together and help to resolve the conflict for the good of the team.

It is fair to say that many coaches have little patience for the humanistic style. To these individuals, effective coaching entails a "tough," highly assertive approach. Perhaps. But if done right, the proper use of humanistic strategies can add significantly to the quality of team member satisfaction, reduced anxiety, and better performance.

Advantages of a humanistic coaching style are as follows:

1. *It builds the athlete's intrinsic motivation.* The desire to play and improve comes from within, from personal gratification and feelings of competence and self-direction.
2. *Player concentration and attentional focus are improved.* This is because the humanistic coach helps players resolve personal issues so that they can focus totally and clearly on performance-related tasks and not be distracted by thoughts and emotions that can reduce concentration.
3. *Personal maturity and growth occur.* The humanistic coach can help players deal more constructively with the stressful aspects of competitive sport.
4. *Humanistic coaches develop player loyalty.* Often, stories will circulate about coaches who are highly assertive toward their athletes. Readers of these stories believe that athletes react best to an aggressive coach. What readers do not see is the time and energy these coaches give their athletes off the field or court. Coaches may have a "hard" and aggressive exterior but often demonstrate a much more sensitive side away from the sport venue. Basketball coach Bobby Knight and the late football coach Woody Hayes are high-profile examples of coaches who made sure they developed a strong bond with their players. In turn, the athletes felt admiration and loyalty toward their coach who treated them with respect and integrity.
5. *Humanistic coaches like to win, but sport offers so much more.* Sage (1980), in reflecting the humanist philosophy in sport, asserts that "using victory as the only end, the goal of sport competition, is too limiting, confining, shallow, and short-sighted for humanism. . . . The end in sport is the joy, exhilaration, and self-fulfillment that one obtains from movement" (p. 226).

Disadvantages of a humanistic coaching style are as follows:

1. *It is incompatible with the needs and expectations of elite level performers.* Humanistic leadership might be incompatible with the requirements of advanced athletic competition. Chelladurai and Arnott (1985), for instance, found that highly skilled athletes prefer an autocratic leadership style when the coach is perceived as having the necessary information to make the best decision, or when the type of decision to be made is based on a complex issue. Relatively little time is available for meeting the personal (and often complex) needs of each individual elite athletes.
2. *It minimizes the importance of game outcome; winning is not a priority.* A humanistic coaching style should not make the athletes' satisfaction and meeting more important than playing to one's potential and winning. This seems incompatible with the nature and objectives of competitive sport. Concern for personal feelings and emotional problems will not, by itself, lead to successful game outcomes. For coaches who view the final score as the most important outcome of sport competition, the humanistic approach offers relatively little gratification.
3. *The lack of performer success may lead to dissatisfaction and dropping out.* If meeting the personal needs of each athlete is more important to the coach than winning (an example is making sure that all players on the team play in every game, regardless of the score), and as a result the team tends to be unsuccessful, players might lose interest and quit the team. After all, the primary goal of sport competition is to win, especially at higher-skill levels. Therefore, although being sensitive to individual needs is a part of winning, coaches should seek a balance between meeting individual needs and ensuring the positive reinforcement that comes with team success.

Here are a few coaching suggestions for using a humanistic leadership style:

- *Interact with the athlete in a warm, trusting manner.* This doesn't mean that less pleasant emotions should never be expected to enter the relationship, because after all, the parties are human. But mutual trust, respect, and sincerity result in mutual admiration.

- *Respect individual differences.* Effective coaches do not treat all players in the same way. They understand that some athletes are more sensitive and need more patience than others. Athletes also differ in the manner in which they prefer to prepare mentally for a game.

- *Engage in off-season interaction.* Humanistic coaches care about their players' welfare year round, not just during the season. Issues such as school grades, physical conditioning, and perhaps the player's social or family life might need input or reinforcement from the coach. The key here is a genuine concern for the total individual, a person who's more than just a sport competitor.

- *Take an active part in practice.* It's very common for coaches to "bark" their commands from a designated point and rarely become actively involved in the practice or conditioning program. At least in the early part of the season, the coach should take an active part in practice. He or she might put on workout clothing and lift weights or run a few laps with the team—a closer identification with the performer's results.

- *Promote mass participation.* Coaches and players alike want to win. To do so often means playing the team's best athletes. But it's clearly a mistake to ignore substitutes. To raise team morale, the humanist attempts to have as many team members as possible participating in the game or to at least provide nonstarters with regular instructional feedback. In fact, substitutes should be given tasks in practice as a technique to help them to feel more closely responsible for the team's game preparation and performance—and to improve their own skills if possible.

Democratic Coaching

Any team with elected captains is exercising a democratic (also called delegative) leadership style. Holding team and individual player discussions prior to making rules that will affect the participants also employs a democratic philosophy. Is this an effective way to govern? It is, according to researchers who have found that when group members desire participation in decision making, their performance and group member satisfaction is affected either positively or negatively, depending on whether this need is met. But whereas the authoritarian leader is efficient and decisive, democratic leadership can be viewed as slow, inefficient, and lacking team focus. Slow because allowing a group of individuals to make decisions or policies takes time and patience. Inefficient because groups can make decisions that are counterproductive and not well thought out, decisions that meet short-term needs at the expense of long-term benefits. And lacking focus because a coach who does not act decisively is not viewed by the players as "in control" or knowledgeable, which can cause player anxiety. Nevertheless, this leadership style can be inconspicuously effective, especially if employed judiciously.

The democratic leader need not leave all decision making to the team. Decisions may have to be made quickly and without input from players and assistants, for example, in the rapid deployment of game strategy. Usually solving complex problems, especially during competition, requires rapid decision making by the coach. In fact, under certain circumstances, the players prefer that the coach make decisions, deferring to his or her apparent knowledge and past experience.

Examples of democratic strategies in coaching include allowing participants to nominate and elect team captains or cocaptains, selecting members of the league's all-star team, or recipients of individual player awards or making decisions about certain team policies, which the coach is prepared to support. For example, whether the players can bring a partner to the team party might be a negotiable item, but whether team members should be allowed to smoke or attend a party the night before a game may not be negotiable.

Advantages of a democratic coaching style are as follows:

1. *It is nonthreatening to athletes.* The coach who follows a democratic style is typically more approachable and a better communicator to players than coaches who follow other styles. The reason is simply that democratic leaders are good listeners; they respect the views—even the criticisms—of subordinates, and they offer advice only when it is either solicited or absolutely necessary. Not surprisingly, this type of coach is perceived by players as being nonthreatening.
2. *Individual initiative.* Players feel that they have some control, either directly or indirectly, in the team's operation. The coach informs them that their input is appreciated—at the proper time. Consequently, they are more apt to volunteer ideas, to demonstrate independence (presumably for the good of the team rather than self-focused, although this is not always the case), and to feel less dependent on the coach in stressful situations. Athletes often cope with stress more successfully when they feel in partial control of a situation.
3. *Greater flexibility and risk taking.* When players are in the midst of game competition, sometimes they need to know that it's okay to take a chance. A batter can bunt if the third baseperson is playing deep, or a player can pass instead of taking the shot. Players adapt more quickly to new and different situations if the coach's style says, "Go ahead, take a chance—but also take responsibility for the outcome." Players should not be overprogrammed to perform in a certain manner because the obstacles that lie ahead can change.

Disadvantages of a democratic coaching style are as follows:

1. *Learning from failure.* Adherence to strong democratic principles demands a philosophy of noninterference. Interference might impede the progress of the group toward its goals. Sometimes, a democratic coach must have the ability to stand by and watch

a degree of team or individual athlete failure and suffering without imposing on the situation. Democratic leaders must not be more loyal to one individual than to the group. For instance, a player or assistant with a violent temper might have to be favorably recognized because of their contributions to the team despite having unpleasant personality traits. Examples include players who produce outstanding results yet do not relate well to teammates, athletes who tend to argue with game officials, or team members who are chronically late for the team bus.

2. *Slow decision making.* It's highly doubtful that a coach would call for a team vote with only seconds available to make a decision about game strategy while the game is in progress. For the most part, making decisions on a group basis is certainly slower than other leadership approaches. Thus, the coach should be careful that when a group decision is warranted, sufficient time is granted for this process.

There are common ways to contradict a democratic coaching style:

1. *The sham democracy.* When is a democratic approach to governing a group not a democracy? When the group leader does not live up to his or her end of the bargain. Let's take voting as an example. Just because the team votes on a decision does not mean the process is democratic. The vote outcome must be supported and carried out by the leader. Even authoritarian leaders may use voting to support certain decisions. How democratic is it if the coach does not approve of the players' choice for team captain and appoints a different choice?

> **Here are some examples of sham democracies:**
>
> *Law enforcement.* The chief of police of a city in the southeastern United States was given funding to purchase five new police cars. The chief first asked the department if they agreed with his car selection or if they preferred another car style, instead.

> The officers were unanimous in voicing their preference for a different, bigger car that would be safer to drive and was used by most other city police departments. The chief's response was "Well, too bad, I'll buy the car that's more affordable and you'll have to get used to it." At that point, the chief lost all credibility with his officers. The chief made his own decision, ignoring his officers' preferred alternative despite soliciting their opinions as part of the decision process.
>
> *Sports.* A basketball coach asked the team to nominate two individuals to serve as co-captains for the season. The coach offered no criteria for the characteristics of team captains he was seeking. He then left the locker room. After prolonged discussion among team members covering a two-day period, two names of two players to serve as co-captains were provided in writing to the coach. The next day, after practice, the coach announced his own choices for these positions. Both these names differed from the players' suggestions. The coach then usurped the players' choices and named his own two players as season co-captains. The team quickly lost their enthusiasm for respecting the coach's choices and never believed the coach's words again; he had lost all credibility.

Bottom line is this: Leaders/coaches must not ask for a vote or for input from others if they intend to make the decision anyway. It undermines the leader's integrity. This is an example when arrogance in leadership can undermine group member loyalty and when the leader becomes less effective in influencing thoughts, attitudes, and behaviors of group members.

2. *Intimidation.* Using voting for team captain as an example again, what if the coach were to list all the qualifications for team captain, thereby effectively eliminating 80 to 90% of the team? This is not a true democratic process. If the coach says, "This is what I believe" just prior to a team-related decision,

the players will not feel comfortable in deciding against the coach's expectations or wishes.

Perhaps effective coaching is a function of the "right" person coaching the "right" athletes under the "right" conditions. This means that team leaders do the following:

1. Choose to coach sports that are compatible with their personality, expertise, and past experience
2. Work with athletes who can respond effectively to the coach's leadership style
3. Use an approach to leadership that is most effective for the type of sport and the situation
4. Individualize their treatment of athletes based on the player's needs and expectations

As Mitchell (1979) contends, "successful leadership is contingent upon a variety of factors and what we must determine is the best match between leaders and the situation" (p. 265).

1. *Use the appropriate style.* A coach's leadership style should be compatible with the situation. Coaches of elite athletes, usually in high-pressure situations in which winning is an expectation or even a mandate to keep their jobs, should not use the same leadership style as the coach of a team consisting of younger, nonelite competitors. The needs and expectations of athletes in these situations differ. A related leadership style is called leading by example, or dependent leadership style.
2. *Meet situational needs.* Effective coaches can alter their leadership style to meet the needs of a given situation. In addition to age and skill level, effective leaders respond in a manner that is compatible with situational demands. Attending to an injured athlete or a team member having personal difficulties (e.g., academic problems, depression, questions about limited playing time) requires a humanistic leadership style response.

3. *Make the job fit the person.* The coach should seek a position that is suitable to his or her personality or natural leadership style. According to Fiedler (1964), compatibility between the coach's personal characteristics and the sport type, conditions, and situations under which he or she will lead (e.g., an aggressive/assertive personality being more compatible as a football or basketball coach than a golf or tennis coach) may be the most realistic approach to being an effective coach. Further, the coach's personality may be more compatible with leading a smaller group of players than governing a large group of players. In that case, coaching golf, archery, and other sports with relatively few participants might be a better choice.
4. *One style does not fit all!* Effective coaches have learned when to alter their leadership style. A coach's disposition to act in a certain way under particular circumstances need not necessitate nor predict his or her behaviors. People can choose to control their actions and methodically apply a particular leadership style in a given situation. Making rapid decisions during the competition may call for an autocratic style, while a decision of whether to have a team social event may warrant a democratic style. The mentality of "I am who I am" rather than a willingness to adapt to various environments and situations has very limited validity in effective leadership.

Managing Stress and Anxiety

Stress and anxiety, which are not the same (discussed later), are common in competitive sport. Is there anything coaches can teach athletes about coping effectively with stress and anxiety that occurs before or during the competition?

- A college head men's basketball coach does not favor a pregame fiery speech as a motivational tool. "You don't win games 20 minutes before the game," he claims. He feels that catch phrases and watching certain video clips before coming out of the locker room have more motivational value.

- A college head football coach asks his players to focus on each play and not to think about the game's end result: Avoid "what-if" statements and focus on the immediate play. He also teaches his athletes to handle adversity in practice by remaining in control of the situation. Routines are developed in practice in reacting to adversity that might be experienced in games. His team practices responses under different game scenarios.

- A veteran college head track and field coach reminds his athletes to avoid external pre-meet distractions, "Don't worry about anyone, including me (your coach), but yourself, and never think about who is watching you" he reminds his athletes. Athletes are better prepared mentally if they rehearse pre-meet activity, knowing how to handle waiting time, and focus internally on their own mental plan. Mental readiness builds confidence and avoids worry and self-doubt, he contends.

- In this day and age of online communication options, a college women's soccer coach maintains a policy and reminds his soccer athletes that they should not receive phone calls from anyone before or during the game. They are a distraction and may cause a loss of concentration and increased stress at the worst possible time. He endorses a policy of not using the phone at least within 2 hours before coming to the game venue.

- A college head coach claims that coaches have to "tell the truth" to their athletes. Mondays (following a weekend football game) is designated as "tell the truth day," in which coaches review game video and give athletes a balanced assessment of their performance on a scale of 1 ("poor") to 10 ("excellent"). "Stay positive," he says, "but be honest and tell the truth. If you are going to improve, then I must do my job as your coach and be bluntly honest with my feedback." Truth telling, often—but not always—delivered in private and confidentially, gives the coach more credibility among the players, especially if you praise and criticize concrete behavior, not empty statements that have no instructional value for the athlete (Ginott, 1965 The coach includes a humanistic coaching style in his leadership role because he or she appears credible, authentic, and recognizes player competence. These impressions, in turn, promote team loyalty.

There is no "best" way to lead for all situations and under all conditions. Coaches in golf and basketball differ markedly as to the leadership style that best fosters athletic performance. Coaches should make critical assessments of their unique situations and surroundings prior to charging "head on" into a style that may or may not be compatible with other team members (e.g., assistant coaches, athletic trainers, school officials).

Effective coaches take the time to listen and react to the feelings of their athletes. Members of any group—and sport is no exception—tend to feel greater identification with group goals if they have played a part, however minor, in creating and carrying out these goals, along with supporting team rules and expected behaviors.

Successful sports coaching is challenging, sophisticated, and consumes enormous time, energy, and skill. When applied appropriately, these coaching styles can effectively influence athletes' thoughts, emotions, and behaviors. Influencing behavior—in this case, sports performance—is what great coaching is all about.

chapter three

Great Coaches are Great Teachers

Undeniably, great coaches are also great teachers. The primary objective of this chapter is to provide insight into high-quality teaching of sport skills, with particular reference to highly skilled athletes. While most coaches of organized sports teams have excellent knowledge of tactics and strategies of their respective sport, sometimes their talent is wasted—unless they can provide solid teaching skills and promote skill acquisition and retention.

The framework of this chapter will be applying the information-processing model (IPM) for meeting two objectives: (a) explaining the model, and (b) providing a list of "do's and don'ts" at each stage of the model. Ways that coaches can promote high-quality instruction and athlete learning and remembering of sport skills will be provided. Over the years, numerous information-processing models have been developed and tested. The model reviewed in this chapter reflects a compilation of most of these previously published models and has the greatest application in sport settings. The existing models are fundamentally similar.

The Information-Processing Model

The information-processing model (IPM) consists of describing the way we take in, process (think about or manage), and respond to information in the environment. When a basketball player runs toward his or her opponent's basket, a number of thoughts are being processed at a very high rate of speed. "Where should I be located—my correct position on the court as we move the ball toward my opponent's goal?" "What is the play or strategy?" "Where is my position to receive the rebound?" "Where are my teammates located on the court?" "What is my defensive position if my team makes the basket?" "Be sure to filter (block) out the crowd and any other events that occur off the court that might distract me." Sometimes the athlete has to recall the strategy used in practice settings, which can be quickly recalled and performed automatically. The answer to each question needs to be rehearsed repeatedly until it can be executed in the virtual absence of thinking.

There are several processing stages occurring between the onset of a stimulus and the athlete's response. Presenting a stimulus initiates a sequence of processing stages, with each stage operating on the information available to it. The information is transmitted in visual, verbal, and tactual form, all these senses accompanied by emotion. In addition, there are pre-performance and post-performance conditions that influence performance quality, both immediate and eventual. Perhaps the most common IP models related to sport have been generated by Marteniuk (1976), the learning model and the performance model. The learning IP model includes the various mechanisms needed for information rehearsal, storage, and retrieval. The performance IP model, on the other hand, describes rapid cognitive (thinking) and motor (movement) responses. Similar, though not identical, stages of the IP model are experienced for novices and for individuals with superior motor skills. The whole information-processing system begins with the performer's detection of one or more stimuli.

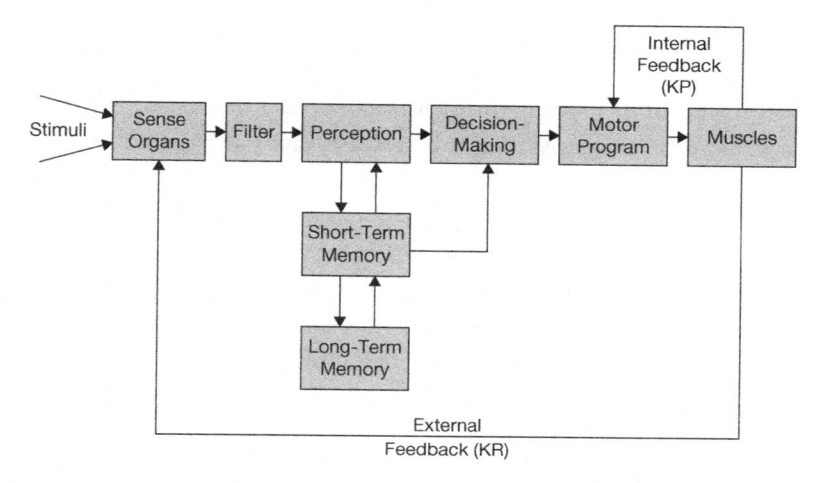

Figure 3.1 Information processing model

Stimuli. Processing information starts with external stimuli entering our nervous system, collectively called our sense organs through our eyes, ears, and sense of touch. An athlete will rely on one or more of these components to detect a ball in flight, a teammate's or opponent's actions or words, the coach's instructions, or regulating emotional intensity. The novice and expert differ at this first stage. A novice takes longer to detect stimuli and is poorer at anticipating this stimulus, whereas an expert rapidly anticipates and is mentally prepared to locate, anticipate, and interpret the stimulus.

Coaching and teaching strategies would include (a) assisting the athlete to review and anticipate performance tendencies and strengths of opponents and (b) generating an action plan to quickly react to the external stimulus. For example, "Your opponent likes to serve (the tennis ball) toward the midline"; "(Ice hockey forward) number 58 likes to shoot at the upper right-hand corner of the net and rarely takes long shots from the blue line."

Filter. With so much information being initiated and processed so quickly, it's necessary to reduce the amount of information load by helping the athlete concentrate only on the most relevant input. The IPM "filter" allows the performer to ignore or eliminate less important ("busy") stimuli that reduces the performer's response time. The filter is far more efficient in separating relevant and meaningful information for more advanced athletes than for the novice. Younger, less-skilled athletes are easily distracted and lose concentration, particularly when under stress, anxiety, and pressure. The less-skilled athlete is more easily distracted by meaningless and irrelevant information, while not focusing his or her full concentration on the most relevant and meaningful stimuli input.

Coaching and teaching strategies would include assisting athletes to select and react to the most important incoming stimuli to which they are exposed (e.g., the laces on a fast-pitched baseball; the position of a volleyball player before she receives a pass from her teammate from the baseline), and identifying the tendencies of opponents so that their performance can be anticipated to help athletes focus their concentration.

Perception. Perception represents how the athlete interprets/classifies new information that has passed through the filter. Major league baseball hitters, for example, claim they detect a pitcher's curve ball by observing the spin of a ball's laces, perhaps the angle at which the pitcher delivers the ball, and other characteristics that the batter perceives. Hitters may also detect a specific throwing motion that "tips off" the hitter about a certain pitch being thrown.

Perception is optimal when the athlete is familiar with the task demands (e.g., increased movement speed) and external conditions (e.g., the weather, a highly skilled opponent). This occurs during practice, in which game conditions are replicated.

Coaching and teaching strategies may include adjusting the pace of the practice environment. The practice environment should be slowed until the athlete is ready to increase performance speed and their familiarity with task demands improves—eventually becoming automatic. This is called "game simulation."

One effective teaching strategy for improving perception is to control as many external conditions as possible. The athlete can then focus on and react to as few distracting movements as possible. An example of an athlete's thought process spelled out might be, "Opponent's ball is hit to my left; respond with a backhand stroke." Or the coach calls "play x," which means, "perform x run pattern."

Short-term memory (STM). Sometimes skilled sport performance must be executed automatically and with minimal thinking. STM one of the most important stages in the model and separates higher- from lower-skilled performers. This stage partially explains why athletes need to focus their attention to the most important information while ignoring less important information.

The primary role of STM is to think about and remember incoming information STM also assists the performer in making accurate decisions about immediately responding to a stimulus, such as a ball in flight or the location or actions of an opponent. In addition, STM is the mechanism that performers use to transfer information into long-term (permanent) memory (LTM). Learning is not possible unless STM is functioning properly. Thus, incoming information is acted on in STM and sent forward to the next stage, the decision mechanism (DM).

A coaching and teaching strategy that may enhance an athlete's STM includes reducing environmental demands to allow athletes to incorporate new information and to deal with new external demands. Novices, for instance, should master fundamental (basic) movements and skills before being exposed to a competitive environment. In addition, with skill mastery, the environment should replicate real-world conditions, going from slow to moderate, to fast-paced tasks. Each of these stages should allow the athlete time for rehearsal (repetition). Strategies include a process called positive self-talk, which is initiated at the early stages of learning a sport skill. Athletes need sufficient time to mentally practice the movement pattern just before and during its execution. This process begins purposefully slower than when the actual skill is executed, then performed with increasing speed or velocity as the movement pattern is improved over repeated trials. For instance, this process is similar to throwing a baseball underhanded to a novice baseball hitter, then over time and with repeated practice, the throws become overhand and at slightly greater velocity. It is important to remember that STM, like any other aspect of the learning process, takes time. Therefore, for sport skills that require rapid decision making and physical responses, STM is a process that may have to be ignored.

Long-term memory (LTM). LTM consists of remembering past events, skills, and experiences. For learning sport skills, LTM allows us to build on—rather than forget—previously learned skills. Do you recall how to hold a tennis or badminton racket? The routines you use when you step into the batter's box in baseball or when standing on the free throw line in basketball? Our pre-performance routines are stored in LTM. The athlete initiates the series of movements and routines that were learned and remembered prior to performing the current task. This is why learning is more efficient if we can link past learning to new learning.

One source of information that has been stored in LTM is what was rehearsed in STM. This means that repeated and prolonged rehearsal of information or skills in STM will result in the transfer of this data into LTM. This information remains in LTM and is accessible to the performer who taps into it at a later time, a process called *recall* or *recognition*. The data (or skill) will be maintained in LTM where they will be permanently stored for future retrieval. It is the coach's role to assist athletes to tap into LTM to execute previously learned skills.

When it comes to coaching and teaching strategies, because LTM has unlimited storage capacity, coaches need not be concerned about "too much" learning or over-practice of sport skills. Coaches should help athletes link new skills and learning conditions to "old" learning skills and conditions—what the athletes already know how to perform. The athletes need help transferring what they already know and can perform competently to what they need to know. For example, remember how we hold a badminton racket ("that" way)? We hold a tennis racket differently—"this" way.

Decision making. Not surprisingly, making decisions while learning new skills requires time. Performing complex skills properly depends on accuracy or speed. The coach needs to determine whether slowing down the speed of making decisions when performing a sport skill will result in improved accuracy and, thus, better performance. The decision-making mechanism carries out the decision in response to visual, auditory, and tactual input., respectfully, what the athlete observes, hears, and feels. for instance, there is very little available time to plan and think about a strategy for hitting a fast-pitched baseball in which response execution is usually automatic (which partially explains why elite-level baseball batters swing at pitches thrown in the dirt). Golf, bowling, wrestling, and archery, for example, are examples of sports in which there is sufficient time to plan, strategize, and then execute the skill.

The decision-making stage is an area that separates higher- versus lower-skilled performers, which has implications for providing high-quality instruction. When coaching athletes in sports that require rapid decisions, the following strategies can be employed:

1. There should be a performance goal for each practice session that indicates what the athlete/learner should be able to do at the end of the session (or some other time frame such as "week," "season," and "game")
2. The mechanics of the skill that requires rapid decision making must be practiced, mastered, and performed before it is executed during an actual competitive event
3. At initial stages of learning there should be as few external distractions as possible
4. The focus of instruction should be on developing an *action plan* based on existing required skills and external conditions that the athlete carries out when experiencing particular situations. An action plan consists of a predetermined set of thoughts, emotions, and behaviors that are carried out in a specific sequence that results in desirable performance outcomes. This means that athletes should be able to detect and interpret the movements of the opponent and to execute specific cognitive strategies (e.g., positive self-talk, visualization, anticipation, mental rehearsal) during actual performance to promote the probability of a successful outcome.

In addition, and of particular importance, the athlete should practice under game-like conditions, a teaching strategy called *game simulation*. Conversely, the athlete should think about game-like conditions experienced in the actual competition so that his or her mental state in practice (e.g., less anxiety and perceived pressure, anticipation, cueing, use of coping skills, greater relaxation) can be transferred to the competition venue. Finally, the coach needs to assist each athlete develop *preperformance routines*, perhaps as part of the athlete's action plan, in preparation for the actual contest. The key outcome of teaching rapid decision making is to assist athletes to make decisions prior to performance execution so that the skill(s) is/are performed automatically, such as swinging a baseball bat, tennis racquet, or golf club—all performed automatically after the response is initiated.

Decision making for *slower* sports skills allows the athlete more time for planning and using mental skills, focuses more on accuracy and less on speed, and develops routines and action plans prior to and during skill execution. Golf, for instance, allows time for pre-shot routines. But, again, the goal in decision making is to plan, anticipate, and execute the primary skills: "Plan, strategize, then execute!" When this sequence is repeated often, it becomes a motor program.

Motor program. This mechanism is usually defined as a well-coordinated sequence of movements that operate together to control movement and is not dependent on internal or external feedback. A proper swing of a baseball bat forms a motor program, for example. Motor programs are movement patterns that are represented in the central nervous system. When specific physical responses are practiced repeatedly, they become remembered (retained). Thus, the ability to perform two motor tasks simultaneously (e.g., skating and shooting or passing a hockey puck or simultaneously dribbling, passing, or shooting a basketball while traveling toward your opponent's basket) means that at least one set of actions can be performed without (or minimal) thinking.

Coaching and teaching strategies for building and carrying out a motor program should be focused on repetition. A motor program takes time and repeated attempts to develop a sport skill and to perform it in the virtual absence of thinking. For example, baseball batting can be divided into component parts. The novice baseball batter needs to execute two sets of movements, upper body and lower body, if he or she decides to swing at the pitch. If the decision is to swing, the batter must perform some or all of the following sequence: (a) visually follow the flight of the ball, (b) make the decision to swing or not swing, (c) if the decision is to swing, then execute numerous mechanical processes that must be executed almost simultaneously. Some of these automated actions include rotation of the hips and forward momentum of the body, in which the forward leg is extended forward toward the pitched ball, and the bat swing is in rapid motion. These movements must be repeated and practiced so that eventually they become automatic.

Due to the high speed of most pitched baseballs, hitters must commit themselves quickly to initiate the swing, but not necessarily complete the swing. This "commitment to swing" must be determined early in the batting sequence or else the pitched ball will occur too quickly and the swing will be completed too late. The ball will pass the hitter. Researchers have determined the precise timing of the hitter's reaction to a pitch thrown at high velocity. The batter must commit—or not commit—to a full swing within a half second of the pitcher's release. The key ingredient to building a motor program is purposeful (intentional) repetition of the to-be-performed skill or sub-skill.

Feedback. The primary purpose of the feedback mechanism, consisting of both internal and external processes, is to provide information to the performer concerning the quality of performance outcomes. Information garnered from both types of feedback provides the performer with the degree of accuracy versus error, with implications for a change in movement quality.

Internal feedback consists of internal sensations that are received after the performed task or skill. These sensations are stored in the brain, commonly referred to as "muscle memory." (Please note that muscles do not store movements; memory of skilled movements are stored in the brain). This process of storing information is referred to as *error detection*, or *knowledge of performance* (KP). Internal feedback is especially needed if the movement is continuous (nonstop), such as basketball or soccer, rather than discrete (segmented), such as archery, bowling, and golf.

External feedback consists of providing verbal and/or visual information to the performer about movement quality. External feedback provides a basis from which to change and improve performance. Information given to athletes about their performance quality is called *knowledge of results* (KR). *Receiving KR is essential for learning sport skills* because information from KR is compared to previous trials and allows the athlete to make adjustments with each new attempt. This is the root of learning sport skills.

You can have an athlete make numerous attempts in performing a sport skill and fail to detect even a fraction of improvement in the absence of KR. An example would be to inform the athlete about specific high- and low-quality performance. An example of high-quality performance is "Chris, good anticipation of your opponent's move," whereas an example of low-quality performance is, "Terry, when you perform 'x' shot, anticipate that your opponent will often respond with a 'y' shot."

KR should be given intermittently, not constantly. One caveat of KR effectiveness is that the coach not overload the athlete with too much information before the athlete can take in, process, and practice it. In addition, KR should be delivered in verbal (what the coach says in providing meaningful feedback), visual (what the coach demonstrates, or models, for the athlete), and tactual forms (e.g. what the coach asks the athlete to do) when possible.

Coaching and teaching strategies for feedback. For KP (i.e., internal feedback), the athlete needs to experience correct movements, such as watching a model with similar physical characteristics perform the skill correctly. Coaches should allow the athlete to observe highly skilled teammates or opponents perform the skill and point out areas of correct form and how the mechanics of the skill are executed.

What should the athlete be feeling while carrying out the skill? Use tactual feedback so that the athlete feels proper skill execution. KP includes assessing correct and incorrect movement quality. Performers want to associate movement sensations with a desirable outcome; the learner attempts to repeat similar sensations in future attempts. Higher-skilled performers are better able to use a combination of KR and KP for skill mastery.

For KR, athletes require additional time to process the information so that feedback is retained and stored in LTM for future use. Here is how not to provide KR. A college football coach, in practice, had his receivers—about six of them—line up and receive a pass from the quarterback during drills. After catching the pass, the receivers went to the back of the line to wait their turn to receive the next pass. No verbal nor visual feedback was offered, perhaps because, in part, the turn-around time between passes was only about 15–20 seconds, not enough time to integrate or mentally rehearse the experience of the previous pass. Examples of external feedback (KR) are "Did the receiver run the correct pass reception pattern?" "Was the pass caught?" How about including an "opponent" during the drill so that receivers become familiar with catching passes closer to game-like conditions? KR can also be delivered in nonverbal form, a strategy called *modeling*, discussed next

Motor/sport skills must be modeled (demonstrated); coaches and PE teachers need to "talk less and show more." One reason for the need to model sport skills is that visual information requires so much less information for processing, as compared to verbal information. Requiring the learner (athlete) to observe how a sport skill is performed (e.g., "Watch how I do 'this' with my hands while I do 'that' with my feet") requires far less processing (rehearsal) of information in STM, storage in LTM, and faster and more accurate decision-making time. Routines are performed automatically and more quickly by visual input than by verbal messages—the "show more (through modeling) and talk less" model.

It is crucial that the model demonstrate the skill correctly—perfectly, in fact. Performers should be able to duplicate the model's movements and turn these observations into improved performance. The athlete should be able to visualize the model's performance under game-like conditions. If the model stands 6 feet, 5 inches and able to dunk the basketball but the observer stands 5 feet, 6 inches and not physically able to dunk, the exercise is for naught.

Implications for Instructional Strategies

As indicated earlier, great coaches are great teachers. Here is a summary of what coaches can do to ensure that their knowledge of the game is transferred into actual athletic performance.

Learning conditions. In early stages of skill acquisition, keep the environment "simple" and as free as possible of extraneous stimuli (i.e., noise, visual distractions, even the presence of observers if you prefer individualized instruction). In the early stages of learning, have novice performers focus their attention on only one or two opponents rather than on all opponents. Again, keep the conditions of initial learning stages simple, then later add more opponents and speed to the environment.

Pre-performance factors. Help the novice athlete attend to as few stimuli as possible; direct his or her attention to the most relevant stimuli. Direct the athlete's attention and concentration. For example, how do you avoid being faked out when defending against a speedy receiver? What are the visual cues a defender should use when the opponent is approaching "your" goal? What should the player be able to anticipate from an opponent before committing himself or herself to initiating a response? Learn and *slowly* employ predetermined cognitive strategies such as mental practice (also called "visualization"), pre-cueing, cueing, positive self-talk, and attentional focusing. Avoid giving an athlete too much to think about too soon in the learning process. Also, have learners focus on only one or two other players (i.e., small groups) rather than trying to engage with the whole team, which may lead to information overload.

Practice conditions. The following strategy cannot be emphasized enough—*game simulations*. There is a concept in the sport pedagogy/motor learning literature called the *principle of specificity*. It means that what a learner practices should be as transferable as possible to actual game conditions. What we learn in practice settings is best transferred to actual game conditions when there are strong associations between practice behavior/practice conditions and game behavior/game conditions. For example, learning to hit a curve ball in baseball is best learned under conditions that approximate an actual game. The pitcher stands the same distance from the hitter under both game and practice conditions, the pitch is overhand, not underhand (as in softball), the pitch's speed in practice is consistent with the athlete's batting skills and level of competition, and so on. Practice can incorporate improving specific skills; however, transfer between practice and game conditions is optimal when the athlete experiences game-like conditions and performance demands.

One big difference between practice and game conditions is the extensive use of KP and KR in practice. KP and KR require time, a condition that is not usually available in a game condition. After several practice conditions, the coach should provide information feedback. This includes reminding the athlete about his or her posture and focus of attention. "Remember, Sally, to have the bat sitting in your fingers when waiting for the pitch," or "When standing on first base, lean toward second, putting weight on your right leg, in order to get a faster jump on a ball that will move you to second base and beyond more quickly."

Teaching cognitive strategies should be easier and more effective in a practice setting than teaching during competition. Cognitive strategies take time to learn so that they are performed automatically and properly during the competition. (see chapter 7 on applying mental skills to sport). The challenge for coaches who learn the proper use of cognitive strategies is over-teaching them. Learners, including skilled athletes, can easily be overcome with too much thinking, resulting in what is called *paralysis by analysis*. Instead of automating one or more mental skills, athletes are asked to do too much thinking, which slows down their reactions to stimuli. They take too much time to make decisions. Practice is for learning and practicing mental skills, including which ones work best under which conditions.

Movement mechanics should be automated, that is, carried out with minimal thinking, either *before* or at the same time cognitive strategies are introduced, depending on the type of cognitive strategy. For example, let's take a cognitive strategy called *pre-cuing*. The athlete wants to focus on learning—in fact, overlearning—the mechanics of high-quality performance demonstrated in practice. After skill mastery has been achieved, the cognitive strategy of pre-cuing can be introduced without interfering with carrying out the skill. Pre-cuing consists of observing or detecting a stimulus in the environment *before skill execution* that will enhance physical performance. It is well known, for instance, that a defensive lineman in football will look at the knuckles of his offensive opponent. If the offensive lineman's knuckles are white, this is interpreted as placing weight over the knuckles in anticipation of moving forward quickly—a running play. Red knuckles signal a forthcoming pass play because the offensive lineman's weight is back in anticipation of pass blocking. Detecting the offensive lineman's knuckle color represents a pre-cue. The main point, here, is that cognitive strategies are introduced in the later stages of the skill acquisition process.

Another example would be the use of visualization, also called mental practice or imagery, in which the learner mentally visualizes performing the skill intermittently during physical practice trials. The combined use of physical and mental practice has been shown to improve learning a sport skill better than using either strategy alone.

Sometimes a teacher or coach will introduce too many cognitive strategies at one time, thereby confusing the performer and inhibiting the learning process. Each strategy should be learned and executed flawlessly before a new strategy is introduced *unless* two or more cognitive strategies are very similar and/or are performed when executing the same skill or in close sequence. Pre-cuing and positive self-talk may be used in close proximity, and so can cueing (i.e., looking for environmental cues immediately after the play is initiated) and anticipation or pre-cuing and psyching-up. In summary, in the early stages of sport skill learning, the environment should remain stable/predictable and clear of interfering/distracting stimuli so that athletes may focus on mastery of movement mechanics and using performance-improving strategies.

For example, teaching a new skill to an athlete in the presence of other athletes might inhibit performance. Observers can be a distraction to athletes when being observed by others. Reminding athletes that a certain individual is watching them perform (e.g., "A scout from the Red Sox is watching our game today") is another source of poor performance. Knowing and informing athletes that they are being observed by others who are "important," such as a recruiter from a college or other elite level of competition raises anxiety and reduces concentration. Under these circumstances, sport skills are performed more poorly due, in part, to the athlete's increased anxiety.

One time, I observed a coach inform the team's best batter (who had a batting average over .350) that a major-league scout was attending "today's" game so the player had better perform well. Due to that distracting information, the player struck out four times in that game. The likely explanation for this poor performance was that the player was thinking and worrying too much, while not executing skills automatically. Coaches should attempt to reduce the amount of verbal instruction—verbalize the basics—and rely on visual stimuli (e.g., modeling, visualization, movement at reduced speed).

Post-practice tasks. This is the time to generate verbal, visual, and tactual sources of feedback to determine the extent to which practice has improved performance. It is also the time for assessing and critiquing performance outcomes and for planning future goals and tasks for continuing to perform better. What still needs work and what should remain as part of future expected performance quality? This is the time for coaches to both praise and criticize the athlete's mechanics, KP, and outcomes, KR. Here are some specific suggestions on delivering feedback:

1. *Avoid distractions.* Find an area—indoor or outdoor—that is void of distractions before delivering feedback to athletes. This is especially true with respect to other team members. The feedback session should be conducted with privacy, if possible. The one exception to this guideline is that several athletes can benefit from this particular area of instruction. Having a group feedback session with players for whom this information or area of practice would benefit results in lower player self-consciousness and less distraction. The intended recipient of instruction would focus and concentrate on the information.
2. *Avoid time delays.* Do not delay the time when to offer feedback. Schedule it in advance of the practice, if possible, and as soon as possible after KR has been offered. Coaches want to link performance with feedback with as little delay as possible. The period between receiving KR and the next practice trial is called the "delayed KR interval." This interval should be brief.
3. *Have direct eye contact with the player during instruction.* Eye contact increases the player's attention to important information. Similarly, speak directly to the athlete so that he or she hears you clearly. Do not talk away from them. I once observed a football coach facing the football blocking sled, and his players were behind him. They could not hear a word he was saying; I asked.
4. Combine different forms of feedback, linking verbal (e.g., "Rotate your hips when you swing"), visual (e.g., "See how the ball rolls off my fingertips when taking the shot?"), and tactual forms (e.g., "When kicking, follow through, that is, kick 'through' the ball; don't hold back when you contact the ball").

5. After providing the player with a summary of the feedback, have the player engage in several more trials of the to-be-performed task that incorporates the feedback. Be sure that sufficient practice trials are offered so that the skill is mastered and the practice session ends on a positive note.
6. Give the athlete verbal confirmation and recognition of improved performance with statements such as "It's looking better; nice effort," or "Your focus on the ball is improving. Develop a routine before the next serve/pitch/attempt by going through your mental checklist that we discussed."
7. Due to our limited capacity to take in and process information, it is important to communicate slowly and to keep your content relatively simple, at first, especially to the novice. Each concept or subskill should be practiced one at a time, especially if the skill is relatively complex and consists of several subskills. In many team ball skills, for instance, a sport skill may consist of being in the correct position, executing correct movement (e.g., run, walk, jump) in the proper sequence, observing the competitive environment (e.g., location of teammates and opponents), setting up strategies to execute offensive and defensive players, and listening for instructions given by the coach and teammates.
8. Have the athlete "teach" the skill or strategy to you—the coach—or to a teammate to ensure there is full understanding and mastery of the skill.
9. Follow up on the new (and, hopefully improved) skill at the next practice. Usually, mastering a new skill takes repeated attempts and additional coaching.
10. Include the team's nonstarters. There are numerous reasons that teaching new skills and strategies to nonstarters are advantageous to the team: (a) Remember that a nonstarter is only one injury away from starting status. (b) Also, the nonstarter has his or her own strengths that will be needed during the competition. (c) Nonstarters need the coaches' attention and will be

motivated to play to their potential if they see the coaches are investing time and effort into their development.

I have observed nonstarters sitting on the bench in a very relaxed and unmotivated posture. They "knew" they would not enter the competition if called on. They would not be mentally ready to compete and their skills were undeveloped. Their coach ignored them throughout the season. Developing the skills of nonstarters is an investment for a high-quality substitute if the situation requires.

11. *Avoid combining skill instruction with negative emotion.* Coaches become frustrated and angry like everyone else. While there are desirable ways to express anger (see chapter 4 on communication), it is imperative that coaches (and anyone else who teaches a sport skill or strategy) should not teach when angry. Athletes, like other learners, require full concentration and as few distractions as possible. Learning a sport skill or strategy requires psychological readiness to learn, react, and execute. Coach anger usually raises the athlete's sense of threat and worry. If the coach is upset, feelings should be expressed briefly, then take a deep breath, relax, and speak in the lowered voice.

In summary, it is essential that the coaches' instruction result in improved performance—both quality of mechanics and performance outcome—and that the athletes can identify positive results that show improved performance over a predetermined period of time. It is one thing for coaches to say "Nice swing" or "Your velocity is improving," but it is more impressive to say "Your free throw accuracy has improved 60%" or, "Your passing accuracy is an impressive 85%" or, "Your pitching speed is now improved to 85 miles per hour." The goal of every coach is to build an athlete's *perceived competence*, a strong characteristic of intrinsic motivation. Coaches want their athletes to maintain their motivation and to feel hopeful about further improvement. The motivation of your athletes will increase if at least one message they take from the instructional session is "I'm getting better" and "I feel good about my ability to compete."

Finally, coaches should keep the learning and teaching environment positive and not punitive. Learning a sport skill and improving performance should be an enjoyable experience. Athletes, who regularly confront failure with every performance attempt during competition, need positive feedback. An overcritical coach creates a poisoned learning environment and considerable anxiety among the athletes. This is not necessary nor desirable.

Balance critical feedback with positive statements. What are they doing right? What has been improved? What can they do successfully on a regular basis? Are the coaches' expectations of athletic performance realistic, or is the learning environment filled with impatience, criticism, perfectionism, and negativity? Is the coach a perfectionist, and if so, is that realistic? What does "competence" look like? Athletes of all skill levels have similar needs—their coaches' recognition and approval, which is a normal human need.

Fitts-Posner Three-Stage Model

One approach to describing differences between high- and low-skilled sports performers that has strong implications for coaches is Fitts and Posner's (1967) three-stage model. Though published many years ago, the model identifies that learning motor (sport) skills occurs in three stages: The cognitive stage (highly verbal), the associative stage, and the autonomous stage, respectively. One reason this model is important for coaches is to provide insights into the process of helping each athlete achieve and sustain stage 3, the autonomous stage.

In the *cognitive stage,* the athletes are relatively unskilled and engage in a considerable degree of thinking about proper movement technique, strategy, and self-talk. This is one reason that coaches want to *slow down the environment* early in learning new sport skills. Learners should be allowed to take the needed time to slowly learn new sport skills. Coach feedback on performance should not occur after every practice attempt. Time is needed to analyze movement properties of speed, timing, location, and precision during the early stages of learning. After subskills have been performed well with consistency, it's time for the next (associative) stage.

The associative stage focuses on proper practice conditions and the use of information feedback in mastering the skill. Learners address the tradeoff between speed and accuracy, whether the whole skill or just parts of the skill should be practiced. This is the time that considerable feedback—verbal, auditory, and tactual—is offered to achieve skill mastery.

The autonomous stage is the most advanced level and addresses performing skills with "regular" (required) speed and a minimal amount of conscious processing. This final stage reflects a well-learned skill that is performed "on automatic." It may involve some degree of planning prior to skill execution, but the skill is overlearned and executed in the virtual absence of thinking.

Coaches want to help athletes reach and maintain the third (autonomous) stage by having skills and strategies executed with a minimum amount of thinking—at least minimal *during* skill/strategy execution. This is accomplished by having athletes engage in multiple trials of the skill using game simulation conditions. In baseball, for example, many athletes warm up or practice without a hat or helmet. This is not the condition under which the athletes will perform the skills in game conditions. Football quarterbacks practice throws during pregame warm-ups, but, of course, wear their helmet during the game. Still, the quarterback is not practicing under game-like conditions and, therefore, is susceptible to performance failure when practicing without a helmet. They key issue, here, "game simulation," was discussed earlier.

Building and Teaching Confidence

Sport confidence is among the most important mental states for high-quality performance. Confidence can be taught. While there are many sources of confidence in sport, perhaps the most influential source is the athlete's coach. Coaches can—and should—play a central role in building the confidence of each competitor. Here are a few suggestions:

1. *Build sport skills.* Confidence comes, primarily, from exhibiting sport performance. Teach athletes new skills and strategies.
2. *Provide ample positive feedback.* Look for reasons to offer compliments that recognize the athlete's effort, performance quality, and outcomes.
3. *Reflect on previous successes.* All athletes have a history of quality sport performance. If you have self-doubts about the present situation, reflect on those past successes, even if they occurred in practice.
4. *Teach the proper use of cognitive strategies.* Mental techniques such as positive self-talk, mental imagery, thought stopping, and others contribute to building confidence. Thought stopping, for instance, serves to prevent athletes from engaging in negative self-talk, a response that should not be allowed.
5. Interpret—or reinterpret—anxiety as a sign of enthusiasm, readiness, and the proper arousal level, not to feel fear and avoid challenges. Essentially all quality athletes feel anxious before the competition. It is the interpretation and management of this feeling that separates highly successful from less successful competitors. Rather than "pretending" that anxiety does not exist, interpret these feelings of worry and threat as a positive sign, a display of readiness and confidence.
6. *Practice under game simulation conditions for optimal readiness.* Nothing builds self-confidence like good preparation. Practice hard under game-like conditions.
7. *Have fun.* One of the most effective pregame thoughts an athlete can have, especially prior to high-pressure competitions or in tense situations, is the thought of enjoying the competitive experience—having fun. I've seen athletes play their best games against their most superior opponents when their coach reminded them to "go out there and have some fun." While

humor is not always appreciated by many coaches, especially when providing instruction and the athletes must be fully engaged on the task at hand, at appropriate times, humor relaxes and distracts the athlete away from unpleasant thoughts.
8. *Know your opponent's strengths and weaknesses.* Fear, intimidation, and threat about the *perceived* superiority of opponents is a major obstacle to self-confidence. All opposing players and teams have weaknesses. Athletes should know them, and through their competition plan, exploit them.
9. *Combine game simulation with vigorous physical training.* In general, athletes should practice under game-like conditions, train year round and be in excellent physical condition.

Measuring sport confidence. Here are a few questions that allows the coach to measure an athlete's level of confidence. If the athlete has a confidence problem the coach can help improve this area of thinking. Use a scale ranging from 1 (very low) to 5 (very high).

1. How confident are you before you compete in most games?
2. How confident are you that you will win the next game the day before you compete?
3. How confident are you when you feel the pressure to win?
4. How much pressure do you feel to win based on statements coming from your coach?
5. How confident do you feel of performing successfully against your next opponent?
6. How confident are you to succeed in changing your strategy after the competition has begun?
7. How confident are you to bounce back after experiencing failure either in the game or in your next game?

Expectations for success. One reason for upsets in sport is that the more successful teams—athletes who are expected to win easily—do not perceive their opponents as threatening to their continued success. Their expectation of success is too high and the amount of effort they give is too low. Success expectations and athletes' motive to achieve are influenced by athletes' perceived ability of their opponents. In many cases, low expectations of success become self-fulfilling prophecies. In the opposite direction, high-quality athletes have a very high expectation of success: They expect to win—and they often do.

There are some sample questions to ascertain an athlete's expectation to succeed and other anticipated outcomes. There is no right or wrong answer; however, coaches may want to have individual conferences with athletes who score very low on these items in terms of future expectations for success.

On a scale of 1 (*very low*) to 10 (*very high*) answer the following questions, with 50 points the maximum total score

    a. How certain are you that you will beat your opponent?
    b. How certain are you that you will perform at a very high level today?
    c. How strongly do you feel the team will perform today?
    d. How strongly do you anticipate you will win today?
    e. How high are your expectations to perform successfully today?

Mental toughness. This is a disposition, not a personality trait, and it is not inherited; it's learned. Mental toughness is defined as reaching and sustaining high performance under pressure by expanding capacity physically, mentally, and emotionally. Mentally tough competitors are self-motivated and self-directed; their energy comes from internal sources; it is not forced from the outside. Mentally tough athletes are in control of their emotions. They cope effectively in response to frustration and disappointment, and they remain calm and relaxed under fire. Rather than avoiding pressure, they are challenged by it. They are capable of long and intensive periods of full concentration and have a strong belief in their ability to perform well.

Building Mental Toughness

Thoughts, dispositions, and tendencies of mentally tough athletes. These are high self-esteem, commitment, self-discipline, a strong desire to succeed, personal accountability (i.e., feels responsible for performance outcomes), competitive, high but realistic self-expectations, no (or minimal) fear of failure, high goal orientation (i.e., motivated by and places great value on setting and meeting goals), and hardiness/resourcefulness (i.e., able to deal with adversity; good coping skills).

Thoughts and actions of mentally tough athletes. They mentally plan (pregame and game) the competition demands and skills; maintain emotional control; have optimal mental arousal for any given task and situation, high confidence, strong feelings of competence, optimism, controlled (managed) anxiety, concentration and attentional control (alert and mentally focused); perform most skills automatically; use proper situational appraisals (having thoughts of being challenged, not threatened); have good coping skills (i.e., deal effectively with sudden or chronic adversity); project a positive attitude (positive body language); and feel enjoyment in the competitive setting.

Sample pre-competition mental skills checklist

This can either be completed by the athlete or completed jointly by athlete and his or her coach for comparative purposes:

On a scale ranging from 1 (very low) to 5 (very high) rate the following, with 25 points as the maximum total score:

1. I have qualities that set me apart from other competitors.
2. I am committed to completing the tasks I have to do.
3. I calm down and plan my next strategy when things do not go my way.
4. I confront sources of pressure rather than become a victim and fall apart.
5. I know my strengths and weaknesses and use that information to win.

Ability to regulate (cope with) acute and chronic stress. The ability to remain calm under situations of tension and stress is one quality of elite athletes. The key strategy in competitive sport is not to eliminate stress, but to regulate it by using proper coping techniques. This regulation process is called coping.

Coping has been classified in the sport psychology literature as "approach" (i.e., physically or mentally confronting the source of stress; actively dealing with it for the purpose of reducing its intensity or removing it) and "avoidance" (i.e., mentally or physically escaping the source of stress so that it becomes dismissed, irrelevant, or quickly forgotten). Elite, better-skilled athletes are more capable and likely to employ avoidance than approach coping to maintain attentional focus and to get past the unpleasant event.

Coaches should be careful not to overreact to an athlete's mistakes, thereby creating additional stress for the athlete. Competitors may (improperly) concentrate on not making further errors rather than on focusing their attention of the proper environmental cues and emotions.

**Sample questions for determining an
athletes' use of coping strategies:**

Think of a time—called a stressor—when you felt high stress intensity. What was your coping strategy following this stressful experience?

Reactions may include the following:
- Kept on task
- Ignored the situation and concentrated on the next task
- Physically confronted the source of stress
- Did not take the situation too seriously
- Became increasingly intense and felt the need for revenge
- Became upset but kept going

- Got into an argument
- Other _____

2. Think of a second stressor of high intensity. How did you cope with it? _____

Fear of failure (FOF). Most high achievers, including skilled athletes, possess a disposition called fear of failure (FOF). FOF, also referred to as the motive to avoid failure, is also defined as a disposition to avoid failure and/or a capacity for experiencing shame or humiliation as a consequence of failure. FOF is the belief that attaining desired goals is not likely. In addition, failure is associated with social and familial rejection, an expectation of punishment, and a sense of reduced social value. Athletes who suffer from FOF do not believe that they will attain desired goals. Sadly, athletes with high FOF are likely to promote failure by avoiding training and preparation. This self-destructive thought process helps ensure their failure and reinforce their belief system, a self-fulfilling prophecy of future failure.

Researchers and practitioners tend to view FOF as a form of performance anxiety, which has implications for coaching athletes. Failure provokes fear to the extent that its consequences are perceived as aversive. FOF is related to low levels of optimism, high levels of worry, somatic (physiological) sport anxiety, and disruptive thoughts. Thus, FOF is more likely for athletes whose self-esteem is dependent on successful sport performance and/or successful outcomes (e.g., winning and other desirable performance results).

For instance, when young children fail or lose in competitive situations, adults may respond in ways that have negative emotional and psychological consequences. Following failure, the child begins to expect a negative evaluation. Even professional and Olympic athletes have this psychological disposition. Most are able to control it. Less effective performers feel, perhaps subconsciously, "If I don't try, I can't fail." This is the worst possible result from FOF because it often leads to quitting sport. The athlete may decide to withdraw from the competitive situation, either physically by quitting the team or mentally by reducing the effort needed to compete at the level of his or her capability.

Coaches and parents need to define success and failure broadly. Success in sport is more than winning and losing. Even when an athlete or a team loses a competition, an individual athlete, or the entire team, may have performed successfully, even good enough to win. One's definition of failure should be restricted to specific events or unmet goals, such as missing a particular basketball free throw or failing to break a personal record in track.

Think of three questions that an athlete can be asked that indicates the degree of FOF. Place each question on a scale ranging from 1 (very low) to 5 (very high). What can the coach conclude concerning the responding athlete's FOF?

Fear of success (FOS). Do athletes, whose prime objective in sport is to be successful, actually fear achieving that success? Perhaps. Attempts to consciously or, more likely, subconsciously, undermine future success may be due to a psychological characteristic called fear of success (FOS). According to clinical sport psychologists, there are five syndromes that may explain the development of FOS.

1. Athletes' fear social and emotional isolation that accompanies success. An athlete may feel that performing at a level far superior to that of teammates or peers will result in social discomfort, even ostracism.
2. Athletes feel guilt from self-assertion in competition. Some athletes are uncomfortable about exhibiting aggressive behavior, especially at the "expense" of an opponent's physical and/or mental well-being. These athletes would likely score low on any measure of competitiveness.
3. Athletes protect themselves from competition because they fear discovering their true potential. Thus, fears about succeeding are derived from fearing failure: FOS and FOF are two sides of

the same coin. Why should this athlete even engage in competition? Perhaps they shouldn't. Withdrawing from competition is a defense against this fear.
4. Some athletes might be intimidated or anxious by breaking a record previously held by a highly respected or admired athlete. They may also feel that others (fans, teammates, coaches, and media) may also resent the broken record.
5. Some athletes prefer not to deal with the pressure to constantly match or exceed their previous best performance. This expectation is exacerbated by the media who regularly critique each athlete's performance. Trying to live up to the expectations of fans and the media can place an extensive amount of pressure on athletes to reach or exceed their previous best performance. Failing to achieve this standard may be perceived as disappointing or even as performance failure.

In a personal interview (Anshel, 1986), the late Charlie Lau, a well-known major league batting coach, said that a fear of performing well is one reason why many hitters with major league skills do not become consistently successful at hitting. Incredible as this may sound to some people, Lau cited anecdotal evidence from his personal experiences—over 25 years at the (baseball) major league and triple-A levels—that some athletes are fearful of living up to the expectations of others after they have demonstrated competent performance. They feel too much pressure to maintain high standards and are not able to deal with criticism from others, notably the media and fans, after performing below previous achievements. So, what happens? They retain their mediocrity as athletes, sometimes subconsciously. For them, this is a safer, less risky approach.

Think of three questions that coaches may ask their athletes (in private and confidentially) that measure FOS on a scale ranging from 1 (very low) to 5 (very high)? What do these answers tell a coach about the athlete's FOS level?

The 10 "Commandments" of Effective Communication in Sport

Clearly, effective communication is a necessary part of quality coaching. Based on my observations of coaches and discussions with athletes as a sport psychology consultant and researcher, over the years I have formulated a set of "do's and don't's" in this area—what I call the 10 "commandments" of effective communication in sport (Anshel, 1987). The term "commandments" is a metaphor to mean "essential components" or "very important guidelines" for being able to accomplish a very difficult goal—to change the feelings, emotions, and behaviors of individuals and groups (teams) for the purpose of experiencing a winning outcome. These guidelines reflect the skills and habits of talented and effective leaders in sport and other areas that require sustained, high-quality human performance.

Effective communication consists essentially of 10 guidelines. These recommendations are so important in the process of affecting athletes' attitudes, feelings, and behaviors that I refer to them as "required" practices for effective communication. They are (a) be honest; (b) do not be defensive; (c) be consistent day to day; (d) be empathetic, (e) avoid sarcasm; (f) praise and criticize behavior, not personality or character; (g) respect the integrity of others; (h) use positive nonverbal cues; (i) teach skills; and (j) treat all team members consistently when enforcing team rules and policies.

I. Be Honest

If coaches are to be effective, they must have credibility to be taken seriously by others. Dishonesty destroys credibility. Being untruthful may also occur by accident. For example, a coach may make a promise to an athlete (e.g., "You'll get in the game if 'player x' is injured or we have a comfortable lead") that later cannot be kept due to a game situation or is simply forgotten. Athletes may perceive this inconsistency as dishonest or deceitful.

Examples of inconsistent or dishonest coaching

A. Nancy was the starting catcher on her high school softball team. She started the season batting fifth, but after 10 games her hitting fell off. She was leaving too many players on base and not batting in runs, stranding too many runners. The coach moved her into the ninth batting position. The coach, trying to justify this decision, told Nancy that he (the coach) wanted more power at the end of the line-up. No one had to tell Nancy that the reason she batted last in the order was her poor batting. The coach was not being truthful. The coach could have told Nancy that together they would try to work out of her slump and that he was moving Nancy lower in the order to take some pressure off or that they would improve her hitting mechanics and then he could return her to the fifth spot. Her confidence faltered and she almost quit the team.

B. Jon, a linebacker on a university (U.S.) football team, sustained an injury after tackling an opponent. He left the game and did not return. His injury required missing three games. He was replaced by a teammate who had similar football (linebacker) skills but was not the team's starter. Jon's coach told him that he would return to starting status as soon as he obtained medical clearance. Jon was ready to play in the fourth game, but his replacement was playing well. The coach told Jon that he would resume playing as the starting linebacker if the substitute player made mistakes and needed to be replaced. No plan to return to the linebacker position was offered nor was there any verbal contact between Jon and his coach about changing Jon's playing status. Instead, Jon played exclusively on the special teams (i.e., punting, kickoffs). Jon was so heartbroken that a few days after the season ended, he informed the coach that he was quitting the team to play football at another school. The team lost a talented athlete with potential to be among the best players on this team.

Abusive honesty. Sometimes a coach, or anyone in a leadership/managerial position, can be *too* honest and hurt an athlete's self-esteem and confidence. When the school member of the track and field team asked his coach to assess his jumping technique and how much further he must jump to compete in the track meet, his coach said the following:

> "Well, to be perfectly honest with you, Frank, I think you're about as good as you are going to get. I doubt you'll ever be as good as Ed. He jumps further than you and I do not see that changing. He's the better jumper. So, if I were you, I'd forget about starting and just be happy to fill in when we need you. Injuries do happen and we need someone to compete to replace injured participants." Frank was devastated by his coach's words and quit the track and field team two weeks later.

Why is this form of communication by the track and field coach destructive? When can honesty be taken too far? *The coach's role is not to predict an athlete's future level of performance, especially if the forecast is a pessimistic one.* I call it "playing God." Good coaches, truly effective coaches, include a heavy dose of skill and strategy instruction to teach skills to athletes and to promote performance improvement.

Coaches, parents, and everyone else should avoid predicting any athlete's future or potential in sport because it is difficult to know to what degree an athlete will develop, grow, and improve. No one can predict the future about the athlete's growth and development (see Anshel & Lidor, 2012, for a review of talent identification literature). If all signs lead to the conclusion that this sport participant will never break into the starting line-up, never make it to the pros, coaches should not feel obligated to break the news. Voltaire said, "Truth is a fruit which should not be plucked until it is ripe." Honesty is necessary if the coach is to be credible (i.e., believable) and if he or she wishes to gain the athlete's loyalty. However, honesty is also a matter of timing and tact. In the words of the French philosopher Marquis, "Honesty is a good thing, but it is not profitable to its possessor unless it is kept under control."

II. Do Not Be Defensive

Defensive individuals are persons (a) who feel the need to explain the reasons something did not turn out successfully but not take personal responsibility for the undesirable outcome; (b) who need to "be right" where everyone else is wrong,: (c) who need to justify their decisions and actions, however "good" or "bad," and (d) who feel threatened by individuals who have a difference of opinion about a given situation. A person demonstrating a defensive posture, for example, will rarely admit to making a mistake, will contend his or her strategy or his or her action was the correct one, even if it lead to failure, and rarely demonstrate contrition if he or she is proven wrong. In other words, defensive individuals are often too insecure—or arrogant—to admit fault because it threatens their self-esteem and creates a sense of uncertainty about "being right." In fact, often, a defensive person will be too insecure to even solicit the views of others, or ignore those views that differ from his or her own. For these reasons, defensive individuals do not grow intellectually nor learn from mistakes because they "know all the answers."

Instead of feeling the need to be right and to know more than anyone else, that is, to repress the insights of others who have valuable past experience, the head coach should encourage participation of analyzing the issue at hand. Be receptive to the opinions of others. Instead of cutting off and preventing subordinates from lending their views in trying to explain—or prevent—a problem, coaches should encourage subordinates (e.g., assistant coaches, athletes, colleagues, sport psychologist) to provide feedback, suggest new ideas, or make changes to the current operation. Coaches must reveal their receptivity and appreciation to feedback.

III. Be Consistent

Trusting others requires knowing that they will be consistent and positive during a given interaction. They will be the "same person" each day; there will be no betrayal about how they will respond to your feelings, needs, and requests. The coach demonstrates consistency from day to day. For example, Fred, a college tennis player, was speaking with his tennis coach about the use of certain strategies against his next opponent. The conversation ended as the coach told Fred to see him anytime he had any questions or concerns related to tennis or anything else. Fred felt great, having a sense of closeness, mutual respect, and trust toward his coach. Then two days later after practice, Fred asked the coach to look at a few of his serves with which he was having some difficulty that day. To Fred's complete surprise (and disappointment), his coach retorted, "After the practice you had today, young man, you need to work on much more than your serve." Fred was devastated. Where was the coach with whom he had such close rapport, respect, and trust just two days earlier—and before that? Fred felt betrayed and did not feel comfortable approaching his coach for any reason for the rest of the season. Fred kept his concerns about his tennis game to himself and maintained an emotional distance from his coach.

The confidence, trust, and security that athletes feel toward their coach can be destroyed by inconsistency, demonstrating various behavioral patterns on different days. If the coaches' actions toward their athletes are unpredictable, most often they will choose to ignore the coach altogether to the detriment of receiving proper skill instruction and performance feedback. An important objective of coaches who are truly interested in fostering communication is to be consistent in the manner in which they come across. If coaches invite their athletes to visit them in their office yet close the door on them (literally or attitudinally) when they arrive, or greet an athlete on Monday then choose to ignore the same person on Tuesday, they are giving mixed messages.

Here are a few guidelines for showing consistency in coaching:

1. Avoid letting an opportunity pass to say a kind and encouraging word to or about someone. Praise good athletic performance.
2. Always recognize the greetings of others. Saying "Hi" with a smile or wave, and addressing the athlete by his or her first name, will help establish your reputation as a good, considerate person. Athletes will avoid contact with a coach who demonstrates extreme and sudden mood swings.
3. If you have an open-door policy for your athletes and assistants, show that you are sincere about it. Gil visited his coach during the office hours that were designated for athletes. Upon Gil's arrival, the coach looked up from his notepad with a look of annoyance and said, "Yeah, what can I do for you, son?" Gil was turned off immediately. "Sorry to bother you, Coach," he said. "See you later at practice. Bye!" Gil never felt comfortable about visiting his coach again. The coach should restate his or her sincerity about having an open-door policy. Make an appointment to meet with the athlete again, soon.

IV. Be Empathetic

How many times have you heard the phrase, "How would you feel if . . . ?" Well, how would it feel for anyone to be ignored, deceived, rejected, blamed, teased, and teased? Inversely, how does it feel to be recognized, praised, accepted, applauded, depended on, popular, and admired? The answers are obvious, aren't they? Yet, some people in power abuse their position of control by showing disrespect to those in less powerful positions. The ability to place oneself "in the shoes" of another person is referred to as *empathy*. The ability to both understand and respond to the feelings of others is a characteristic that will pay the coach many dividends. Sadly, this personality trait is often missing from the repertoire of techniques and strategies used by individuals in power (e.g., coaches, managers, supervisors).

The print media reported that an angry parent confronted his son's baseball coach in an angry manner about his son's lack of playing time. The coach did not respond with a sense of urgency or importance. Instead of taking the parent's complaint seriously, he dismissed the parent's concerns and told the parent to contact him at another time to discuss the matter. What was lacking in the coach was a sense of empathy toward the parent's feelings. Communication is always more effective if the person who has more decision-making power in the given situation (i.e., the coach, in this case) shows empathy toward the less powerful person's emotions and statements (Ginott, 1965, 1969). A reaction such as, "I can understand how you feel" or "I'm happy to discuss the matter with you, but let's meet privately at another time when I can devote more attention to this matter" would likely have reduced the tension created by the parent's deep frustration which, no doubt, had been building for days or even weeks.

Effective coaches remember how they felt when their feelings were hurt as athletes. The secure team leader says, "I don't want these athletes to be hurt and suffer the way I did as an athlete." Ineffective (insecure) coaches say, "If it was good enough for me, it's good enough for them." Was it really "good enough" then? Could it ever feel "good" to be upset and feel powerless toward changing the present situation?

Finally, as Pennsylvania State University sport psychologist, Dr. David Yukelson (2010), says, "[T]o truly understand or comprehend another individual's perspective, people need to be adept at the art of listening" (p. 151). Yukelson also claims that "the foundation for effective communication skills is having credibility in the eyes of their athletes, and having developed trust and respectful relationships" (p. 152). This process creates and maintains the coach's credibility. To Yukelson, "credibility is reflected in the athletes' attitudes about the trustworthiness of what you—the coach—say and do" (p. 152).

V. Avoid Sarcasm

Webster's Dictionary (1984 defines "sarcasm" as "a taunting or caustic (i.e., biting) remark" (p. 529). Psychiatrist, Dr. Haim Ginott (1969), calls sarcasm "a sound barrier to learning—a serious mental hazard" (p. 67). Sarcasm, according to Ginott, "erects sound barriers for effective communication" (p. 67). Coaches who use sarcasm ("Nice play, rubber hands") do not usually win games, partly because they erect a sound barrier to effective communication with their athletes. Sarcasm, if used repeatedly, destroys their athletes' self-confidence and self-esteem. An athlete who is physically fatigued should not be called "lazy." A participant who asks a question about the team strategy must never be labeled "brainless."

Here is a true example. Coach Fred was observing his team run through several trials of a new play on a university football team. He turned to his left and saw the team punter talking with a female student. "Hey, Lance," he yelled within earshot of several team members, "if you want to fool around with the ladies, do it on your own time. Pay attention to what we're doing on the field. Maybe you'll learn something." Lance was embarrassed by the coach's words, of course. Several players and other observers were also embarrassed for him, as was the lady with whom he was talking. There was no inappropriate behavior. The coach, in the meantime, lost the respect of this athlete and diminished any chance of establishing a strong and trusting communication link for the future.

Here is another example of the destructive effects of sarcasm in coaching. Fran was running wind sprints with her softball teammates. Suddenly, she felt a sharp pain in her side and could not continue. "What's wrong, Fran, you out of shape?" the coach bellowed. "Too many pizzas, huh?" This sarcastic response from the coach angered the athlete because she was in pain and was not trying to remove herself from the drill. Fran, in fact, was in very good condition. Further, Fran perceived from the coach's remarks that her discomfort was not being taken seriously. "Perhaps she was faking," the coach might be thinking. In any case, sarcasm diminishes the chance for building mutual respect and constructive dialogue between athlete and coach.

The unpleasant consequences of sarcasm are exacerbated if the coach uses sarcasm to the player in the presence of other team members. That's a sin in the eyes of an athlete that is almost unforgivable and certainly unforgettable. Two primary guidelines about the use of sarcasm are helpful. First, coaches, parents, and officials should avoid making sarcastic remarks at all times, even when the intent is humor (called *gallows humor* in Ginott, 1965). Such statements are never humorous, whether or not nervous laughter follows the statement. In fact, the targeted person's laughter after a sarcastic statement usually serves as a defense against embarrassment. Laughter in this context is almost never genuine.

The second guideline is to use statements that convey sincerity. After observing a player fall and scrape her knees on the floor, the coach should simply ask the player if she is all right or initiate first aid procedures. The coach should not laugh and say, "Hey, nice balance" or make some other remark that would embarrass the athlete. In another example, after a coach explains the strategy for the second half, a player may ask the coach to repeat something. The coach should wisely comply, rewording his or her original statements so that the athlete is certain of the strategies. The coach should not say, "What's wrong, Al, I just explained our strategy. Weren't you listening?" Sincerity says, "I care about you," and it is inherent in effective communication. Sarcasm says, "I don't respect you."

VI. Praise and Criticize Behavior, Not Personality

It's not surprising that leaders in any area of performance need to be positive to get the best out of group members. This is particularly important in sport with respect to influencing the thoughts, emotions, and behaviors of athletes. One would think that any form of positive feedback is a good thing. And, yet, sometimes both praising and criticizing athletes can be ineffective, even counterproductive. There is, in fact, a right way and a wrong way to praising and criticizing the performance of others. One of the most common and counterproductive errors in providing others with praise and criticism is to address the person's character or personality, not his or her performance Ginott (1965, 1969).

Praising and criticizing character or personality is never constructive. This is because it offers listeners no information and, therefore, does not allow them to make a realistic judgment about their actions. Yet this is often the most common form of feedback that coaches give athletes.

The correct use of praise. The proper use of praise is challenging to most of us—especially teachers, parents, and coaches, each of whom is placed in the position of instructor and critic. In addition, we—as a culture—don't offer praise as often as we should, and when we do, often it is based on over-the-top emotions of excitement and happiness.

The soccer coach was very pleased about Susan's defensive skills in a recent game. Certainly, praise was in order, but it was not of a personal nature. The coach avoided saying, "Susan, you're a wonderful athlete." Instead, the coach described what Susan had accomplished: "I liked the way you stayed with your opponent. You prevented her from scoring at her average. Nice going."

There are two types of praise that should be avoided. The first type is called *personality-based praise*. Praising the athlete's character or personality ("You are a great guy/girl," "What a good team player you are") is vague and abstract and may not be compatible with the athlete's personal view. Such statements may even be perceived by the player as insincere. Praising personality tells sport performers that they are accepted and liked only when they act in accordance with the expectations of others but are not deserving of such recognition when they don't. These expectations may be very difficult for the player to meet.

Another reason statements that praise character are best avoided is because they create dependence on the coach for approval. The athlete might conclude, "If the coach says I'm good (or the best), then he (she) likes me." Inversely, if the coach does not give the athlete similar praise on a given day, the competitor might feel differently about the coach: "I guess the coach doesn't like me today." This is often what happens when praise becomes personally based rather than behaviorally based. Personal feelings about an athlete should not be based on the person's sport skills; this disrupts team unity.

The second type of praise that should be avoided is called *judgmental praise*. Telling athletes that they (a) are "the best," (b) played a great game, (c) are better than someone else, or (d) did a "super" job might make an athlete feel good for the moment, but such statements fail to reinforce the *behaviors* (performance) that were responsible for the desirable outcomes. Judgmental praise may create anxiety and evoke defensiveness. It does not lead to the athlete's sense of self-reliance, self-direction, or self-control. Applauding the athlete's efforts with superlatives such as "great" or "the best" brings on feelings of discomfort, especially for younger competitors. The athlete gains little understanding about what he or she did to deserve such a comment. Praise of this nature also *may* be incompatible with the athlete's self-image or perception of the situation. Ginott (1965) suggests, "Avoid praise that attaches adjectives to [an athlete's] character" (p. 106). He further states that avoiding praise that judges character or evaluates personality allows the person (athlete) to feel more secure in making mistakes and taking risks without fear. This, in turn, raises self-confidence.

The cardinal rules of praising are (a) describe without evaluating; (b) report, do not judge; and (c) let athletes evaluate themselves.

Is it possible to be "too honest?" Yes, it is. If you feel an athlete does not have what it takes to become a top-level athlete, or at least to meet performance expectations at a particular position, be *very* careful about being over judgmental and attempting to predict the athlete's future. Sometimes athletes need time, instruction/coaching, confidence, less anxiety, and other factors that can be learned and nurtured and that will significantly improve performance. On the other hand, if a coach is relatively certain that the athlete is better off going in another direction, perhaps playing another position or even switching sports, then perhaps the coach can meet with the athlete in private and discuss the situation. Coaches will also want to be open with the athlete's parents if they seek a meeting with the coach. This is not the time to ignore an open and honest conversation with all parties, especially if the athlete will be devastated by the coach's decision. Coaches must be sure to provide specific, behavioral examples of the athlete's actions that have led to this conclusion.

Constructive criticism. Sadly, we criticize others based on the words used with us as children, words used by our parents, coaches, teachers, and friends. We, in turn, use similar messages in the way we criticize others. But rather than offer feedback, too often the goal is to hurt the feelings of another person, and we succeed in this goal frequently.

In coaching, criticism is often used to give feedback on performance or to express anger or frustration. It isn't that criticism is so bad in itself, but rather that the manner in which it is communicated can have negative ramifications. Most critical remarks bring on anger, resentment, and a desire for revenge. When an athlete is criticized, particularly if the criticism is constant, he or she learns to condemn himself or herself and to find fault with others.

Janice, a high school volleyball player, hit a spike stroke out of bounds, resulting in victory for the other team. The outraged coach reacted, "What the hell did you do that for, Janice? What a dumb mistake. If you can't hit the ball where you're supposed to, get off the court." The player's feelings were terribly hurt. This form of criticism condemned Janice's attempt to risk an offensive shot that could (and often does) score a point. In the future, she may well concentrate on merely returning the ball in bounds with a weaker, less risky shot. But winners are risk takers. Chronic criticism reduces risk-taking behaviors in sport.

Some words are so damaging to the listener that perhaps they should be deleted from vocabularies of all human language. Words such as "stupid, dumb, fool, idiot," and "jerk" serve one purpose—to hurt the feelings and lower the self-image of others. They are terms that say nothing about the inappropriate behavior of the person but instead focus on degrading the individual's character and personality. They never serve the purpose of offering information. As Ginott (1969) suggests, "When a person is drowning, it is not a good time to teach him to swim, or to ask him questions, or to criticize his performance. It is time for help."

VII. Respect the Integrity of Others

The 18th-century German philosopher Johann Friedrich Herbart once said, "He that respects not is not respected." To be an effective communicator, the coach must show respect when interacting with the players. Respect is not a sign of weakness or a shift in control and power. It entails an awareness of the athlete as a unique and distinct individual whose opinions, feelings, privacy, maturity, and unique skills are to be recognized and appreciated. Dishonesty and a lack of communication are examples of disrespectful ways of relating to others. Respecting the integrity of each athlete develops loyalty toward the coach and the desire to support team goals. To use a cliché, "all hands are on deck" in supporting the team's—and the coach's—mission.

Expressing anger. Anger is a fact of life. Anger is used to "release" strong emotional feelings and tension, and this venting of feelings might, surprisingly, relax the person. Of course, many coaches use anger as a way to arouse, motivate, or condemn. Does it work? It depends. There is a right way and a wrong way to use and express anger.

Typically, anger is based on irrational statements and behaviors. The angry coach will insult, "hit below the belt," fly into a rampage, swear, and perhaps (albeit very rarely) physically strike at the source of his or her irritation; interestingly, corporal punishment—striking an athlete—is actually allowed and common in many Asian countries (based on my direct observations and conversations with Asian coaches in their respective home countries).

Anger does have its time and place. In fact, failure to express anger at certain times during practice or a game would convey to the athlete indifference. In one example of using anger effectively, a coach was meeting with his basketball team at halftime. His team was not using the defensive patterns that they had practiced during the week. He was genuinely angry that the athletes seemed to forget what they had spent hours practicing in preparation for the game. The coach told them, in no uncertain terms, the following in this order:

1. The specific performances that he had observed so that the athletes were made aware of the same situations and events as the coach
2. What he had observed during the first half of play that was contrary to what they had practiced
3. His feelings of anger and frustration about the incongruence between what the team must do on defense to win and what it had been doing in the first half
4. What the team had practiced in preparation for this game and how these plays related strongly to the necessary strategy during the game
5. What the team had to do to counter the opponent's offense—position by position.

The coach did two things that made his halftime talk effective. First, his anger (which, by the way, was justified) was directed at specific behaviors of the athletes. He engaged in no name calling and no hollering just for effect.

The second effective strategy used by the coach occurred after his expressions of anger. He told the athletes of his confidence in their ability to perform according to the plans. "I know you men can do it because I saw you do it beautifully this week in practice," he asserted.

The players felt more confident leaving the locker room. The coach's anger was expressed before he offered instruction and was not the last message he verbalized before the team left the locker room. Had the coach's message ended on a down note—that the players were doing a terrible job and had no business being out on the court or winning the game—the team would have been undermotivated, less confident, and more forgetful of the instruction.

Guidelines for the constructive use of anger are as follows:

- It's fine for the coach to express angry feelings provided the athlete's character and personality are not attacked. Sarcasm, name calling, use of destructive adjectives, and physical abuse are never appropriate.

- The first step in handling emotional upheaval is to identify feelings verbally by name. "I am annoyed with you. I am very, very upset. I'm furious." Sometimes the mere statement of feelings changes behavior, according to Ginott (1965). Most athletes fully realize the rationale behind the coach's angry emotions.

- The next step, not always necessary, is to give the reason for one's anger by stating inner thoughts and wishful actions.

For effective communication, the integrity of all individuals must be respected. Even in a state of anger, the coach must appear sensitive, informative, intelligent, and emotionally mature.

VIII. Use Positive Nonverbal Cues

Over the years, there have been some great coaches in sport who would say relatively little to their athletes. Nonetheless, they were inspiring and produced a tremendous sense of player loyalty. How could this be? In many cases, the coaches with relatively poor verbal skills were able to communicate nonverbally and, thus, could produce in their players the desired psychological benefits and performance outcomes.

Touching behavior. In recent years there has been considerable media attention to instances in which coaches, athletic trainers, and even team physicians have been accused of sexual harassment. While complete descriptions and media stories go beyond the scope of this chapter, all team staff (i.e., nonathletes) should be very cautious before touching an athlete. Patting someone on the back or placing an arm around a player's shoulders is usually harmless and nonsexual. Unless complete trust between coach and athlete has been firmly established, it is best for coaches to "proceed with caution." And, yet, touching conveys one of the most sensitive, caring, and trusting messages that two people can communicate—nonverbally—to one another. Sadly, touching can convey the wrong message or be misunderstood by the person who is touched.

Coaches must use common sense about when, how, and where to make physical contact with an athlete—if at all. Touching may convey good feelings toward the other person, but it also must be accompanied by deep trust. Trust takes time to build. Common sense should prevail, but when in doubt, it is better to refrain from an action that may be misinterpreted. Therefore, most clinical and school psychologists agree it's best that coaches and teachers (i.e., individuals in authority positions) avoid physical contact, however well intended, with athletes and students.

Eye contact. The tendency to look the intended listener in the eye makes a different impact on the sincerity and intensity of the message than speaking to, while simultaneously looking away from, the person. Of course, eye contact can be a glance, a glare, or a gaze, each denoting a different message.

For example, *the coach should not raise his or her voice in an angry manner when giving information to the athletes.* The participant will become conscious of the coach's angry feelings and, either intentionally or more often unintentionally, will filter out the coach's message. Anger and providing information should be separated if the information is intended to be remembered. The player concentrates on and remembers more of the message when it is communicated calmly than when it is communicated in a highly aroused manner. The key issue is to make the best use of nonverbal communication through positive rather than negative channels.

IX. Teach Skills

Good coaches are good teachers. Teaching sport skills and strategies is a science referred to in the literature as sport pedagogy (Anshel et al. 1991a). Techniques for teaching skilled athletes differs from instructing novice athletes, but less than one would think. Basic guidelines of effective instructional techniques must be applied if skills are to be learned, remembered, and applied in a game situation (see Anshel 1990d, 1990e). Some of these techniques include the following:

- *Having a goal.* Communicating the goal of the instructional session (what the athlete has to be able to demonstrate)

- *Learning by imitation.* Modeling the skill in correct form so that a visual representation of the skill is used by the athlete during practice to compare his or her performance with that of the "perfect" model

- *Eliminating information overload.* Reducing the amount of information taught at one time, then allowing time for athletes to mentally rehearse, plan, and review their performance. Highly skilled athletes can learn and remember skills with which they are familiar better than the novice can, of course. But information overload is still possible when new information is transmitted, especially in verbal form

- *Simulating game conditions in practice.* Allowing skills and strategies to be learned in practice before they are used in a game, a concept referred to as game simulation. It is necessary to allow for numerous repetitions to improve retention of the information or skill. Due to the athlete's psychological state during competition, entailing anxiety and high arousal, teaching new skills should not be attempted during the game, although changing game strategy using similar skills remains an option

- *Giving learners feedback on their performance.* Informing the athlete as to which skills are or are not being performed correctly is more than a matter of shouting, "Nice catch, Jack." The timing of such feedback, its content, the manner in which it is communicated, and allowance for repetition of the skill are just a few of the considerations that need to be applied for conditions of optimal learning

- *Avoiding premature judgments.* Perhaps one issue that some coaches need to address and to do more thinking about is their tendency to make conclusive, long-term judgments about an athlete's skills and abilities based on initial, brief observations of performance with little regard to the benefits of skill instruction. All athletes need to learn and to improve sport skills, no matter at what level of play and expertise they begin the program. In addition, differences between individuals in their present skill levels, their desire to learn, and other psychological characteristics make it impossible to predict to what degree a player will improve or how he or she will perform during the competitive event.

X. Interact Consistently With All Team Members

Goethe, a philosopher, said, "Treat people as though they were what they ought to be, and you help them to become what they are capable of being." A coach will receive maximal effort, concentration, commitment, and loyalty from virtually all players on the team if those players believe that the coach is interested in them, both as athletes and as people/students/professionals. Probably the best way for coaches to communicate these feelings is to interact with all team members—starters and nonstarters, high skilled or less skilled—on a consistent basis.

A few definitions of terms will help to clarify this recommendation. First, consistent and constant interaction mean different things. *Consistent* interacting in the present context refers to demonstrating an ongoing, predictable pattern of communication with others, whereas a *constant* communication style requires interacting with others on an almost nonstop basis. The coach should not attempt to speak with all team members (starters and nonstarters) *all* the time, particularly not with large teams as in football. This would not be practical nor the best use of the coach's time.

What is suggested is that the coach "keep in touch" with all team members on a regular basis to (a) be aware of each athlete's improvement and progression, (b) point out the ways in which the athlete has shown improvement, (c) acknowledge specific skills that have been demonstrated efficiently, (d) remind individuals of the skills that they need to improve further, and (e) offer compliments to performers based on some aspect of their play from the recent past or the same day. The contact may also be based on a more personal level.

To give a true example of needing to treat team players consistently and showing no favoritism is the case of an unnamed (now retired) National Football League all-pro and starting player who refused to attend off-season workouts during the past season and indicated unhappiness with plans of his coach to change the team's defensive alignment. The player had signed a large multi-year contract. According to numerous media reports, the player showed up at preseason training camp out of shape and unhappy. The coach's response was not to allow this athlete to participate in drills until the he—the player—passed the team's rigorous fitness tests. To make matters worse, the athlete had recently sustained a leg injury, making his progress in training and season preparation even more difficult.

The main point for this communication guideline is that head coach is treating this player, last year's starter and previous all-pro, like any other team player. According to the *Tennessean* newspaper (Author, 2010), "[This player] has to practice if he wants to play. [The player] has gotten away in the past with playing without practicing, [the coach] said. That will not happen under this regime. If he's going to play, he's going to practice, and that is the same with every player here. The days of him playing without practicing are over" (p. 3C). This coach is treating the well-paid so-called "star player" in the same manner he treats all other players. He is being consistent, and that will increase his credibility with other team members—no favoritism. Effective coaches commit time and energy toward interacting with nonstarters as well as starters, all of whom have had, and will continue to have, an impact on team success.

chapter four

The Psychology of Successful Athletes

A well-studied and published area of sport psychology is understanding the psychological characteristics of highly skilled athletes. Coaches and sport psychologists want to identify the most common features associated with high-quality/elite-level athletes so that these characteristics can be identified and taught to less-skilled competitors. In addition, studying the characteristics of elite-level competitors can help teams select competitors—talent identification (discussed later)—who have the potential to perform at the highest level.

For instance, at the elite sport level administrators often ask clinical sport psychologists to assist with testing and examining the psychological features of players who have entered the league's draft. Teams need to decide which players have the potential to become successful at the elite level. While physical skills are certainly self-evident based on the players' performance statistics, less is known about the performers' *mental* skills and psychological characteristics. A team clinical sport psychologist is hired to identify players through psychological (paper and pencil) testing to determine who would make a valuable contribution to the team. Team administrators want to ascertain the athletes' "character" before selecting players in the draft. Some of the key characteristics include the player's self-discipline, training habits, self-motivation to succeed, if he or she was/is a good students and maintains the necessary conscientious study habits as part of game preparation, if he or she is a good team player, and if he or she maintains fitness year round. The problem with psychological testing in sport is that these tests—collectively called *talent identification*—have been shown to be poor predictors of an athlete's future sport success.

Attempts to understand the psychological factors that can either explain or predict the performance of highly skilled (elite-level) sports competitors has been an important mission of sport psychology researchers and practitioners for many years. Coaches and sport psychologists continuously try to predict an athlete's future success based on his or her responses to a psychological inventory.

Predicting sport performance has been attempted by numerous sport scientists over the years who have claimed to determine the personality profile of elite-level competitors in various sports, and to separate player personalities based on their position during competition. Receivers in U.S. football, for example, might have a different personality profile than running backs or linemen, males different from females, athletes from nonathletes, and so on. If individuals make claims about predicting future performance without research support, the benefits of describing and predicting an athlete's psychological profile are minimal.

Personality Traits vs. Dispositions

It's important for coaches and sport psychology consultants to know the differences between personality traits and dispositions/styles/orientations because each category of characteristic represents a different way to measure and interpret scores. By definition, *traits* are not changeable to training and are stable across situations. *Dispositions*, also called styles or orientations, are amenable to change, instruction, training, and to specific situations and conditions. More formally, personality traits are defined as a person's distinctive and enduring (i.e., cross-situational) thoughts, emotions, and behaviors that characterize the person's reactions to life situations. Personality traits and dispositions should not be used interchangeably. The following are personality traits that are common among elite athletes as detected by a psychological inventory:

- Elite athletes prefer to have their coach present during the warm-up period if the coach is perceived as supportive and as a source of inspiration.

- There is a difference between acknowledging the strengths, weaknesses, and tendencies of an opponent and being consumed with these thoughts and worrying about them. Skilled athletes are not worriers.

- They are a little tense like most athletes; however, they manage these unpleasant but predictable emotions successfully by the use of pregame routines. Their stress management and coping skills are superb. It is desirable to control arousal level.

- They use self-statements that reflect their readiness and eagerness to compete. Elite athletes sometimes use behavioral techniques, such as low-intensity aerobic work (e.g., brisk walking, jogging) as a form of relaxation. Another example is to use positive self-talk to overcome self-doubt and other undesirable thoughts and emotions.

- Elite athletes will typically regain their composure if they become troubled, stressed, or too excited, a condition called "overarousal."

- They engage in visualization, as they mentally review images of their successful performance before the actual competition, a form of mental practice. This routine reduces pre-competition anxiety and builds confidence.

- They can concentrate on the upcoming event during competition preparation (warm-up). They focus intently on the demands at hand—they are in the moment—and are not preoccupied with their opponents and the pressure to win during this time.

- Athletes can deal with unusual circumstances and distractions before and during the event. They do not allow unpleasant or unexpected circumstances to break their mental preparation. Examples include enduring a delay in the competition, a change in weather conditions, and pre-event harassment.

- Most elite-level athletes have a higher tolerance, or threshold, of pain than non-elites, but typically, successful elite athletes can focus their attention externally on the task at hand.

- They can withstand and deal with events that are beyond their control such as "poor" officiating, opponents' success, bad luck, or bad weather.

- Skilled athletes handle the pressure of a competition's final stages. They do not succumb to pressure. High-skilled athletes develop and carry out a mental plan, which prevents "choking" in high-pressure situations, manages anxiety, and maintains optimal arousal levels. See Appendix C for a measure of sport anxiety—the *sport anxiety scale* developed for this book.

The High-Need Achiever

Athletes who are *high-need achievers* (as determined by a paper-and-pencil inventory) (a) usually experience considerable pleasure following success; (b) have fewer and weaker physiological symptoms of arousal (e.g., increased heart rate, respiration rate, or sweating), so high-need achievers react to stress less harmfully (feel more challenged) than low-need achievers in pressure situations; (d) feel responsible for the outcomes of their own actions; (e) prefer to know about their success or failure as soon as possible after performance; and (f) prefer situations that contain some risk about the result, with a 50-50 chance of failure to obtain optimal motivation to succeed.

High-need achievers will be strong supporters of coach instructions, adhere to the team doctor's or athletic trainer's rehabilitation program, properly—mentally and physically—prepare for each competition, and give 100% effort during the contest. There is no substitute for individual and team success for the high-need achiever.

Mental Toughness

Mental toughness (MT) is usually defined in multiple ways. It concerns having the *natural* or *developed* psychological edge that enables the athlete to cope better than opponents with the many physical and psychological demands of sport. MT also is reflected by an athlete's consistently high quality performance (e.g., determined, focused, confident, in control under pressure) as opposed to their opponents. MT also consists of demonstrating emotional resiliency by bouncing back from "emotional hits," such as making a physical error, reacting to successful performance by opponents, receiving a "bad" call from the referee/umpire, and other sources of sudden stress. Under pressure, MT athletes are passionate and have the capacity and ability to recruit optimal levels of emotional intensity under the most stressful circumstances. Scholars contend that MT is learned, not inherited. We are not born with an "MT gene." It's developed over time and from various experiences.

There is an array of mental skills that are learned and reflect mentally tough competitors. Bull, Albinson, and Shambrook (1996) list the most important components of developing MT. They (a) have a strong desire to succeed; (b) stay positive in the face of challenge and pressure; (c) control what they can control and forget or dismiss the factors that they cannot control; (d) are committed to giving 100% effort in preparing for the competitive event and maintaining emotional control; (e) maintain a high level of self-belief; and (f) possess a positive body language (i.e., they "look" confident (e.g., chin up, shoulders back, eye contact when communicating with another person), committed, and self-assured in reaching their destiny; project a positive attitude; avoid hanging their head, sloping their shoulders, or going about their training with a "defeated" appearance). There are mental skills that result in each of these outcomes.

Mindfulness

Rather than dwelling in the past or contemplating the future, mindfulness is a technique that consists of helping the athlete remain in the present moment in a less reactive, less judgmental manner. Only in the present can an athlete possess the power to make changes to the situations that affect them. Nothing can be done to alter the past, and athletes can only prepare for, but not guarantee and control, the future. Only in the present can an athlete attempt to predict what is going to happen in the future. Mindfulness teaches that stress increases when there is a discrepancy between what the athlete wants and what is actually occurring. The athlete can choose to see things as they are and accept them as they are, and then work to improve the situation, if possible. Future research is needed to test the effectiveness of mindfulness in sport settings. Due to the vast array of high-quality resources that are available online, readers are asked to visit Google and insert two words, "mindfulness" and "sport," separated by a comma ("mindfulness, sport").

Personality Inventories: Pros and Cons

Many psychological inventories were not constructed with a sport application in mind. With the exception of licensed mental health professionals, most people don't have the training required to accurately read, interpret, and apply the data from a psychological inventory. Can a personality profile describe the desirable characteristics of highly skilled athletes? The answer appears to be yes and no.

There are psychological features that elite athletes share that coaches would like all their athletes to aspire. Just a few examples include high levels of competitiveness; confidence; self-esteem; coping skills; resourcefulness; mental toughness; positive perfectionism (e.g., having high but reasonable standards, handling some degree of, but not persistent, self-criticism); self-expectations of success; high, challenging, but realistic goals; pain tolerance, concentration; stability; dominance; and self-control. Elite athletes should include low levels of anxiety, fear of failure, fear of success, chronic stress, and expectations for failure. Some scholars would say that just because various individuals have promoted their sport instrument does not mean the psychological inventory can separate skill levels and predict future sport success. What about the value of physical training, skill instruction, proper equipment, high-quality coaching, the use of mental skills, and the athlete's normal maturation and development? Might these factors supersede scores obtained on a psychological inventory?

Often, personality profiles have been used to predict the probability that an individual will achieve sport success. However, researchers have shown that inventories can predict elite-level athletic skills and success only 8 to 10% of the time. The primary shortcoming about determining if there exists a set of personality traits among athletes is that there is no defined body of literature on which to base comparisons between athletes and nonathletes, males and females, or elites and non-elites.

Also, sports—and the individuals who play them—vary markedly concerning to the mood state that is "most desirable" or predictable for their own successful performance. For example, tension and anger are usually undesirable mood states for optimal sports performance but have been linked to performance success in cross-country running, karate, and other sports. Researchers contend it is not uncommon for athletes to perform well despite having theoretically "negative" profiles." Most composite psychological profiles of elite athletes reveal people who are physically and mentally healthy, mature, and committed to excellence. Certainly, these are factors toward which all athletic participants should strive.

Here are a few psychological characteristics—not personality traits—that have been shown to be relatively common among highly skilled athletes.

Risk taking. One psychological characteristic of highly successful competitors is risk taking. The term, "risk," is defined in most dictionaries as a dangerous element or factor, possibility of loss or injury, hazardous speculation, danger, or peril. In sport, risk has been associated with physical injury experienced during the competitive event.

Sport scientists have studied the tendency of highly skilled athletes to engage in more risk-taking behaviors—actions that can lead to bodily harm or failure—compared to less-skilled competitors. Highly skilled competitors will rarely perform tasks for which they are not well trained and physically fit. As much as high-quality athletes want to win, no one wants to get hurt, or worse. Sport competition is, of course, inherently risky for all performers. But the elite athlete, more than others, seems to thrive on and to prefer the excitement of engaging in risk-taking behaviors. These behaviors occur most often during situations that require solving problems and making decisions.

Competitiveness. In the current context, competitiveness is the desire to strive for success (in sport competition, to have a strong need to win and establish and maintain high, challenging goals). Highly competitive athletes view success more toward the quality of their performance than toward the competition's outcome. The implication for coaches is that quality performance deserves at least as much recognition as the competition's results.

Self-confidence. Sport psychologists, coaches, and researchers agree that self-confidence is one of the most important mental states for success in sport competition. Self-confidence, also called sport confidence in the sport psychology literature, is the athlete's belief about his or her ability to be successful in performing a desired skill. Self-confidence is the athlete's belief that one can successfully execute a specific activity in meeting performance goals. Sport confidence is the athlete's belief in his or her ability to be successful in sport situations and his or her general optimistic belief about his or her future sport success. Highly confident athletes are more likely to have high self-expectations and to anticipate successful performance outcomes.

Maintaining high confidence is accompanied by positive emotions; however, this mental state does not occur automatically. Coaches and the athletes, themselves, must employ mental strategies that induce self-confidence.

chapter five

Using Mental Skills to Regulate Thoughts and Emotions

Emotions are an integral part of competing in sport. While different types of emotion vary in intensity (e.g., arousal, anger) and content (e.g., anxiety, stress), athletes rely on controlling emotions to perform at their ideal performance state. Of constant concern to participants (and to coaches) is reaching and maintaining the proper emotional state that will contribute to reach their performance potential. As this chapter will reveal, coaches play a crucial role in helping athletes perform at their best. To reach this objective, they must regulate at least three emotions that play primary roles in performance: (a) cognitive and somatic (physiological) types of *arousal level*, (b) chronic (long-term) and acute (short-term) *stress*, and (c) chronic and acute/cognitive and somatic forms of *anxiety*.

Regulating athletes' emotions is often more difficult and challenging for coaches than we think. Attempts to "psych up" an athlete too often, unfortunately, results in "psyching out" the individual. For example, coaches differ on the content and intensity of a pregame talk, even in sports that demand a high level of energy, aggression, and intensity (e.g., contact sports). Many leaders foster an exciting atmosphere before the competition, while others use a low-key approach. There is a certain intensity in preparing for competition for any given sport that meets the athlete's individual needs.

The athlete's "ideal" emotional status and the coach's actions in trying to help athletes reach it are often dependent on four factors: (a) the type of sport, (b) the position within a sport, (c) the situation within a particular competition, and (d) the athlete's personality. A football coach will tend to "fire up" the players because relatively high levels of both cognitive and somatic arousal are needed for a relatively long period of time. Baseball coaches, however, know that players have to stay loose and maintain relatively low excitement before and during the game. If the manager is low key, the players will more likely relax. Let's examine the properties and underlying sources of stress, anxiety, and arousal, beginning with the premise that they are not the same thing.

Perhaps at the heart of the field of sport psychology is the use of *mental skills*, also referred to as *cognitive strategies, behavioral strategies, or cognitive-behavioral strategies* if both types of performance-enhancing techniques are used as part of the same intervention. "Cognitive strategies" refer to the conscious application of a mental technique—not directly observable—for the purpose of improving performance outcomes. "Behavioral strategies" consist of the deliberate and planned use of observable (i.e., behavioral) techniques that also serve the purpose of enhancing sport performance. Cognitive-behavioral strategies, then, combine the athlete's thoughts and actions usually as a single intervention to improve sport performance. Strategies are planned and purposeful.

For years, researchers have attempted to determine the thoughts, feelings, and emotions of high-level (elite) successful athletes before and during the competition in contrast to their less successful and lower-skilled competitors, sometimes in comparison to nonathletes. What are the thoughts and emotions of highly skilled athletes that help them attain and maintain their best performance? Under what conditions do they have certain thoughts, and what effect does this have on their mental preparation and performance? Many coaches have, understandably, limited knowledge and experience about the proper use of mental skills.

The primary purpose of this chapter is to provide a brief overview of interventions and both cognitive and behavioral strategies that have been developed and studied by researchers, educators, and practitioners in applied sport psychology.

One issue of the journal *The Sport Psychologist* (1990, vol. 4, no. 4) was devoted to the experiences of sport psychology consultants who worked with professional and Olympic-level athletes. Despite the extensive passage of time since this publication, many of the issues and limitations raised in this 1990 journal issue still persist today. One consistent observation, for example, was that athletes know very little about the existence and proper application of mental skills. Female athletes seem to be more receptive to mental skills programs than their male counterparts.

Even frequent users of mental skills differ widely on which techniques work best for them and when they should be employed. For example, some athletes engage in too much thinking. That is, positive self-talk and thoughts that build self-esteem, and improve the athlete's attentional focus and confidence, can actually hinder their concentration and ability to respond automatically during the competition. It is clear is that "one size does not fit all." What may be effective for one athlete, or one type of sport or sport situation, may not be effective for other athletes and sport types and situations.

It is also imperative to state that some athletes, coaches, and sport psychologists attempt to learn and apply too many techniques at one time, thereby compromising their effectiveness. These techniques are skills and, like any skill, they must be taught slowly and under the appropriate conditions. Before describing some of these mental skills, let's first define what we mean by a mental skill (or cognitive strategy), a cognitive-behavioral program, and an intervention.

What are interventions? Interventions, mental skills, and cognitive/behavioral strategies are often used interchangeably, but they are not the same concepts. Interventions encompass all the mental skills programs that are intended to change behavior. Singer and Anshel (2006) define an intervention as "the process by which sport psychologists attempt to influence the thoughts, emotions, or performance quality of sports competitors and teams" (p. 63). The authors further describe sport psychologists as persons who "intervene" by positioning themselves between the athlete and the competitive environment and then provide information and instruction to athletes about the proper use of mental or behavioral strategies that are intended to facilitate a particular outcome. The objective of using interventions is to alter the athlete's thoughts, emotions, or actions. Strategies consist of various types of thoughts (e.g., positive self-talk, visualization) and behaviors (e.g., pre-performance routines) that, when applied in sport-related situations, form one or more interventions. Sport psychologists and coaches are "outsiders" who come between performers and the environment, or the situation, to enhance physical performance and performance outcomes.

Before interventions are suggested, however, most coaches and sport psychologists will determine the athlete's limitations (e.g., "I do not perform well under pressure"), concerns (e.g., "I cannot be consistently successful and reach my performance potential unless I relax and feel confident prior to the event"), and future aspirations (i.e., "What must I do to overcome my limitations and concerns?"). One or more mental and behavioral skills may then be offered. The concept of interventions will further be described later in this chapter.

Key Emotional States

Stress, anxiety, and arousal have been used interchangeably—and incorrectly—by researchers in scientific literature, sport psychology, the media, and coaching for many years. Clarification is needed as to how these concepts are defined because each of these concepts do not share the same emotions and feelings; they are caused, measured, and treated differently. Consequently, they require different techniques to regulate them.

Stress refers to present *bodily* (i.e., physiological, somatic) or *cognitive* responses to an environmental demand. This demand can be interpreted as positive or negative. *Anxiety*, on the other hand, reflects *only negative*—never positive—feelings of worry or threat about a *future* event. Whereas stress has both positive and negative properties, *anxiety is always unpleasant*. There is no such thing as "positive anxiety." This is not to say that anxiety is warranted, even necessary, in sport—in life we always look both ways before crossing the street due to our anxiety of being struck by a car. Successful athletes experience anxiety, but they know how to control (manage) it better than their less successful counterparts. Anxiety management is a cognitive (thinking)-behavioral (acting) skill.

Arousal, sometimes used interchangeably with the term *activation*, is a natural, ongoing state that consists of neural excitation on a continuum from very low (e.g., comatose, sleep) to very high (e.g., extreme excitement or aggression). Arousal is responsible for harnessing the body's resources for intense and vigorous activity. Arousal includes somatic (i.e., physiological) and cognitive (thoughts) dimensions. While arousal is *related* to anxiety and stress, they are not the same. This is important for coaches to know because each type of emotion differs on its sources and warrants various interventions to improve and regulate performance. Stress and anxiety, for instance, are not the same thing (see next section).

Stress

Stress is probably one of the most misunderstood concepts in sport psychology. For example, stress tends to be viewed as undesirable, unhealthy, and negative, something to be avoided at all times. This is not necessarily true, especially when examining definitions of stress. Stress is the arousal of mind and body in response to external demands. A *stressor* is any situational sudden demand on the mind or body, while a *distressor* is any demand resulting in harm to mind or body. Thus, while most demands—physical, mental, or emotional—that are made on us are harmless, even positive, these demands can turn negative. Stressors, then, can become distressors. When an athlete, for example, perceives a stressor as predictable and manageable (e.g., receiving physical contact or successful performance by an opponent, booing from the crowd), they become less threatening and produce less anxiety. Stress, then, should *not* be avoided. It is both desirable and necessary in life—and in sport competition. In fact, as described later, there exists an emotion called "positive stress."

Traditionally, stress has been defined as a particular relationship between the person and the environment that is appraised (interpreted) by athletes as taxing or exceeding their resources and endangering their well-being. The environment or the situation each play an important role in experiencing stress. An athlete can compete in a stressful environment or in a nonstressful one. This means that managing stress includes attending to environmental factors that cause or contribute to it. A good sport example is to have the team practice in the same environment and facilities as to be experienced in the actual competition.

An example of how *not* to follow this advice occurred when a (U.S.) team in the National Football League team from a warm climate played their next game in a much colder climate in a snow storm. The visitors traveled only 2 days before the game was scheduled; players clearly did not have sufficient exposure to the colder, harsher weather conditions. Result: Home team beat the visiting team 59-0.

A very important concept related to understanding sport stress is *appraisal*. Appraisal is an *interpretation*, or *perception*, of the environmental stressor. This means that stress is controllable, since athletes must first perceive a stimulus or situation as taxing or exceeding their resources (e.g., confidence, mental toughness, positive emotions, proper emotional intensity) to deal with the stressor. In other words, if the athlete perceives a situation as challenging or harmless, rather than as threatening or harmful, ostensibly the athlete should feel less stress.

Successfully managing sport stress, then, primarily consists of three processes: (a) managing the environment (if possible, and it usually can be done), (b) building resourcefulness (e.g., confidence, optimism, self-control, mental toughness, resilience, coping skills), and (c) influencing the athlete's interpretation (appraisal) of situations including harm, threat, and challenge. Elite athletes apply challenge appraisals more often than their less-skilled counterparts.

Positive Stress

To many coaches and athletes, stress is never beneficial or positive. They feel that the words, "positive stress," are an oxymoron—a contradiction in terms. How can stress be positive? Based on how we typically view the concept of stress, the two words simply do not seem compatible. However, as discussed earlier, stress can be positive, productive, helpful, and even desirable. Positive stress can improve athletes' attentiveness and energy for meeting deadlines, entering new situations, coping with emergencies, achieving maximum performance, and meeting new challenges.

How is stress beneficial to athletes? If stress is viewed as anything that causes energy to be expended—physically, mentally, and emotionally—then stress is a form of "positive energy" because it produces growth and achievement. Stress is experienced physically, mentally, and emotionally. For example, physical stress occurs when exercising; mental stress occurs in response to thinking and concentrating (cognition), while emotional stress is energy expenditure following certain negative feelings (e.g., anger, fear, sadness, frustration, anxiety). Emotional stress, however, can also consist of more positive content (e.g., happiness, relaxation, enthusiasm).

There are two important points about positive stress. First, without taxing the system—physically, mentally, or emotionally—athletes cannot reach nor maintain their ideal performance state. Growth takes place in response to stress, that is, the expenditure of energy. The second important point is that the problems associated with stress can easily be alleviated when stress is balanced with what is called *voluntary recovery*. Recovery is anything that causes energy to be renewed or recaptured—physically, mentally, or emotionally. Voluntary recovery is planned in content, time, implementation, and duration. *Involuntary recovery*, on the other hand, consists of the biological breakdown of the human organism (e.g., sickness, disease, depression). If an athlete has a planned recovery strategy, he or she is likely to experience *positive stress* and deal with it productively. This is why deficiencies in athletic performance, especially if experienced over a prolonged time (e.g., a batting slump in baseball, repeated missed basketball free throws) might benefit from taking time off to recover rather than continued play despite repeated failures. The batter might overcome his or her hitting slump by sitting out for a few games and reducing the tension and stress that comes with repeated failures (time for recovery).

Recovery consists of two characteristics. First, recovery has a reenergizing effect, so that after the recovery period, the person feels more invigorated and refreshed. Second, the recovery strategy must distract the performer from the task at hand. Thus, a baseball/softball player would not recover from batting practice by immediately taking ground balls. Instead, he or she would "disconnect" physically, mentally, and emotionally by moving to a different location and remain inactive for a brief period of time—even minutes. Recovery tasks might include drinking water, having an informal conversation, or just relaxing and thinking about something else. Athletes will benefit by balancing stress and recovery. The human organism needs an occasional "time out."

Positive stress is usually defined as arousal that promotes health, energy, satisfaction, and optimal performance. When stress or anxiety are experienced occasionally and in moderation, performance can actually improve. Examples include preparing for an upcoming difficult task, remaining alert over time, concentrating on the task at hand, not being distracted by extraneous, irrelevant thoughts, and overcoming obstacles. Stress, then, can be desirable—even necessary—in sport, and in life. The most important factor for coaches is not to prevent or eliminate all sources of stress, but rather to regulate and manage them.

Anxiety

The word "anxiety" is not about feeling eager and excited in a sport context. As indicated earlier, anxiety is about feeling worried or threatened. Sources of worry and threat are inherent in sport competition, so this chapter will address these sources and what coaches (and their athletes) can do about controlling these feelings. Anxious feelings are very common and even expected among athletes of all skill levels, genders, and sport types.

Sport competition is inherently threatening because, by definition, someone must win and someone must lose. Losing, for many competitors, is threatening to one's self-esteem and expectations. Sport environments may increase athletes' perception of threat *if they are aware* of being judged and are attempting to meet the expectations of others (e.g., parents, coaches, spectators, media). It is not surprising, therefore, that one of the primary sources of poor sport performance is anxiety.

Anxiety is an emotion that reflects an athlete's interpretation, or perception, of a situation as threatening—real or imagined. If a person imagines a situation as threatening, then it is—to that individual. Perceptions are real; they reflect the person's interpretation as truth. A person who is worried about an upcoming exam and consequently has trouble sleeping is anxious.

Whereas anxiety is traditionally defined as an unpleasant emotion, arousal, on the other hand, can be either physiologically or psychologically based. This is because arousal is not automatically associated with either pleasant or unpleasant events. You might be highly aroused after scoring a point during a sport event or be equally aroused by learning that a teammate was injured on a play during the game.

In sport, anxiety reflects the performer's feelings that something may go wrong, that the outcome may not be successful, or that performance failure may be experienced. Sport competition, after all, is all about demonstrating superior performance than an opponent.

Losing reflects failure, and failure directly inhibits self-esteem, the lack of achievement.

Perhaps the performer views an opponent as superior or knows that a member of the audience—a judge, family member, friend, teammate, or the coach—is evaluating the quality of his or her performance. This can be threatening, particularly for individuals with relatively low self-confidence, low self-esteem, or a lack of previous success. Such individuals are sometimes referred to as "practice players" or "chokers." They have a tendency to "freeze up" and to perform more poorly during the competition, especially in pressure situations, than in practice. They rarely experience their performance potential. This is not to say that anxiety is always undesirable. To succeed in sport, athletes must be aware of potentially threatening situations.

There are two recognized types of anxiety, state and trait. *State anxiety* (A-state) is transitory in that it fluctuates over time between situations. Competitive state anxiety consists of conscious feelings of apprehension and tension due mainly to the individual's perception of the present or upcoming situation as threatening. Often, though not always, anxiety is accompanied by activation of the autonomic nervous system, which is why it is confused with arousal, which also is closely associated with the nervous system. Still, researchers commonly measure state (not trait) anxiety by its somatic (physiological) and psychological (cognitive) properties.

Trait anxiety (A-trait), unlike state anxiety, is a relatively stable disposition, often depicted as a personality trait. A-trait predisposes an individual to perceive a wide range of nondangerous circumstances as threatening or dangerous. Further, the individual with high A-trait tends to demonstrate A-state reactions beyond what is necessary, given the present sense of danger. Thus, high A-trait athletes are more susceptible to state anxiety before a competitive event than low A-trait performers (Anshel, 2005). Trait anxiety can be measured like any other cognitive (trait) measure—with a psychological inventory.

It is often reported in the sports media that some athletes become literally sick to their stomach before every game (so much for the value of a proper pregame meal). It is likely that athletes who experience acute illness before a competition, a sign of extreme state anxiety, have high A-trait. Pregame nausea or vomiting is an example of why high A-state is never desirable. The pregame meal is needed to produce energy and to sustain physical activity. In addition to negative emotional and physiological ramifications, anxiety has also been shown to have a deleterious effect on motor performance. Studies have shown through electromyography that muscular coordination in skilled movements decreases when the performer has high A-state. This is likely due to increased muscular tension.

Probably the most important factor that contributes to feeling anxious or worried in a sport situation is the athlete's interpretation, a process called *appraisal*. Appraisal consists of the athlete's interpretation of a given situation or event and directly influences his or her psychological and physiological responses. For example, a stress appraisal will elicit a different set of mental and somatic responses than an appraisal considered irrelevant or positive. Stress appraisals are further categorized as positive/benign, harmful, threatening, or challenging.

Sources of anxiety. State anxiety is not an automatic response to sport competition; it is learned. Researchers have attempted to ascertain the sources of state (also called situational) anxiety. How an athlete appraises (perceives or interprets) the situation often predicts an anxiety response. A coach's reprimand, for example, may cause the athlete to feel considerable anxiety *if* the event is appraised as threatening to the athlete's self-esteem (i.e., the athlete feels devalued, perhaps humiliated). Similarly, experiencing pain or injury will likely elicit an appraisal of harm or loss, which is also considered threatening. However, if events, such as remarks by others or spectator booing, are stressful, but are interpreted by the athlete as a challenge rather than threatening, then the performer is more likely to feel the incentive to increase emotional intensity (arousal) and feel less anxiety. Hopefully, performance improves. Former major league hitting star Barry Bonds told the media that he considered spectator booing a compliment to his skills and achievements. The disapproval of fans did not bother him at all, he reported.

Similarly, athletes may view the success of an opponent as irrelevant or harmless early in the game, but change that interpretation near the game's end with a close score as more stressful and threatening. These different appraisals usually elicit different types of coping responses. Personal dispositions (e.g., trait anxiety, self-esteem, achievement motivation) and emotional states (e.g., confidence, optimism, and performance expectancies) also influence the individual's appraisal of a situation.

Skill level is another factor that contributes to interpreting a situation as threatening (i.e., feelings of anxiety). For example, Jones and Swain (1995) found that elite British cricket players interpret their anxiety levels as significantly more beneficial and less debilitative to their performance than their less-skilled counterparts. Anxiety can be good, or have a positive influence on sport performance, if it is perceived as facilitative.

The key finding in this study was that elite competitors revealed more positive interpretations of their anxious feelings about their future performance (i.e., higher positive expectations, ability to overcome worry and feel confident) than their less-skilled counterparts. Therefore, an intervention to improve the management of anxiety should create challenging (not threat) appraisals of the situation and require athletes to rely on skills and strategies that have been learned and practiced. As most coaches already know, it's all about good preparation.

In sport, coaches and athletes want to regulate, not necessarily eliminate, state anxiety (A-state) at manageable levels so that it *helps* rather than hinders performance. To do this effectively, it would be helpful to know the sources of sport anxiety.

Anxiety About Success and Failure

Athletes of all ages and skill levels are often under great pressure to perform well and win. Their need for approval and to meet the expectations of others, which are normal feelings, is often linked to their self-worth, which contributes to a sense of pressure to perform successfully. Not surprisingly, state anxiety is generated from the possibility of performance failure. Conversely, anxiety may also be experienced due to the pressures and expectations following *success* (e.g., "They're not as good as they used to be," "Why can't he or she perform as well as last year?"). The psychological outcomes of these feelings are called *fear of failure* and *fear of success*, respectively, and both are common in competitive sport.

Clinical sport psychologists generally contend that the most common sources of anxiety in athletes are fears of failure (e.g., losing, poor performance), followed by social disapproval (i.e., others won't like me) and rejection (i.e., not feeling relevant toward team success). One of the less fortunate aspects of sport competition is the pressure that athletes feel to meet the expectations of others—especially persons whose opinions the athletes value. The more an athlete succeeds, the more those expectations rise, and the more the pressure increases to match the expectations of others. But how well and accurately can most coaches detect excessive state anxiety in their athletes so that they can help the athlete manage it effectively? Can coaches estimate their athletes' anxiety levels?

An area requiring future attention by researchers is determining the athlete's optimal anxiety level. Whereas the concept of optimal arousal has been studied extensively, the thought that a modicum of anxiety is actually desirable—anxiety has life-saving properties when driving a car, for instance—has escaped most scholars. The exception to this tendency, of course, would be Jones and Swain's (1995) work on facilitative anxiety in which the content and interpretation of anxious thoughts can actually improve performance. Determining optimal state anxiety and understanding the cognitive strategies and situational factors that can control it and facilitate its occurrence remains an area for future research. One outcome of prolonged state anxiety in sport occurs when the athlete is consumed and distracted by negative thoughts and self-doubt prior to and during the competition. The result is the undesirable condition called chronic anxiety, which, in turn, can lead to a state called under-arousal.

Arousal

Traditionally, arousal has been interpreted and measured strictly as a physiological process on a continuum ranging from very low (sleep) to very high (excitation) intensity. Arousal is often determined by changes in heart and respiration rate, sweating, blood pressure, and other physiological measures. However, scholars have measured *emotional* (cognitive) aspects of arousal, including positive feelings (e.g., excitement, happiness) and negative feelings (e.g., fear, embarrassment, and depression).

Hanin's Individualized Zone of Optimal Functioning (IZOF)

Hanin (1980, 2000) attempted to explain the arousal-performance relationship based on the contention that athletes' state anxiety differ extensively. In particular, Hanin contends that rather than identifying a single optimal level of state anxiety, athletes possess a zone, or range, of optimal functioning just prior to competition. This zone, what he calls the *individualized zone of optimal functioning* (IZOF), consists of an optimal state of arousal that is unique for each individual athlete. This arousal zone will be much higher for some athletes than others. It is up to athletes (perhaps with help from their coach) to determine this zone, and then be able to reproduce this "optimal" arousal state consistently from one competition to the next.

The IZOF has its critics. For instance, Landers and Arent (2010) doubt the IZOF's validity because "the IZOF model has only been operationalized with measures of anxiety. The questionnaires employed do not measure arousal per se" (p. 235). To lend further credence to this point, Arent and Landers (2003) found that physiological measures of arousal were twice as likely to predict performance, as compared to psychological measures, which Hanin uses exclusively in the IZOF intervention. A second criticism of Hanin's model is the use of psychological measures of anxiety rather than arousal. As indicated earlier, these are different constructs and are defined and expressed differently in self-report measures. While the IZOF model provides interesting insights into understanding and measuring optimal arousal, more research is needed that combines both somatic and cognitive measures. The IZOF, however, remains a plausible measure of establishing an athlete's optimal arousal level—for now.

The Arousal/Performance Relationship

One cause of poorer performance when arousal is too high is in response to the athlete's thoughts and emotions. Individuals with either high arousal or anxiety tend to exclude too much information when performing. Overly excited competitors may not use all the information available in scanning the field before making a decision to react. An inaccurate judgment could result. This is referred to as an over-narrowing of attention (Landers, 1980).

In summary, the key issues concerning arousal for coaches and athletes are (a) determining the level of arousal that is *optimal* in a given situation to establish the point of diminishing returns and (b) learning the proper techniques for controlling it. Determining the level of optimal arousal at some pre-determined point during the competition is challenging, partly because what is optimal for one athlete may be too low or too high for another athlete given the same situation. When it comes to feelings of excitation in sport, more is not always better.

Determining Optimal Arousal

What is the "best" arousal level for a particular situation or for a given individual athlete? How can the appropriate or customary level of arousal be ascertained? These are challenging questions for sport psychology researchers and practitioners. It is apparent that generalizations about the "right way" to do something are rarely valid for all participants. To individualize the prescription and treatment for optimal arousal for each competitor would be more desirable. An athlete's customary performance quality is associated with his or her customary arousal level.

Competitors' current arousal level immediately prior to and during the competition should be compared with their subsequent performance. Then, after the competition, the coach and athlete should jointly determine whether changing the arousal level before or during future competitions is desirable.

One possible approach to determining optimal arousal—the difference between feeling "up" as opposed to feeling "uptight"—is to pose questions that help the performer to identify certain feelings. These questions are intended (a) to self-monitor feelings and physiological responses prior to and during competition, (b) to identify athletes' feelings accurately, and (c) to remind them to use appropriate physical and mental strategies that can favorably affect mental status.

Counseling sport psychologists typically ask athletes (a) to identify the time or game in which they felt they performed at their best and at their worst, (b) to describe these performances as accurately as possible, and (c) to describe their feelings and mental attitudes during this time. Specific questions include "What were you thinking about during this event, if anything?" "Was your concentration easily attained, or did you have to work hard to concentrate?" "Were you relaxed or tense, and why?" "Describe your focus of awareness: To what were you directing your attentions?"

Based on an athlete's responses to these questions, coaches or sport psychology consultants suggest mental strategies that the performer can use to alter levels of arousal and anxiety to improve his or her mental preparation for competition. The coach's or consultant's objective in asking these questions is to identify athletes' feelings associated with desirable and undesirable performance and to recall their perceptions of physiological responses they experience at the time of competition.

This approach was used by Orlick (1986) in his "mental plan" model. Briefly, Orlick asked athletes to identify certain feelings (e.g., self-confidence level) and emotions (e.g., anxiety, arousal) on a scale from 1 (very low) to 10 (very high). This self-monitoring technique encourages athletes to become more aware of their mental status at any given time. But perhaps more important, athletes' increased awareness allows them to compare the kinds and intensity levels of feelings/emotions that accompany good performance outcomes with the feelings and emotions linked to poorer performance outcomes. In this way, when conducted over several competitions, the athlete's best (optimal) arousal state can be identified.

Choking

Performing under pressure is inherent in competitive sport. The ability to perform according to one's skill level and in accordance with previous performance quality often creates anxiety (worry; threat) and pressure that is thought to be responsible for what has been called "underperforming." That is, athletes do not meet performance expectations in high-pressure situations. This phenomenon is called *choking*.

Choking is defined as the inability to perform up to previously exhibited standards. This decreased performance occurs in pressure situations. Pressure is defined as any factor or combination of factors that increases the importance of performing well on a particular occasion. Choking in sport, then, consists of reduced performance quality under pressure circumstances, the inability to perform up to previously exhibited standards, suboptimal performance despite incentives for optimal performance, and performing more poorly than expected given one's level of skill.

To many sports fans, any player or team that does not perform to its own expectations have been labeled "chokers." Examples, based on media reports, include the 1998 San Diego Padres or the 1990 Atlanta Braves baseball teams, each of which lost four games in a row to the New York Yankees in their respective world series. More recently, the 2008 Chicago Cubs baseball team won more games during the season than any other team in the National League (NL). Yet, they were swept in three games in the semi-final playoffs against the Los Angeles Dodgers, who were a wild card team. In fact, the Cubs made five errors, one by each infielder, in the last of these games. Only months later did their manager, Lou Pinnella, disclose to the media that the players were "tight" and put under tremendous pressure to win the 2008 World Series, not only because they had the best win-loss record in the NL, but because 2008 was the centennial anniversary since the Cubs last won a world series. This incident is a good example of choking.

Whether these major league baseball teams actually succumbed to pressure in the world series is far from certain. The only way to measure if sports competitors actually succumb to pressure—if they "choke"—is to determine their perceived level of pressure, among other feelings and emotions through psychological inventories or interviews. Only responses from the players can determine if their thoughts (cognitions) and emotions lead to below-par performance.

Therefore, ostensibly, players with high perceived pressure and anxiety who also perform poorly would have to be operationally defined in such a study, such as striking out with players in scoring position, poor pitching in a game that the pitcher's team was supposed to win, making mental and physical errors; athletes in these situations might have choked.

Before we automatically label an event or outcome as reflective of choking, perhaps the successful teams (players) had better skills, in the case of baseball, superior pitching and better talent, than their opponents. Rather than choking, the opposing national league teams simply lost to a more talented team—at least during the world series. Can choking be identified and explained?

The causes of choking are both internal and external. Internal causes of choking include overarousal, appraising situations as highly stressful, the athlete's perceived loss of self-control, and expectations of failure. External causes of choking include crowd pressure (high expectations of spectators and low to moderate expectations of the athlete) and fear of success (the pressure to maintain what the athlete perceives as unrealistically high quality of performance). Other external causes are expectations and actions of the coach (expressing the importance of winning or attaining a certain performance level) and external pressure from the demands and expectations of teammates, spectators, and the media.

Why does choking impede sport performance? Because the feelings and emotions that accompany choking are similar to extreme anxiety: heightened narrowing of attention focusing and slower information processing. A narrowed attentional focus, similar to high state anxiety, is undesirable when task demands require the athlete to scan the competitive environment, looking for the location of opponents and teammates and planning strategy. Slower information processing is manifested by being easily distracted from the task at hand, poor attentional shifting between internal (thinking) and external (scanning) directions, slower and less accurate decision making, more thinking and less reliance on automatic responses, and making performance errors.

Choking can also be accompanied by physiological changes such as increased muscle tension, sweating, higher heart rate, nausea, and stomach cramps, any of which can directly influence energy level and sports performance.

Overcoming "The Choke"

Choking in sport is not inevitable. Some athletes, in fact, seem to thrive under pressure. Others, however, succumb and do not meet performance expectations. There are mental and behavioral techniques athletes can use to prevent perceived pressure and to react to expectations by others with confidence rather than with anxiety. Here are a few suggestions:

1. *Practice under game-like conditions.* This allows the athletes to learn to adapt to actual pressure in realistic conditions experienced during the competition. Athletes will perform more comfortably if they can recall performing skills and strategies conducted in practice settings.
2. *Improve and maintain the athlete's self-confidence.* This is the coach's job. Teaching and mastering fundamental skills and strategies, together with positive, tangible information feedback on performance quality, improves self-confidence.
3. *Keep expectations realistic.* Choking is partly due to external pressures that, in turn, are generated by high expectations of coaches and other observers. Keeping expectations in accordance with past performance will reduce pressure and lessen the likelihood of choking. Coaches need to avoid setting team and individual goals that competitors feel are unrealistic.
4. *Put the competition—and sport in general—into perspective.* As indicated earlier, sport is not a life-or-death situation. Athletes compete to win, but it's also true that sport should be fun to play. This is a cliché, but nevertheless it's only a game. There is always tomorrow – and the day after that.
5. *Coach, avoid pressure statements.* "We have to win this game"; "The game is now in your hands"; "We're counting on you"; and other statements that induce guilt coming from coaches and, to a lesser extent from parents, teammates, and spectators add considerable pressure for success and contribute to choking.
6. *Focus externally.* Choking is a reaction to aversive thoughts. Athletes should reduce the time spent thinking about scenarios that begin with "what if" or "I hope 'this' happens (or doesn't happen)." Instead, focus on external features in the sport environment, develop and practice pre-competition routines, and remember past successes. I know one elite athlete who focused on advertisement signs in the stadium before the game; it relaxed him. Talking with teammates about topics that have nothing to do with the competition also relaxes the athlete.

7. *Develop performance routines.* Linked to external focusing is engaging in one or more thoughts and actions that prepare the athlete for action. This is called a "mental plan." Many other sport psychology researchers have suggested using specific mental and physical routines prior to skill execution or before the competition that will act as a tension reducer and confidence builder. Examples include specific thoughts and actions before and immediately after entering the batter's box, between tennis serves, or just prior to a golf swing. These routines should be automatic to avoid external distractions.

Cognitive-Behavioral Strategies: The Foundation of Self-Regulation

It would take considerable time and energy for coaches to continually guide an athlete's thoughts and actions in teaching physical and mental skills. Instead, great coaches teach athletes how to generate these thoughts, emotions, and actions independent of external commands by using their own initiative. Athletes must initiate, maintain, and control their own actions to feel responsible for their success. The bases for executing treatments and interventions in sport psychology is a process called *self-regulation* (SR).

The process of helping athletes manage their own actions is at the heart of SR. SR is the framework by which we use mental skills. We self-regulate our actions throughout our waking hours, from the time we wake up until the time we go to sleep. We develop and perform daily routines and actions that maintain proper health and meet biological needs. We carry out tasks to meet short-term and long-term goals. Athletes realize they must maintain proper fitness and engage in other tasks that prepare them for sports competition. Injured athletes realize they must engage in daily specific rehabilitation tasks at a given location to return to competition, a process called adherence (discussed later). All these are examples of SR. Thus, SR concerns a person's initiatives to engage in and maintain goal-directed behavior by using certain thoughts, emotions, and actions. Self-regulating athletes are managers of their own actions engaging in voluntary (i.e., conscious) action management. Sports coaches mentor their competitors concerning the proper SR strategies. SR is the foundation of using mental skills and developing other types of routines in sport because athletes must manage their own actions in carrying them out properly.

Researchers have confirmed the effectiveness of SR in numerous previous studies on highly skilled athletes. Sample items on most SR checklists include the following:

- "I am able to calm down quickly if something upsets me by taking a deep breath and planning my next strategy,"
- "If I feel upset or nervous, I am able to calm down by thinking about past successes."
- "I will have a detailed plan of my swimming races."
- "I will use mental imagery during half-time in the locker room."
- "I arrive early or on time for my injury rehabilitation program."
- "When I run as part of training, I remember that it's good for my health as well as for my performance endurance."

As indicated earlier, SR strategies in sport consist of goal-directed behavior, that is, voluntary thoughts and actions over time that are intended to help athletes perform at a higher level. This includes the use of mental skills and other interventions that athletes must initiate, monitor, sustain, and complete to achieve desirable outcomes.

Coping With Stressful Events

Stressful events are part of the fabric of sport competition. Making a physical or mental error, receiving a "bad" call from the game official, success by an opponent, poor weather conditions, and experiencing pain (discomfort) are examples of short-term, or acute, stress. The process for reducing the intensity of short-term stress and overcoming adversity is called coping. It is important that athletes be taught proper coping skills and stress-management programs that allow them to overcome the psychological barriers after experiencing stressful events during the competition.

Coping is a skill but not necessarily an effective, automatic response to stress. Coping skills, therefore, must be learned and practiced. In addition, coping is not always effective. An athlete's use of a coping strategy for reducing perceived stress, particularly in response to frustration, can be ineffective. At times, coping attempts can produce more stress, not less, and can lead to highly undesirable outcomes. Examples include receiving a penalty, being dismissed from the competition, increased anxiety, slower processing of information, which may lead to poorer performance, and even losing the competition. Coping strategies may be used in isolation or as part of an intervention package, or program. The coping literature uses different labels and frameworks from which to choose in the attempt to cope effectively. One popular framework in the coping literature is "approach-avoidance."

Approach-avoidance coping. The coping process consists of using one or more types (categories) of coping. One common way to categorize the many types of coping strategies used in competitive sport is "approach" and "avoidance." Approach coping consists of an athlete's thoughts and actions that are directed at the source of stress. Approach coping can be effective (e.g., receiving information/instruction/feedback on ways to reduce stress) or ineffective (e.g., arguing the call, nonstop thinking about the stressor, which interferes with the athlete's concentration and anger).

Avoidance coping, on the other hand, concerns thoughts or actions that help the athlete become mentally or physically distant from the source of stress. Examples of mental avoidance coping would be psychological distancing, ignoring, or minimizing the importance of a stressful event. Physical avoidance could entail walking away from or not taking seriously a stressful event. Humor would be another example of either mental or physical avoidance coping. Researchers have found that elite athletes cope more often using avoidance than approach coping strategies. They are better at putting the stress event behind them and moving forward. Sometimes the coping process can best be learned by incorporating specific strategies into a program. The COPE model is an example.

The COPE Model

Anshel (1990) developed the COPE model to help athletes handle acute (immediate) forms of stress caused mainly by negative input from others (e.g., coaches, spectators, opponents). As an intervention, use of the COPE model has assisted athletes to overcome unpleasant verbal feedback on sport performance.

COPE is an acronym that describes four cognitive-behavioral strategies that can be used to handle unpleasant input from others. Athletes implement these techniques immediately on receiving the undesirable input. The four stages of the model are as follows:

C = control emotions. The immediate reaction of an athlete's mind and body on exposure to hostile input might be to feel uptight and tense. This response is known as the "fight-or-flight" reflex in the sympathetic nervous system, and the athlete feels the rush of adrenaline being pumped into the bloodstream. *The model requires taking a few deep breaths and regaining composure.* By controlling emotions at this stage, athletes can remain aware of and receptive to any important information that will contribute to better subsequent performance while reducing muscular tension. This is *not* the time to use relaxation techniques that slow somatic processes and inhibit rapid thinking and reacting.

O = organize input. The objective here is for the athlete to *deal rationally* with the stressful episode. One tendency of skilled performers is that they know the difference between important and unimportant (or redundant) information. A coach who yells, "You fool! How many times do I have to tell you . . ." is providing an important message: "Don't do 'such and such' in certain situations."

But the coach is also including a less constructive message when using name calling and ridicule. To maintain the proper mental and physical readiness after exposure to uncomplimentary input, the athlete must be able to decide what is worthy of attention and what should be ignored or discounted.

One practical use of the COPE model in response to negative statements from the player's coach who admonishes or reprimands the athlete comes from author, John Feinstein, in his best-selling book *A Season on the Brink* (1986). Feinstein describes how members of a Division I college basketball team were able to cope with unpleasant input from a coach who had a reputation for his temper and making angry statements toward his athletes. The players knew that their coach had a volatile temper when he was angry and that the only way to deal with that was to ignore the words of anger and listen to the words of wisdom—the instruction and feedback component of his message. The advice most players understood, according to Feinstein, was "When he's calling you a (jerk), don't listen. But when he starts telling you *why* you're a (jerk), listen. That way you'll get better (p. 5).

Another approach to organizing negative input is to integrate the complete message and then decide what has validity ("I can use this information") and what does not ("The person is angry; the message, if there is one, is inaccurate or based on the person's emotions, so ignore it"). Psychologists often refer to this process as *cognitive reappraisal*. Although to ignore stimuli that serve no purpose to the listener would be very efficient, it is also very difficult to do. A more practical approach is to integrate all of it and then develop skills to separate what is desirable and consciously filter out, perhaps by discounting, ignoring, or stopping the rehearsal of undesirable input as quickly as possible. The best ways to do this are (a) stop thinking about the stressful episode, at least temporarily during the competition, and (b) quickly refocus on environmental task demands.

P = plan response. At this point, the coach's hostilities or other forms of stress are history. The last thing an athlete should do is to focus on his or her own unpleasant feelings and quickly get rid of them. Focusing internally on negative information prevents athletes from maintaining a state of optimal readiness for the next response. Instead, the performer must quickly begin to plan upcoming actions based on recent feedback and experiences. Athletes might acknowledge the opponent's strengths, strategies, or tendencies or concentrate on correcting their own performance. At this stage, athletes' thoughts must go from integrating information to using it.

E = execute. All skilled athletes move with the appropriate precision and speed almost automatically and in the absence of cognition. This is especially important after experiencing an unpleasant event. An athlete who has been intimidated or upset by the discouraging remarks of others, particularly a person who controls the environment (e.g., coaches, parents, observers, and teammates) will hesitate, take fewer risks, and lack self-confidence in subsequent performance. The objective at this stage is to execute purposeful movements with the appropriate level of assertiveness, arousal, and concentration.

Common Coping Interventions

The following cognitive strategies, described briefly here, are commonly used in coping with discomfort and pain in sport.

1. *Positive self-talk.* Elite athletes prepare for pain by developing self-statements and mental imagery that allow them to handle it. Examples include, "Stick with my plan to handle the pain"; "Concentrate on my opponent"; "I can do this"; and "Focus on my technique."
2. *Mental imagery.* Imagery is used for various reasons and to meet different types of goals. Imagery may be used to rehearse and learn new skills and game strategies, to build self-confidence, to develop automated routines during the competition, and to manage discomfort or pain. Imagery begins, then, with thinking about its purpose, followed by taking a few minutes

to relax, closing the eyes, and thinking of the skill or activity being performed perfectly and successfully.

3. *Dissociation.* The important goal in pain management is to disconnect mind from body. This strategy consists of a mental skill called *dissociation*. Dissociation attempts to disconnect one's attentional focus from physical exertion and, instead, focus on external stimuli. Instead of focusing on the discomfort, let's say "tired legs" during a workout, focus on some external stimulus, including music, a workout instructor, or some other environmental cue. Dissociation is often used by individuals engaged in endurance sports or tasks. When athletes focus their attention on an external stimuli (e.g., a ball in play, an opponent or teammate), they are ignoring their own sensations, including pain and discomfort.

4. *Association.* Sometimes an athlete will want to confront (deal with) rather than avoid thoughts of discomfort, as long as a physician has given the athlete approval to compete. To overpower the feelings of discomfort, athletes use self-statements such as "I will get through this"; "Ignore my body and concentrate on my opponent (playing assignment)"; and "Focus on my performance"; or, they use pain as a cue to get "psyched up," the cognitive technique called *association*. One good example of using association is during exertion in weight lifting. The lifter's attentional focus should be on the muscle group used for that particular lift.

5. *Coping with pain at critical moments.* Competitors may "allow" themselves to feel discomfort only at certain times during the competition. For instance, players may focus on their injuries only between plays, but will ignore those injuries when executing movements on the field or when concentrating on their opponents and team strategies.

The key objective in pain-management strategies is to promote feelings of self-control, knowing when to monitor feelings of discomfort and when to ignore these feelings. Some conditions warrant a combination of attending to discomfort and ignoring feelings of discomfort, while other conditions require going in one direction or the other. Typically, however, pain is debilitating and unpleasant, often requiring the performer's attention. The performer, therefore, needs to develop mental skills to manage these feelings of discomfort.

Positive Self-Talk

One of the best ways to maintain self-confidence is to engage in positive self-talk. This is a universal practice among champs. The purposes of self-talk strategies vary. When the technique is used to gain or to maintain self-confidence, focusing inwardly and thinking about one's strengths rather than about one's opponent can generate a sense of self-control and responsibility for a competition's outcome.

Another reason to engage in positive self-talk is to analyze the movement. Canadian Olympic silver medalist (1984), Sue Holloway, in the kayak paired competition, engaged in a post-race analysis by asking herself, "Did this work? Did we do this? Or did we forget about it? How are we going to remember this?" For competitors to take the time to reflect on their performances and the possible causes of the outcomes—whether they are successful—is important. This self-reflection should always be done in a positive manner.

Mental Imagery

Mental imagery in sport, sometimes called visualization, is defined loosely as "seeing through the mind's eye" or creating a mental blueprint of desirable sport performance. Imagery is a mental skill using the athlete's thoughts of vivid images to alter performance. There are some types of imagery that involve physical movements (e.g., kinesthetic, or tactual imagery) and may be categorized as a *behavioral* rather than as mental or cognitive intervention. The benefits of imagery have been studied and applied to a number of situations, including anxiety reduction and learning new sport skills and game strategies. The results of most of these studies indicate that imagery favorably influences some targeted emotion, thought, or other mental state, often resulting in markedly improved performance

> **Sample mental imagery program**
> An elite-level basketball player has been experiencing thoughts that reflects the athlete's anxiety—feelings of worry or threat—while at the free-throw line. The team's mental skills coach writes a script for the player using visual, auditory, and kinesthetic (tactual) senses. Even "hearing" the crowd noise and task location—the free-throw line—is incorporated into the visual image to be as accurate as possible of the actual environment and external conditions. Imagery is increasingly effective when the athlete recalls *vivid* details of the imagined scene. The athlete's mental image should reflect actual performance situations as much as possible.

The goals of most imagery programs, including the one referenced, are (a) to increase the relationship between the athlete's imagined and real performance, (b) to create a mental representation of the athlete's actual competitive condition about which will be imagined, and (c) for athletes to mentally place themselves in the actual performance environment—in this case, at the free-throw line—to work through the feelings that occur in actual competition and address the cause(s) of performance limitations (i.e., better anxiety management). The actual situation should be mentally replicated or else the imagery session will not evoke the same game-like feelings and the imagery strategy will be less effective.

The basketball athlete in this example followed these guidelines:

a. Know the goal of the imagery session. Is it to improve a skill? Manage anxiety or some other emotion? Overcome errors or perceived pressure? Build confidence? Improve coping with in response to a particular type of stressful event?

b. Use one of several types of relaxation techniques, such as progressive relaxation, in which the athlete contracts (while inhaling) then relaxes (while exhaling) each of several muscle groups. The goal is to relax muscular tension and slow heart rate. Relaxation improves the vividness of imagery.

c. Re-enact the environmental (performance) conditions, as well as the athlete's feelings and emotions at the time.

d. Create an image that uses as many senses and is highly vivid (e.g., "I could 'feel' the basketball on my fingertips when taking the shot"").

e. Imagine through the mind's eye, that is, observe the performance condition, in this example, standing at the free-throw line, in the same way it was—and will continue to be—experienced during actual games. The athlete wants to replicate actual competition conditions during the imagery session. To use other terms, the athlete should use an internal, not an external, focus. Internal is far preferred because the athlete is attempting to make a mental blueprint of the actual situation.

f. As the skill is being "performed" mentally, incorporate the actual conditions and emotions that are likely to be included. Replicate real-life conditions.

g. Be sure that the skill is performed in the desired (perfect) manner—no errors—and leads to performance success. Do not image failure. The athlete wants to build the proper, most desirable blueprint of future performance.

h. Successful performance outcomes should be accompanied by a sense of personal satisfaction and gratification—perhaps replicating the external conditions of approval, recognition, and applause that may actually be experienced.

A complete imagery session following the relaxation phase takes only a few minutes and should not be conducted before bedtime (sleeping). The reason is that if done properly, imagery increases arousal level; remember, the image replicates an actual sporting event and that should raise, not lower, arousal.

The athlete should provide feedback to the consultant about the imagery experience, perhaps using a scale ranging from 1 ("not at all" or "very low") to 5 ("extremely" or "very much"). Numerical checklists allow the coach and athlete to compare current with past and future imagery attempts. Improvements can be measured numerically across time.

Assessing imagery procedures. Was the image conducted from an internal or external viewpoint, and did that result in an accurate representation of the actual situation? Was the athlete able to manipulate the images? Were all guidelines followed correctly? Could the athlete relax and concentrate on the skills, and was the skill executed successfully? The athlete should apply this imagery technique at least once daily, but can use other imagery sessions for other purposes (mentioned earlier), and to reach other goals. Imagery, if done properly, has strong research support and should be part of the arsenal of mental skills for every athlete to address personal needs both before and after the competition.

Case study: Pre-cueing to improve soccer goalkeeping

Sport psychology is a field that goes well beyond counseling athletes or teaching mental skills. One rarely recognized dimension is called educational sport psychology. It concerns the factors that help explain how athletes learn and remember sport skills and strategies, sometimes with the help of mental skills. The role of educational sport psychology might observe coaches deliver effective or ineffective instructional techniques. The end result, hopefully, is improving the athlete's performance outcomes. A study by Gabriel J. Diaz published in *Science Daily* (2010) nicely demonstrated the importance of a mental skill called pre-cueing.

Pre-cueing is the performer's detection of an environmental stimulus, or cue, just before initiating the skill that allows that performer to be ready, anticipate, and then perform the skill with the right precision, coordination, and speed. While receiving guidance *during* skill execution is termed a *cue*, a *pre-cue* is a planned strategy for obtaining this information and guidance *before* the skill is performed. Occasionally, sport psychology consultants can take on a teaching (pedagogical) role to help athletes use pre-cueing to anticipate the initial moves of their opponents, which results in faster response times and improved performance speed and accuracy.

Diaz attempted to explain how some top goalkeepers are able to stop a penalty kick, diving in the correct direction in advance of the kick. Diaz said his research stemmed from an observation of real-world penalty kicks, in which players aim for the left or right side of the goal while hiding their choice from the goalkeeper. Diaz knew that goalkeepers in penalty situations cannot wait until the ball is in the air before choosing whether to jump left or right; the speed of a well-placed penalty kick will almost definitely get past the goalie. This is why goalkeepers jump before the foot hits the ball. So, the research question is whether the goalie is making a pre-planned, "educated" choice about which direction to jump or if the direction of their jump better left up to chance (50/50).

He found that in the split second before foot meets ball, a soccer player's body betrays whether a penalty kick will go left or right. The result is that skilled soccer players were able to predict the direction of the kick before the foot strikes the ball.

Indicators such as the angles of the kicking foot, kicking upper-leg, and kicking shank were movements of a specific, or "local," area of the body highlighted by coaches and sports psychologists. Two of these, the angle at which the non-kicking foot is planted on the ground, and the angle of the hips as the kicking foot swings forward, are reliable indicators of kick direction.

Dissociation

The use of dissociation entails focusing one's attention on external features of the environment, as opposed to attending to internal feelings and sensations. Exercising in synchronization to music, for example, serves a dissociative function that focuses the performer's attention externally on the musical input and away from the physical responses to vigorous exercise. This technique can also help injured players keep discomfort from interfering with the cognitive demands of the competition.

Association

As discussed earlier, elite athletes tend to use one of two mental techniques in coping with physical discomfort, *association* and *dissociation*. The objective of association is to mentally be "in touch" with one's body and to maintain the necessary effort and motivation to meet physical challenges and personal performance goals. *This technique demands an internal focus.* For example, elite distance runners might concentrate on planting each foot with every step. Weight lifters "associate" with the same muscles used for optimal effort during a particular lift. Elite long-distance runners, golfers, and weight lifters, among others, consciously use an association strategy.

Association, however, can backfire. Athletes focusing internally on an injury may be misfocusing their attention and exacerbating their discomfort. Sport psychologists have found that one reason injured athletes do not return to their former (pre-injury) performance level, despite an apparent full physical recovery (as determined by a physician), is that their attention is incorrectly aimed toward the injured area rather than on environmental factors such as teammates, opponents, and objects.

The sport psychology literature contains a vast array of cognitive and behavioral techniques that help athletes reach their ideal performance state. In this section, several of these techniques and programs will be briefly reviewed. It is worth repeating a statement from earlier in the chapter. Each of these techniques are mental or behavioral skills, and like any other skill, they require learning, practice, feedback, and patience until there is full mastery and the skills can be executed with minimal planning and thinking. These are sample strategies. There are books and articles on each of these that are listed at the back of this chapter.

Discounting

Is every distraction, negative statement, or stressor of equal importance? Should athletes take each exposure to negative comments seriously and equally? Discounting is a mental strategy athletes use to reduce the importance of undesirable messages (e.g., an angry coach's remarks) or experiences (e.g., making a performance error). This technique helps organize information as meaningful and nonmeaningful, a message that warrants immediate attention versus ignoring.

Relaxation

Relaxation is the reduction or complete absence of muscular activity in the voluntary muscles. Relaxation techniques are popular among athletes and sport psychologists because they help reduce anxiety and stress, which are common problems in sport. However, relaxation techniques can be misused, especially if the athlete or skill needs to increase, not reduce, arousal. For example, sports that call for relaxation include golf, archery, and bowling. Other sports (e.g., basketball free-throw shooting, U.S. football field goal kicking, baseball pitching and hitting) require sudden reduced arousal. Other sports (e.g., wrestling, boxing, soccer, track and field) are sports that warrant prolonged heightened arousal.

In addition, there are different types of relaxation techniques, each serving a different purpose and meeting individual needs. Examples include progressive relaxation, autogenic training, biofeedback, imagery, centering, and hypnosis. Though full descriptions of these techniques go well beyond the scope of this chapter, all of them serve similar purposes in reducing muscular tension and improving thought processes. Each technique is explained more deeply in various publications available online.

It is important to note that relaxation is not always the proper response to unpleasant thoughts, emotions, and muscle tensions. Some athletes would rather use other cognitive or behavioral strategies, such as exercise, positive self-talk, cueing, pre-cueing, and attentional focusing. In addition, some athletes find relaxation very difficult and stressful in itself. Further, many situations are not compatible with relaxation strategies (e.g., just before or during the competition). However, if used correctly and under the appropriate circumstances, relaxation training is a valid and proven means of preventing or reducing muscular tension and anxiety while improving the athlete's concentration and self-confidence.

Music

The use of music is one of the more effective behavioral strategies that improve the athlete's mental set and helps establish optimal arousal level. Researchers have found that there are advantages of movement to music, especially if the activity is in synchronization to musical accompaniment.

One proper use of exposing athletes to music is based on the preferred level of cognitive and physical arousal. Fast-paced music speeds heart rate and other physiological processes (due mainly to an adrenaline rush), while slow-paced music relaxes the individual (assuming the individual enjoys the particular musical selection). Performance quality improves if the musical pace mirrors that of the pace of physical activity. Thus, activities that are dependent on faster reactions and movement speed should be accompanied by a faster pace (e.g., ice or field hockey, soccer, basketball) while slower, more relaxing music will be prove more beneficial for less intense sports such as golf, archery, and bowling.

The Problem of Overprescribing

One primary purpose of sport psychology consulting is to provide mental and emotional support to athletes to help them reach their optimal performance. Sometimes the form or style of consultation addresses mental health (often called psychopathological) issues, while other times a specific issue or concern is addressed by learning a mental skill (e.g., visualization) or intervention (e.g., mental planning). Growth and development of the research and practitioner literature has resulted in a proliferation of mental skills and interventions that allows consultants to prescribe "the best" remedy that addresses the athlete's unique problem. Sometimes, however, consultants, not unlike some medical practitioners, overprescribe strategies. They offer athletes a "menu" of options to address a particular concern and athletes are overwhelmed with an extensive to-do list. In attempting to follow a consultant's advice, an athlete may get so caught up in using the mental skill or intervention that he or she becomes distracted or less coordinated in performing the task at hand. This problem may be called "paralysis by analysis" in the sport pedagogy literature.

It is important, therefore, for coaches and sport psychology consultants to remember three things. First, mental skills are *skills*, and, like any sport skill, they need to be learned and practiced over time until they can be incorporated during competition. Second, athletes can be burdened by learning and using too many mental skills in a relatively short period of time. It is desirable that the athlete respond to learning a new mental skill or intervention "automatically" with only a minimum of conscious thinking at the predetermined designated time, usually before or during the competition. And third, athletes differ in their need to use certain types of cognitive strategies, but not others. Some mental techniques are applicable to many different sports, while others are effective for certain specific sports only and for a particular problem.

One more important point: Coaches, don't rush it and expect immediate change in your player's thoughts, emotions, or actions.

Learning *anything* takes time, patience, repetition (practice), and measurement, especially under the conditions of sport competition in which there is an antagonist called an opponent who wants your athlete to fail. Learning cannot occur without practice (repetition) and feedback on performance quality.

Here is a true story about the improper use of teaching and applying a mental skill. I was present in the home team's locker room minutes before a Division 1 (U.S.) college football team took the field. I was the team's sport psychology consultant (for three seasons). One of the mental skills I taught each athlete was the proper use of mental imagery. The head coach approved the plan for using this technique. Without consulting me, however, the coach conducted a team mental imagery session in the locker room after warm-ups were completed and the team was about the take the field. He ordered staff to darken the locker room ("lights out!") for a 2-minute imagery session. Then he asked the athletes to use mental imagery to "think about performance success" however each athlete defined "success." This was an example of the improper use of a mental skill. When the lights came on, a few of the athletes started snoring, others were yawning, and all were relaxed—but not prepared to play a football game. Our team fell behind 21-0 after the first quarter and went on to lose the game. Thus, the coach who believed that he possessed the necessary skills and knowledge to administer a mental imagery program to his team just minutes before game time. This example shows why all sports participants, including and especially coaches must be careful about assuming they have the required background and skills to apply a mental skills program without proper training.

One primary role of coaches and sport psychology consultants is to help athletes select, learn, and apply the cognitive or behavioral strategies that best meet their needs. These strategies may be described according to the conditions in which they might be most effective, and when used in combination as part of a mental skills package, program, or intervention. For example, while the mental skill of visualization is often used to reduce anxiety, it can also be applied in combination with learning sport skills and team strategies. Therefore, in this way, visualization can be used to reduce anxiety or to improve sport performance. Perhaps one of the most common use of mental skills has been the competitor's attempt to cope with stressful events experienced during the competition.

Key points. Given the extensive number of strategies and interventions reviewed in this chapter, let's review this material.

- Sport psychology interventions are mental and behavioral techniques, sometimes consisting of one or more mental skills that are intended to favorably influence the thoughts, emotions, or performance quality of sports competitors and teams.

- Cognitive interventions consist of the athlete's *conscious* use of thoughts or emotions that enhance performance quality. Examples include mental imagery, positive self-talk, cueing, and attentional focusing.

- Behavioral interventions consist of the athlete's *conscious* use of actions that improve performance quality. Goal setting, music, social engineering, and light exercise are examples.

- Mental toughness (MT) is common among elite athletes. It is learned, not inherited and not a trait. MT consists of having the *natural* or *developed* psychological edge that enables an athlete to cope better with the stressful demands of competitive sport and allows athletes to overcome adversity while maintaining focus and control of the situation.

- Self-regulation is the foundation of using mental skills and other forms of interventions. It consists of the athlete's ability to initiate, monitor, and maintain specific planned thoughts and actions that are intended to enhance sport performance and other desirable outcomes.

- Some athletes are more responsive than others to certain types of mental skills than others. For reducing anxiety, for instance, some athletes prefer to engage in light exercise, while others prefer using relaxation techniques. Coaches need to be aware of the needs of each athlete and to respect individual differences in how they prefer to mentally prepare for the competition.

An important purpose of this chapter is to inform coaches, athletes, and all other sport participants about a component of sport competition that is often neglected—the mental game. It is said that "sport success is 90% mental." That's not true; you still need superior sport skills to win. However, what *is* true is that the athlete who is aware of and applies mental skills before and during the competition will be more successful versus the athlete who does not use mental skills at least 90% of the time.

chapter six

Coaching for the Competition

We now turn to applying these previously described theories, beginning with the coach. Coaches cannot be expected to reach into the heart and mind of each athlete and cause the performer to feel a certain way. Each player has a different mental approach to the competition and to affect every athlete in the same manner is impossible. The unique needs of each athlete is the problem with the so-called "T-E-A-M" approach, which many coaches support. In this strategy, everyone on the team goes through the same mental and physical preparation before the competition. The sport psychology literature does not always support this approach.

Of course, some pre-competition tasks must be conducted by all team members at the same time. Many athletes at the more advanced levels prefer to prepare mentally for the competition in their own way; some players would rather be alone, while others prefer the company of their teammates, for instance. Here are a few general suggestions that coaches can use in group settings and with individual athletes to help them to manage arousal and anxiety.

Anxiety and Arousal Reducers

Pre-competition emotions are often stressful. Stress is the body's way of preparing for "flight or fight." And, yet, sometimes coaches must help their players to "psych down" and become a bit more subdued. Although arousal and anxiety are not identical and often warrant different techniques, several approaches to reducing both mental states can be used.

1. *Light exercise.* Stress, arousal, and anxiety can all be reduced through light physical activity prior to the competition. In fact, one psychological benefit of the pregame warm-up routine is to relax the athlete. This stress-reducing technique is particularly effective with high state-anxious athletes (Morgan 1979). Low-arousal sports such as golf, fencing, or tennis usually require less intense physical activity (walking, Pilates, or yoga, for instance) to relax the performer than do high-energy activities such as soccer, wrestling, and football.

    There has been some debate about the overuse of physical activity during warm-up. Often, teams seem to exert a game's worth of energy before the competition even begins. There is support in the physiology literature—although more research is needed—that an intensely physical and emotional pregame warm-up might do more harm than good by depleting players' energy and, in a hot, humid environment, lead to dehydration.

2. *Avoid giving the "relax" command.* Coaches commonly tell their players to relax, especially just before the competition. Sometimes this increases the athlete's tension. "The coach knows I'm uptight," the athlete thinks. The coach's request to "take it easy" may be contradictory to the player's preferred mental state of feeling more pumped up. For the coach to say nothing may be more helpful than using verbal messages that try to alter the player's preferred state of mind. Confidence-building messages (e.g., "Just play the way you practiced and

you'll be fine") may be more effective than messages that intend to change the athlete's emotional state.

3. *Develop pregame routines.* Tasks that are familiar to athletes are less anxiety provoking than novel actions before sports events. This is why it is best to have the players follow a regimented and familiar pregame warm-up routine, the night before, on the day of, and just prior to the competition. The night preceding and the day of the competition should be structured and relaxing. The potential for anxiety is heightened when athletes are less certain about the pre-competition schedule and the type of activities prior to and at the competition venue on the day of a competition. Of course, the activities of game day differ from other days. But coaches can decrease athletes' nervousness by conducting game day rehearsals. Some coaches will simulate routines at least 24 hours leading up to the competition, including the times of day that meals are consumed, scheduled practice times, and other conditions similar to the actual competition.

4. *Simulate games in practice.* Athlete anxiety will be reduced if skills and strategies that will be used in the competition are rehearsed in practice sessions until they are mastered. Most coaches contend that the mental preparation for games starts during practice all week. During the game is not the time to teach new, unrehearsed skills.

5. *Individualize mental strategies.* Athletes differ markedly in the ways that they prepare for competition. Some players prefer a sedate atmosphere that allows for self-reflection, mental imagery, and relaxation. Others desire a more vocal, exciting locker room atmosphere. The key coaching strategy here, is, whenever possible, to allow each player to prepare mentally for the competition in the way that he or she finds most comfortable. Athletes who like it quiet but are exposed to a lot of noise become annoyed and distracted, raising anxiety and not preparing properly for the competition.

6. *Have high but realistic expectations.* Anxiety is heightened by personal insecurity, low self-esteem, and the high expectations of others. The athlete perceives the sport situation as threatening. Coaches can increase player confidence, thereby reducing anxiety, not with trite, abstract comments such as "You'll do fine" or "Go after 'em," but rather with informative messages that are based on past performance. Coaches might consider reviewing the player's strengths, weaknesses of opponents, game strategies, and articulating their confidence in the player's skill and effort as a way to promote positive thoughts and reduce negative (anxious) ones.
7. *Keep errors in perspective.* Physical mistakes are an integral part of performing physical tasks. The coach's response to mistakes directly affects the athlete's stress level. Many coaches contend that players take on the personality of their coach whether they remain "cool and calm" or respond to adversity with anger and lose emotional control. To manage anxiety after an error, coaches should remain in control and be the only person who can question or become upset with a call. Players need to keep calm.

    Keeping an error in perspective means (a) remembering that the error is unlikely to affect the competition's outcome directly; (b) keeping the player focused on present and future events and, for the moment, forgetful of past mistakes; and (c) helping the athlete to cope with the error so as to avoid negative self-statements, decreased self-confidence, and undesirable emotions and feelings.
8. *Avoid discussing the team's record.* Thinking about records and outcomes, which are beyond the performer's control prior to the competition, tends to decrease concentration and to increase anxiety. Anxiety is, after all, a response to the chance the athlete will fail, the source of worry. Reviewing the team's losing record or the pressures of maintaining a winning record are counterproductive. Coaches with whom I have spoken are

in agreement that athletes need to concentrate on performance, not outcome, and to let winning take care of itself.

9. *Respond with empathy, support, and optimism to an athlete's injury.* Coaches (and athletic trainers) should be calm, yet attentive and sensitive, to the injured athlete. In addition to the pain, injured players must deal with their fear of surgery and a possible end to their season—or career. The coach's (or athletic trainer's) response to the player's injury will significantly affect the athlete's anxiety level. A supportive, empathetic coach will relax the player, whereas an angry, disappointed coach who ignores or inflicts guilt on the player, even during the rehabilitation period, induces anxiety and resentment.

    Former Western Illinois University cross-country and track head coach, Dick Abbott, considered it part of his job to "supplement the medical first aid that the training room provided with his own brand of emotional first aid" (Mechikoff & Kozar 1983, p. 82). After the athlete received proper training-room attention, Abbott would step in with concern and reassurance that the injury would heal on schedule. Then he would consult with the athlete on almost a daily basis.

10. *Minimize self-focusing.* Results of studies indicate that persons who feel anxious and have unfavorable expectations about an outcome should *not* focus their attention on these unpleasant thoughts. Negative thinking tends to exacerbate anxiety and to disrupt future performance. Sometimes such thinking leads to the athlete completely disengaging from further activity. Instead, athletes should focus externally on the task at hand, the location of opponents and teammates, or anticipate their next move. On the other hand, persons who have confidence, positive feelings, and expect favorable outcomes will benefit from internal focusing. Focusing on positive thoughts improve confidence, optimism, favorable expectations, and less anxiety. These individuals are likely to persist on tasks longer and feel more confident and in control of the situation.

11. *Acknowledge possible sources of stress and anxiety.* Sometimes it is a good idea for athletes to simply ignore feelings and experiences that produce unpleasant feelings, including anxiety. In fact, ignoring negative thoughts is an effective way to cope with stressful events. At the same time, it is not constructive for coaches to ignore athletes' stressful feelings; instead, they should help athletes directly address sources of stress.

Every competitor has different needs and has his or her own unique ways of preparing for the competition. The coach has the very challenging task of knowing which buttons to push for a particular athlete and to create an environment in which the athlete will thrive and play to his or her best. Now we turn to the strategies coaches might use to raise athletes' arousal levels to reach optimal performance levels.

Pre-Competition Arousal Raisers

Athletes cannot be effective if they are not giving optimal effort or seem unmotivated to compete. Their reactions will be slowed and their coordination reduced. The nervous system has to be in an optimal state of readiness; information processing is an active process, from anticipation of a stimulus to evaluating the performance outcome. Sometimes the coach must bring the team "up" to ensure proper effort and concentration. This is more difficult than most people realize. A few guidelines follow.

First, the coach must consider each player's skill level, age, psychological needs, playing position, and the task's complexity. Some players, for instance, require less psyching up than others. Less-skilled players should focus on form, concentration, and planned maneuvers. Therefore, levels of activation that are too high are more likely to disrupt their performance.

Second, the ability to control both positive and negative emotions improves with age. Younger athletes are more susceptible to the deleterious effects of disapproval and negative feedback from significant others (e.g., coaches, parents, peers) than are their older counterparts (Passer 1983). Emotional control in sport is a function of the person's self-perceptions of their skill level, readiness to compete, expectations for success, and causal attributions following sport experiences (i.e., internal attributions following perceived success; external attributions following perceived failure). Each of these factors tends to be more accurate and productive in older, more experienced, and better-skilled athletes. Younger athletes will feel more anxiety when they are scolded or given information that increases the pressure to win the competition than their older counterparts, who can keep these pressures and expectations in better perspective.

Third, some positions and tasks require higher levels of activation than others. As far back as 1970, Oxendine contended that sports skills involving gross-motor movement require higher activation levels than skills that are highly complex in nature. Sprinters should be more psyched up than long-distance runners, for instance, according to track and field coaches.

Another important factor related to increasing arousal is timing. For example, it is not a good idea, contrary to popular practice, to get the team excited the *night* before a game. This only disturbs sleep and concentration. The late Woody Hayes, former football coach at Ohio State University, disagreed with coaches who have their athletes view commercial films that are high in aggression the night before a football game. After all, the game isn't played until the next day. Some coaches will have their team observe videos from sports films (e.g., a pre-game talk or another movie scene) in the locker room just minutes before taking the floor. Therefore, watching a film to increase aggression the night before a competition is ill-timed and may disturb sound sleep.

Visual aids, however, can be effective motivational and instructional tools. Some coaches show the film of last year's competition. Former college football coach and athletic director Dick

Tamburo suggests that if you will face a team at the end of the week that humiliated your team the year before, you may want to show the film of last year's humiliating defeat prior to the start of the game (Mechikoff & Kozar 1983). Rather than forgetting past failures, Tamburo's suggestion might have some merit if the present players are confident and want to prove that they are a better, improved team.

A different approach to visual input is to provide videotapes of the athletes' best previous performances. The purpose of this strategy is to model correctly executed skills, a concept that supports Bandura's (1977) self-efficacy theory. To increase pre-competition arousal, coaches want to instill a sense of self-confidence and optimism in each player.

Athletes have an understandably strong need to be reminded of their good qualities, as well as receiving a few criticisms of their performance. A balanced review of their level of competence will have more credibility and influence to make favorable changes in their future performance than reliance on what they did wrong. To remind athletes of their past successes enhances feelings of reassurance, self-confidence, and expectations for success. Examples include, "Based on how I saw you perform in practice this week, I know you're ready"; "This is a better team than our opponents"; and "Think about what you can do well, and be proud of it. Let's prove we're the better team." If, however, the opponent is commonly acknowledged as superior, the coach might remind the athletes, "This is a good opportunity to compare your skills to theirs." "How good are you? Let's find out!" I was present when a coach simply said "Go out there and have fun" just before competing against a nationally ranked, far superior team. The team played their best game of the year.

Finally, although arousal has an emotional component, coaches can institute certain techniques that predictably increase their players' physiological arousal, again to optimal, not maximal, levels. Examples increasing arousal level include (a) increasing voice intensity; (b) using bright indoor lighting; (c) generating loud noises such as clapping or fast-paced music; (d) using nonverbal cues such as hand or facial gestures, especially when in close proximity to the athlete; (e) contacting the athletes physically, such as holding a player's arm or shoulder (but be careful; abusive physical contact raises anxiety to the detriment of performance and male coaches must be especially careful about the firmness and location of touching a female athlete); (f) using the players' first names, especially when providing verbal recognition for high-quality performance; (g) setting immediate (short-term) performance goals; (h) introducing the players—at least the starting lineup—to the crowd before the competition; and (i) having players engage in light physical exercise, which is customary during the pre-competition warm-up.

If this list of arousal raisers seems too much for one coach to do, that might be true. This means that arousal-raising strategies should also be conducted by other team leaders, too. These team leaders could include assistant coaches or team captains. Less effective coaches appear to forget that coaching assistants and selected players can have a valuable role in regulating the athletes' emotions before and during the competition, and making other contributions to team game preparation. Media stories abound that provide examples of team players giving a pep talk before, during, or after the game. Former head coach of the 1968 U.S. Olympic track team, Payton Jordan, asserts, "If athletes hear you (the head coach) all the time, they will shut you out after a while" (Mechikoff & Kozar 1983).

I call it "becoming coach deaf" when the player stops listening or is "going through the motions" of showing interest in the coach's words, but nothing sticks. With time, the content of the head coach's message loses meaning; athletes "tune out" the person who is constantly offering verbal input or feedback. New voices coming for different individuals increases the athlete's cognitive arousal level, which can increase player incentive and interest. Further, assistant coaches typically establish positive relationships with players, which increases their influence on player thoughts and actions. In fact, in a study by Anshel and Straub (1991), American college football players indicated a preference for greater input by, and the more effective use of, the team's assistant coaches to improve team leadership. Head coaches would be wise to delegate some leadership responsibilities, at least occasionally.

Halftime and Time-outs

Halftime, in most sports, is a period often used for adjusting, regrouping, reviewing plans and strategies, relaxing (recovery), and exchanging information. Athletes should be allowed to remain quiet and to calm down from their first-half efforts. They need to prepare mentally for the second half (or next period), even in isolation if they so choose. They have special physiological and psychological needs during this time-out period to which coaches must be sensitive. For instance, liquid refreshment is essential to replenish energy and body resources, not only between periods but also in small amounts *during* the competition. Here is an example of what *not* to do. As soon as the athletes enter the locker room during a break in game play, some coaches tend to shower them with information feedback. This is a bad idea. After the contest, and even at half time, most athletes need a recovery break and rest, at least for several minutes. After vigorous physical activity and heightened arousal the human organism needs to recover for a short time. Without recovery time, our ability to process and retain information is impaired. Researchers maintain that a disruption in attentional processes may occur if internal/external factors (e.g., fatigue, high arousal) cause an imbalance between an athlete's ability to process information and task demands.

Therefore, two suggestions for the coach are warranted: First, delay offering input to the players for several minutes at the start of a long rest period (half-time, for instance). The players need a little time to relax and to allow their information-processing systems to focus and concentrate on new input. Second, limit the amount of information that is provided when athletes enter the locker room. Coaches may (and often do) have "a thousand things" to tell their players based on their observations. Unfortunately, much of this information will not be remembered and, hence, not used later in the competition. Ignoring the coach's input is not usually intentional, but rather, due to information overload, physical and mental fatigue, and a limited ability to process and retain new, perhaps complicated, information.

Another issue concerning halftime and time-outs concerns providing players information feedback. Effective teaching indicates (a) making one or two key points in one session; (b) trying to communicate *visually*, perhaps using a whiteboard or physical demonstration; (c) summarizing key points at the end of the session to reduce the amount of information to be processed and remembered; and (d) including positive comments—compliments—about earlier performances and having reasonably high expectations about the quality of subsequent performances.

Should athletes be criticized during the competition? Yes, they should if it's warranted; however, coaches should use criticism constructively and selectively without losing emotional control. While critical feedback is essential for learning and altering performance, too much criticism is like too much of any type of information—it is soon forgotten because the athlete feels overwhelmed, and, perhaps, humiliated. Also, critical input should not be communicated in a manner that intimidates or embarrasses the player, such as criticism in front of teammates, if at all possible. A statement such as "You guys were terrible" has less impact on improving performance than "You're waiting too long before taking the shot" or "We're playing too loose on defense; stay closer to your opponent."

What about anger? Isn't it normal for coaches to become upset and angry with poor athlete performance? While coach anger is a common reaction to frustration, anger is rarely effective in providing players with effective feedback and improving performance. Anger can be a distractor. Players get caught up in the coach's anger rather than in the message. Anger reflects a loss of emotional control (for example, name calling, destroying equipment, physically or mentally abusing athletes, or making threats) and is counterproductive.

Athletes become highly stressed and are caught up in the coach's anger rather than in the information he or she is trying to provide.

For successful coaches, the most effective approach at providing feedback is to accentuate the positive when the team is behind at halftime. The message typically is "We are better than this; fortunately, we have 30 minutes left to show it." When a coach comes into the locker room and is visibly upset and projects anger and hostility toward the team, he or she is taking a 50-50 chance on positive motivational results, not good odds.

How NOT to Prepare Athletes for Competition

Some anxiety is a good thing. Mature, higher-skilled players need a sense of concern—even urgency—before and during the competition. While all athletes experience anxiety, elite-level athletes are better able to manage their anxiety than non-elites are. In this way, anxiety is far less disruptive to performance. Still, coaches do not want their players to be more anxious than necessary. Sometimes a coach will use a technique that has the opposite of its intended effect; it unintentionally promotes, rather than reduces, anxiety. Here are some examples of what coaches often do in the mistaken belief that they are helping the athletes:

1. *Teaching before or during the competition.* Studying minutes before an exam is fruitless because the learner is too tense and anxious (worried) to retain information. Learning is severely inhibited under stressful conditions. The same process occurs in sport. The emotions of high arousal and anxiety prevent learning to any significant degree. Similarly, learning new skills and strategies just prior to or during the competition rarely leads to performance success. Coaches must avoid presenting new skills, introducing complicated changes in strategy, and sophisticated explanations immediately prior to and during

the contest. New, unrehearsed plays should be saved for the next practice session and mastered before being included in competition plans.

2. *Making "must-win" statements.* Don't the players already know that? Comments that reflect dire consequences if the team fails to win only add to player anxiety (worry or threat) and fail to build confidence and the proper player mental preparation. Effective coaches focus on reviewing skills and strategies before the competition or between periods—or they say nothing at all.

3. *Using criticism as a motivator.* Critical feedback, if used appropriately, can motivate athletes to think, feel, and perform more effectively. However, too often in sport settings critical feedback is used and expressed wrongly. Critical comments are usually expressed in an angry manner; however, it's the coach's anger that creates negative feelings and emotions in competitors. Too often coaches believe that they need to bring a player "up" by putting the player "down." Athletes need self-confidence in order to succeed; they need to feel good about their ability to perform at their best and win. Criticism of an athlete's character or sarcastic remarks tend to have the opposite effect.

   Wait a minute! What about the player who "rises to the occasion" in response to his or her coach's harsh remarks? True, some players may react with vigor, aggression, and determination, and perhaps improve their performance as a result—in the short term. But the long-term effect is often another story. Verbally abused players will feel resentment, anger, humiliation, and less loyalty toward the coach. The recommendation to coaches is to base criticism on specific performance and not to use it to "play games" with an athlete's mind.

4. *Setting goals incorrectly.* Sometimes a coach will require an athlete to set and meet what the athlete feels is an unrealistically difficult goal. True, players should find challenging goals motivating. But goals that are too difficult, that are set exclusively by the coach without input from the athlete, and that are

based on outcomes (over which the player often has no control) rather than performance, will tend to raise anxiety and inhibit performance. In fact, many athletes will give up or drop out rather than attempt to meet a goal that they consider to be far beyond realistic expectations. The competitor's belief is "If I don't try, I can't fail" or "Why even bother?"

5. *Inducing guilt.* Inducing guilt in the athlete about his or her failure to meet performance expectations hinders rather than enhances sport performance. Statements such as "You guys should feel ashamed of yourselves" or "You mean to tell me that the other team is better than you?" do not motivate athletes or enhance player loyalty to the team and coach. Guilt can contribute to heightened anxiety and is one of the causes of anxiety, both before and following the contest. Instructing a player purposely to injure an opponent or to cheat is an unethical example of attempting to induce player guilt.

6. *Blaming the referee/sports official.* Coaches and athletes often become antagonistic toward receiving a "bad" call from the game official, especially if the call results in performance failure. While blaming the official for performance failure could be an accurate response, the coach needs to be cautious that blame is not misdirected and that the official is not a scapegoat for the team's loss. Sometimes the coach feels that arguing with the arbiter will motivate the team (i.e., create heightened arousal and "wake them up"). The potential problem with this approach is that when athletes feel that the outcome of a competition is not under their control (i.e., its "bad luck" due to "poor" officiating), they feel helpless about their power to change the situation. Consequently, players mentally give up and do not maintain optimal effort. They may even stop trying. Coaches have a right and responsibility to communicate with game officials. But when the interaction is negative and persistent, players feel embarrassed ("I expect my coach to behave in a mature manner"), guilty ("I caused the argument"), or helpless ("We can't win because the ref doesn't like us").

7. *Reminding players who's watching.* Although athletes love a crowd, they seldom respond enthusiastically to being evaluated by persons whose opinions may influence their future success. Judges, scouts, and recruiters are potentially threatening to players. Consequently, awareness of their presence might cause more harm than good by increasing anxiety (which, as you remember, is defined as "perceived threat"). Coaches would be doing players a favor by not mentioning who is watching.

8. *"I don't have to justify my decisions."* So said an assistant college football coach on hearing my suggestion that some players would benefit from understanding the reasons behind certain coaching decisions. Let's face it, the coach is in the driver's seat. He or she is the decision maker, and the athletes can either carry out his or her orders or leave the team. But this does not diminish the fact that players often feel more anxious and even less supportive of the decision when asked to do something without an explanation, especially if the player disagrees with the coach's decision. Why do players have a particular training regimen? Why was a player removed from the game, a certain play called, or a particular strategy used? If coaches want player loyalty, it would be wise to take the time to explain the rationale for making certain decisions, at least occasionally and if it involves a particular player.

   Perhaps the term "explain" is more palatable to the coach than "justify," which may suggest sacrificing power, control, and authority. Of course, coaches don't have the time to explain all (or even most) decisions to the participants. But on some issues and in certain situations, to ask for athletes' opinions before a decision is made and to explain the decision before any action is carried out makes sense.

9. *Applying the starter/nonstarter double standard.* One way to decrease player loyalty to the team and coach is to treat players differently based on their team status. Mistreating the players who are less central to the team's success negatively impacts all team members because athletes need to support

one another regardless of their positions. The team leader may necessarily spend more time with starters than with substitutes, especially on larger teams. But ignoring substitutes or allowing starting players to follow one set of rules and policies while the nonstarters follow another is upsetting and may diminish team loyalty and motivation. Coaches should remember that nonstarters are only one injury away from starting.

10. *Using exercise for punishment.* This practice is one of the great myths in coaching and physical education. Exercise serves the very important purpose of improving one's physical status so that maximal performance can be reached and maintained. For competitors to find conditioning to be meaningful and even pleasant is important. Exercise should be desirable, not something that is a tool to invoke pain or discomfort. In this way, administering exercise as a form of punishment to athletes is a contradiction in terms. Using exercise as punishment turns the athlete away from the very activity that is necessary to promote good performance and health. Coaches should want to keep exercise enjoyable.

Tips for Managing Anxiety

Responsibility for controlling an athlete's emotions rests with the individual competitor. There are many books, chapters, and magazine articles that address the proper use of mental skills for reducing undesirable feelings before and during the competition. Certainly some techniques will work better for one athlete than another, and not all of these strategies are valid under all sport conditions. The following recommendations for anxiety management are derived from applied sport psychology researchers.

1. *Focus on what you can control.* One primary source of anxiety is worrying about uncontrollable factors such as sustaining an injury, playing a superior opponent, or a successful game outcome. Athletes whose thoughts center on "what if's" or "I

hope's" are candidates for heightened anxiety. Quality competitors focus on their performance and reflect on the strategies they practiced in preparation for the competition. Anxiety lies in fear of the unknown. By focusing on what one can control, athletes become task oriented and concentrate on immediate performance demands. Focus on strengths, not weaknesses, and what you can do, not what you can't do.

2. *Think practice.* As a sport psychology consultant, I have found these two words to be the most concise yet powerful message I can give a competitor. If high anxiety is due to the performer's perception of a threatening situation, it makes sense to reflect on the times when sport skills were executed without these unpleasant thoughts. These times are practice sessions. When athletes "think practice," they are reflecting on a relatively relaxed, nonthreatening environment in which their sport skills were performed successfully. If, according to researchers, our bodies cannot tell the difference between real and imagined stimuli, why not play a mental videotape that reflects success, accompanied by positive, desirable thoughts, rather than the "nightmare" videotape?

Authors Dr. Ken Ravizza, the late sport psychologist, and Mr. Tom Hanson, a former professional athlete (1995), reflect on the value of game preparation and carrying out effective practices in baseball. They contend that "the quality of your practices determines your reactions to pressure situations. A quality practice involves doing things with the same intensity and focus you use in a game. Thus, practice what you are going to do in a game" (p. 137).

3. *Remember the worst-case scenario.* The worst-case scenario reflects this simple question: "What is the worst that can happen?" If you were to walk across the street blindfolded, the worst-case scenario is death if you were struck by a car. Consequently, this sort of behavior is unthinkable. Fortunately, not since the early Romans has sport been a matter of life and death. The reasons for competing in sport are the enjoyment,

pleasure, and personal fulfillment it brings to its participants. Even at the level of advanced competition, the worst-case scenario strategy will reduce stress and enable the athlete to maintain emotional control.

Remember that the competition's outcome is not always under the performer's control, so in thinking of the worst-case scenario, you are placing sport in perspective. Sport participation should be fun.

4. *Keep active*. Researchers have found that engaging in regular physical activity reduces anxiety and distracts the individual from unpleasant thoughts. This relaxing effect is one purpose for the pregame warm-up. Physical activity provides a physical outlet for heightened emotions, such as anxiety, rather than bottling up these emotions, and focuses the person's attention externally on performing a physical task rather than internally on undesirable emotions.

5. *Use cognitive strategies (mental skills)*. The sport psychology literature suggests numerous mental skills for managing stress and anxiety (discussed later). Mental imagery, various relaxation techniques, thought stopping, positive self-talk, and numerous cognitive-behavioral mental skills packages have been used successfully to reduce unpleasant emotions. Not unlike sport skills, these mental skills require instruction, practice, and eventual mastery over a period of time. The athlete's "obligation" in using them is to believe in the effectiveness of these techniques and to practice them regularly.

chapter seven

Coaching the Injured Athlete

It is common to experience an injury in sport competition. Because enormous time and energy is invested to develop athletes' skills, it is very important that coaches continue to work with and invest in recovery from injury during their rehabilitation period. This chapter will address the psychological issues associated with experiencing an injury while competing in sport, describe the factors that contribute to and diminish high-quality sport performance after rehabilitation, and suggest ways in which coaches can promote full recovery of the injured athlete—do's and don'ts.

Psychological Responses to Injury

Experiencing a sport-related injury is often very traumatic for athletes. In addition to pain and physical harm, sport-related injuries are uniquely traumatic. Serious injuries may signal the end of an athlete's career in sport or that another player may permanently replace the athlete, spelling the end of his or her career. And then there is the mental side of experiencing an injury. From a psychological perspective, athletes typically feel a strong attachment to their sport participation. The anguish that athletes feel after an injury is partly due to a personality trait called *sport self-esteem*.

Self-esteem (SE) refers to the extent to which a person identifies with his or her unique qualities and values themselves. There are approximately seven sources, or types, of self-esteem, and each source reflects the person's level of self-acceptance and importance. Examples of SE that reflect one's self-value are knowledge (i.e., scholarship, intelligence), social, religious, physical (i.e., physique, or body), and sport. Thus, not surprisingly, this trait is prevalent among highly skilled athletes who most strongly identify themselves related to their sport involvement. Serious injuries that may result in reducing the athlete's skill level and endanger the athlete's future participation in sport directly influences (i.e., reduces) their sport self-esteem.

Most injured athletes experience three phases after an injury.

Phase 1: Grief. Many athletes, similar to nonathletes, have a "Superman complex" and feel impervious to suffering an injury, especially one that will endanger their future participation in sport. Thus, this first post-injury phase consists of a *sudden shock-like state*, in which they do not believe and comprehend that they may have sustained a possible career-ending injury. Manifestations of being injured include anger with their situation—even directed at medical or athletic training staff—denial that the injury results in not participating in future competitions, and "bargaining" with others such as a higher power, medical or athletic training staff, their coach, to dismiss the injury as "nothing serious" when, in fact, it might be very serious and need time for a rehabilitation program.

Phase 2: Intense preoccupation with injury. Because athletes' sport self-esteem has taken a "big hit," this phase of the injury experience includes focusing attention and concentration on the potential for poor outcomes that may be experienced; many athletes may be consumed by this traumatic experience. The results of being preoccupied with the injury include insomnia, mental fatigue, depression, anxiety, crying, and guilt about disappointing the coach and teammates.

Phase 3: Reorganization. In this last phase of the injury experience, the (**non-elite**) athlete feels (and displays) renewed interests in other sports, hobbies, academic outcomes (if the athlete is attending school), while maintaining involvement in the injury rehabilitation program. Life's activities, perhaps including recreational (lower-skilled) sport involvement, are reorganized, while the athlete still hopes for a complete recovery and a resumption of sport competition.

Fear and Anxiety in the Injured Athlete

Experiencing a sport injury carries with it numerous thoughts and emotions that inhibit the athlete's normal mental functioning. There are several sources of fear and anxiety that accompany an injury, particularly if the injury results in missing games, being examined by a medical practitioner, or consulting a mental health professional. Some of the most serious fears, those that inhibit and distract the athlete's normal cognitive functioning, include the following, all of which the coach's actions and words can help in comforting the player.

Not recovering. The injured athlete's self-talk is filled with worry about never being able to compete at the same level prior to the injury, that the injury is permanent and disabling. Later, we will address the likely reasons that athletes do not perform as well after sport injury rehabilitation as compared to pre-injury performance.

Re-injury. If the athlete suffered structural damage and pain, it's understandable they will fear re-injury. After all, even if the rehabilitation went well and the athlete was fully compliant to attend all rehab sessions, there is the perception that healing process did not recapture the same level of tissue health as before the injury.

Perception of weakened tissue will cause many injured athletes to be cautious about going "all out" while ignoring their injured area. The result is for rehabilitated athletes to perform in a more tentative manner, which, ironically, can lead to further injury.

Losing playing time or team status. This issue is of major importance to injured athletes who fear that their substitute teammate will perform well and replace the injured player. This is one reason so many athletes choose to ignore pain and injury and not report their medical condition to the athletic trainer or other medical staff. Losing playing time is based on a medical diagnosis and compliance to the injury rehabilitation program. Losing playing time, however, is a coach decision that will be addressed later in this chapter. Coaches have an enormous role to play in creating an atmosphere for every athlete based on safety and security and for eradicating athletes' insecurities about their future as a team member and resuming their team position.

Not feeling like a productive team member. This is very common among highly skilled athletes. They may feel guilty about not being able to demonstrate their competence and contribute to team success. The injury is also prohibiting them from demonstrating their competence. In their haste to recover and participate, their guilt might lead to premature participation to compete, which, in turn, may lead to further and more serious injury and pain. They are not ready to experience the rigors of performing at optimal levels in competition. The coach has an enormous role here in helping the athlete remain patient to complete the post-injury rehabilitation program.

Disappointing others (coach, teammates, fans, parents). Feelings of disappointing others is the athlete's perception that may or may not be based on reality. Perhaps the athlete is picking up cues from others based on changes in communication—verbal and nonverbal—or comments that the athlete overhears or reads in the media that suggest the athlete's "failure" to meet performance expectations. For example, it is unwise to ask the athlete when he or she will be able to return to competition. That is an issue that only the team's medical staff can answer accurately and might induce further guilt that he or she is unable to contribute to the team. Injured athletes need not be reminded that the coach, or anyone else, is waiting impatiently for their return and that their team role might diminish as a result of their prolonged absence. What the coach can do, instead, is to express support for the athlete's speedy recovery and that the team looks forward to his or her return to competition, even mentioning informally and over the course of the rehabilitation period that the athlete's contribution to the team is missed.

Psychological Predictors of Injury

Researchers have attempted to examine the factors that best predict an athlete's propensity to be injured during the season. If this finding can be verified, it is possible for coaches and athletic trainers to intervene and help present injuries from occurring, at least to a point. Here is what they found.

Life stress. Life stress, consisting of the degree of previous and current change and stress in athlete's life, is significantly related to experiencing a sport injury. Reasons are uncertain, but researchers feel that high personal stress increases muscular tension and distracts the athlete from performing sport skills with optimal coordination. Injury results.

Weapon to induce guilt. A sports injury could be used to send a message to coaches, "You pushed me too hard"; "Now look what you've done"; I am too hurt to play." Psychologically, the injury is intended to either "punish" or induce guilt to the coach.

Fear of success. Athletes may be unable to cope with the pressure of achieving or maintaining high standards. This occurs more common than most people think.

Fear of failure. High uncertainty or low self-esteem, particularly low *sport* self-esteem, which reflects the athlete's self-worth and may justify poor sport performance ("If I am injured I can't try; If I can't try I can't fail"),

Poor coping skills. Lack of social support ("I need my teammates, family, and coach to deal with my concern about future involvement in sport"), personal resources (e.g., confidence, resilience, mental toughness, patience), and the need for attention may contribute to the athlete not performing very well and is (ostensibly) due to the injury and not due to the athlete's low skills.

Returning to Play Post-Injury

All sports participants, especially coaches and the injured athletes themselves, want to know about the factors that influence the duration of an athlete's medical treatment and return to competition. These factors reflect the important role of coaches in addressing why some athletes quit sport after sustaining a serious injury, while others comply with the full rehabilitation process and return to competition as planned.

Sport of secondary importance to athlete. Clinical studies show that a serious sport injury can result in an athlete who reorganizes his or her priorities in life. They might ask, "Just how important is being healthy for the rest of my life, as opposed to endangering my health and well-being while continuing to play and risking a more serious injury?" For some athletes, the injury is a wake-up call to reflect on the importance of playing versus replacing sports participation with other activities. This decision may be situation specific, however, when addressing the loss of a college scholarship or long-term financial stability as a professional athlete.

Fear of long-term disability. Some injuries are life threatening, either in the short term (e.g., a cardiovascular event) or long term (e.g., brain injury). The issue of "to play or not to play" is certainly in the hands of medical staff. The fear of a long-term disability, however, presents its own challenges in terms of reduced concentration, playing with less all-out effort and a more tentative (and less effective) style, and maintaining an internal focus of attention, as opposed to the external, autonomous attentional style as occurred before the injury.

Fear of failure. Experiencing the injury is devastating to many injured athletes. The post-injury psychological consequences, however, are just beginning. One of these consequences is fear of failure (FOF). Sustaining an injury is accompanied by an array of thoughts and emotions that can lead the athlete to conclude that he or she has lost his or her effectiveness and, consequently, is less likely to reach and maintain performance success—the fear of failing to replicate pre-injury quality.

Low self-confidence. No one has ever scored points or competed while sitting in a medical treatment facility. Receiving treatment reduces the athlete's thoughts of invulnerability, or, as indicated earlier, "the Superman complex." The performer's talent, fitness, strength, skill, and mental toughness are replaced by thoughts of failure and low self-confidence. Doubts about a future in sport can result.

Unfair expectations of others. While many injured athletes experience pain and are unable to perform at pre-injury levels, some athletes may feel that coaches and teammates are expecting a rapid return to action. There is the danger that some athletes have been injured on multiple occasions and may be perceived by the coach—and perhaps teammates—as "soft" and susceptible to the deleterious effects of sport competition. The expectations of others may be unreasonable, especially if the injury does not "appear" serious. Again, medical staff are needed to offer complete explanations of the athlete's injury and prognosis to the coach(es). Full explanations, however, are not open to teammates; that is the injured athlete's choice.

Need to win the respect of others. The antithesis of an injured athlete dealing with others' "unfair" expectations of his or her future performance and health status is the need to win the respect of all team members. This may seem like an impossible task and, indeed, may be unnecessary. After all, the injured athlete's priorities are not to appease others, but rather to strictly follow the injury rehabilitation protocol and, at a time to be determined by medical staff, to decide on when—or if—the athlete plans to return to competition.

Low risk-taking and tentative performance. One unpleasant but common manifestation of returning to competition after a sports injury is the failure to regain the feeling of performing at the autonomous level. That is, instead of "letting go" and executing complex skills with relatively little thinking (i.e., stage 3 of the Fitts-Posner three-stage theory, briefly explained in chapter 3), injured athletes return to competition with greater caution about taking risks for fear of reinjury. This common characteristic is one reason post-injury performance is less effective in contrast to pre-injury performance. Getting the athlete to return to pre-injury cognition (i.e., thoughts and emotions) is an important goal of coaches and sport psychologists.

Poor concentration and low readiness (created by mental fatigue and anxiety). Sport injuries have a devastating effect on the athletes' mental readiness, anxiety (i.e., worry, perceived threat), and concentration (i.e., attentional focusing). Rather than focusing externally on the current event or task at hand, the athlete is now consumed by "what if . . ." self-talk. This source of worry about a reinjury reduces concentration and arousal; attentional focus is now divided between projections of future reinjury and mistrust over the effectiveness of the rehabilitation program. "Is every body part, especially the injured and rehabilitated area, really as good as new?" says the athlete's self-talk. This issue consumes the athlete's attention and reduces concentration on relevant stimuli where the athlete's attention *should* be focused.

Pain threshold and tolerance. Both *pain threshold* and *pain tolerance* are conscious reactions to physical discomfort, but at different levels. Pain threshold is the point at which a person first detects pain, whereas pain tolerance is the maximum point at which the person can experience pain, after which time the body signals immediate cessation of the pain-causing stimulus. Pain tolerance renders the painful area or activity nonfunctional. The point at which pain is detected is partly genetic (hence, the reason some athletes experience pain and can overcome it during the competition, whereas other athletes succumb to pain rather quickly and take longer to recover. Coaches must become aware of each athlete's pain threshold and tolerance and of using cognitive strategies such as attentional focusing and mental imagery to help overcome pain. On the other hand, athletes (and their coaches) must heed the body's message that pain signals a danger to tissue and to one's health and well-being. Pain should never be ignored with the exception of a physician's clearance that the athlete may compete.

Anticipation of reinjury. Athletes who have experienced serious sport injury no longer feel impervious to another sport injury. There is no denial (e.g., "I won't be injured") about the feasibility of experiencing another injury. There is a problem, however, with the lack of mental readiness that accompanies another injury, especially to an area or muscle group where the initial injury occurred. Anticipation of reinjury is problematic to future performance because it causes athletes to think too much (i.e., stage 1 of the Fitts & Posner three-stage model, see chapter 3) and not to perform their skills on automatic (stage 3 of the model), where most performance execution occurs. The athlete needs to focus his or her attention externally on the event at hand, not internally where the cognitive stage of the Fitts and Posner three-stage model (i.e., planning, anticipating, and positive self-talk) occurs for less-skilled athletes.

Effects of injury on athletes' cognition and emotion. Athletes are, of course, very active. They train hard and must meet very high fitness standards in reaching strict performance standards. Experiencing a sports injury causes this very active competitor to become sedentary, except for the prescribed exercises of injury rehabilitation. Because physical activity is known to have a very favorable effect on emotion and cognition, the sudden cessation of a regular exercise regimen might lead to unfavorable psychological outcomes. Examples include depression, anxiety, reduced self-esteem, reduced speed and efficiency of information processing, and negative self-talk. Contingent on medical staff approval, injured athletes need to keep physically active during the rehabilitation period. Even fitness testing can be conducted to indicate improved fitness scores.

Reasons for Poorer Performance Post-Injury

It is well known that sport performance often deteriorates after the athlete returns to competition following the rehabilitation program. Why is that? It is essential that coaches execute strategies that prevent a deterioration in the athlete's performance after completing (and adhering to) the injury rehabilitation program. This occurs even after the medical staff have cleared the injured athlete to compete. Here are the likely reasons.

Changes in attentional focusing (from external-broad to internal-narrow). The medical staff and athletic trainer have given the athlete a "green light" to resume sports competition based on completion of the athlete's rehabilitation program. For some "unknown" reason, the athlete's sport performance is poorer, as compared to pre-injury performance levels. This happens often, but why? One plausible answer is the injured athlete's *misaligned attentional focus*.

Athletes visually focus (concentrate) along two dimensions, internal-external and narrow-broad. A typical example of an *internal focus* is self-talk (e.g., "I can do this, so concentrate") or self-monitoring in which the athlete is concentrating on a single stimulus or event, such as a baseball batter who is waiting for a certain type of pitch to arrive. A sample *external focus* consists of focusing visually on the golf ball sitting on the tee or a football player who scans his opponents and determines his strategy before the ball is snapped. A *narrow focus* is to concentrate on a single stimulus or condition (e.g., the location of a teammate to receive a pass in soccer), while a *broad focus* is observing the alignment of all football players on offense or all players on defense before the ball is snapped in anticipation of executing a certain play.

The problem of inferior performance by athletes who have suffered an injury and are ready to compete is that they tend to be over-cautious and tentative in how they approach competition. Instead of going all out and executing automatically, they often fear reinjury. Instead of focusing their attention externally on the task at hand, they are focusing internally on the injured area. In other words, their focus is incorrect; *it should be broad and external*, for the most part, reflecting their pre-injury attentional style, *not narrow and internal*. The athlete must stop focusing on—ignore—the injured (rehabilitated) area and, instead, use the same (normal) attentional focusing style as before the injury. There are mental skills that can assist athletes in correcting their attentional style, which is discussed later in this chapter.

Increased muscle tension. Returning to competition creates muscular tension and anxiety. The main source of this reaction is fear and worry about being reinjured and meeting pre-injury performance expectations, both self-generated and externally imposed by teammates, media, spectators, the coach, and parents, among others. Muscle relaxation techniques have shown to be effective in reducing muscular tension.

Less pain tolerance (more tentative movement, slower response time). Pain sends a message that no athlete (and medical staff) should ignore. Post-injury rehabilitation often results in reduced pain tolerance, the maximum pain a person can handle while still functioning normally. Pain tolerance is partially genetic, but it is also a function of skill level, attentional focusing (the ability to ignore pain by focusing externally on the task), and using mental skills such as dissociation, mental imagery, and psyching up.

Attributing the injury as the primary cause for poor performance. How can a highly skilled athlete explain the reasons for performing poorly after returning to competition, as compared to pre-injury skill levels? Athletes almost never indicate to others that their skills are now inferior and they are simply less competitive then prior to the injury. We do not hear athletes explain their lower-than-expected performance level as due to low ability, poor effort, and being overmatched by opponents. Instead, we may hear the athlete explain poor performance as due to bad luck or, more often, due to an injury. Although pain and injury are certainly possible and accurate explanations, failure due to an injury provides cover for athletes whose skills have diminished. Perhaps more time is needed to "recover" and hopefully (and eventually) compete at a higher level.

Rehabilitation and Compliance: Roles of the Coach and Athletic Trainer (AT)

The coach is the primary agent in the athlete's recovery from an injury, especially a serious injury that requires missing more than one game. In this segment, we review the many roles that coaches and athletic trainers can implement as an integral part of the injury rehabilitation program. Coaches, who carry the most credibility, influence, and control among all team members, may decide which of these strategies may be delegated to the AT and which to implement themselves.

Clearly explain the injury and rehabilitation process. Coaches, ATs, mental health professionals, and all medical staff (e.g., team doctor, surgical specialists) should provide clear details of the injury and rehabilitation process to athletes and, if under 18 years of age, to their parents as well. However, this explanation should be based on whether the athlete wishes to have detailed information. Some injured athletes want to know as little as possible about the injury. Too much knowledge is stressful for some individuals. Ask them what they prefer: full details or a more general description.

Provide the specific rehabilitation plan and the trainer's expectations for compliance orally and IN WRITING. Work with the athlete to schedule rehabilitations sessions—both time and location. Try to have an AT or student AT attending all sessions.

Monitor player attendance and progress and hold player accountable for compliance. The athlete's attendance at all sessions should be monitored, recorded, and submitted to the coach each week to determine the athlete's program adherence. Lack of monitoring player attendance informs the athlete that medical staff and coaches do not take the program seriously, that it is disorganized, or that the rehabilitation program is ineffective.

Teach athletes about proper responses to pain and injury. All injuries of varied levels of seriousness should be viewed as serious and nothing to "brush off" or appear unimportant. This is not the time to display a lackadaisical attitude toward an athlete's pain or injury. Let the team medical personnel dictate the injury's level of seriousness, and do not let the ATs or coaches' view the injury as frivolous. Experiencing an injury and other sources of pain should be a part of team policy. Playing hurt has serious long-term medical and health consequences, especially with respect to a brain injury.

Have former injured athletes talk to the team about their experiences. This should occur during the preseason and part of sharing team policies with all team members. Former players offering their experiences in returning from a serious injury provides confidence and optimism to other players who may be suffering from an injury and have doubts about a full recovery.

Collect and share media stories. Newspapers, magazines, television, and social media all can be used to share stories about comebacks of former players who went on to have brilliant sports careers.

Medical staff and, perhaps, the team's AT should inform the coach about each player's rehabilitation regimen. The coach should express empathy and reassurance of a successful return to competition *privately* to each injured athlete. Receiving the coach's reassurance and endorsement of a return to play sends an enormously powerful message that the athlete is expected to still contribute to the team this season as soon as they receive the "all clear" sign from the team's medical staff.

Know when to refer players to a licensed sport psychologist or other mental health professional. If there is resistance to treatment (e.g., lack of attendance, poor rehab technique, poor attitude about attending and completing each session) the coach should be involved immediately. For athletes under 18 years of age, there should be parental involvement. Inform parents (with athlete's permission at the college level) about rehabilitation treatment and prognosis. Some conditions do not involve psychotherapy, but rather entail learning mental skills with a performance coach. In fact, many athletes and coaches attach less of a stigma to visiting someone who uses the title "mental skills coach" or "performance specialist" than a working with a licensed "psychologist" or a "therapist." In all cases, however, it is imperative that athletes work with specialists who are familiar with the sports psychology literature and, in particular, the proper use of mental skills., and will make a strong contribution to the athlete's recovery from injury.

Obtain full program compliance. All parties—athlete, coach, AT, team physician—must agree with rehabilitation regimen strategies (e.g., location, frequency, travel to the rehabilitation venue, intake of medical prescriptions). The best rehabilitation program in the country won't be effective if the patient (athlete) fails to adhere and commit to the program. This is more likely if all parties—from athletes to the team physician—contribute to the planning and implementation of all segments of the program to help ensure 100% compliance.

Inform the coach about the planned player rehabilitation regimen. The coach should meet *in person* with the athlete (preferably not by social media or a phone call). Personal meetings create a stronger bond and more authenticity between coach and athlete. We would not want our doctor or dentist communicating unpleasant medical test results by phone. This is an injured athlete and compassion is needed to provide the athlete with hope and optimism about the player's future team involvement. Building player confidence is one strong outcome from a personal meeting. In addition, the coach should express empathy (i.e., understanding and compassion) about the insecurities of successfully returning to competition and reassurance the athlete will still contribute to the team.

Inform parents. Sharing information with the athlete's parents about the injury prognosis and treatment requires the permission of athletes age 18 years and older; parental permission is needed in most states for athletes younger than 18 years. Parents form an important source of support to the athlete of all ages. They should also play a role in promoting player program compliance by providing transportation to the rehabilitation venue and giving emotional support to ensure full compliance with the rehabilitation protocol.

Develop pain-management strategies. Several studies have shown promising results on the benefits of using mental skills on pain threshold and pain tolerance when the strategies are used correctly. Examples include dissociation (i.e., thoughts that disconnect the athlete's mind from the body, or injured area), imagery (i.e., making a mental picture of performing pain free and successfully), and attentional focusing (i.e., concentrating on an external event or stimulus while ignoring one's body and any unpleasant feelings). These techniques are an important source of a mental skills coach's repertoire of strategies that psychologists have learned and can teach athletes. Mental skills must be practiced several times per day to be effective.

Provide athlete with strong social support. Social support is perhaps the most important source of social influence that provides comfort, motivation, and the drive to achieve success and to reach one's goals. Social support is formally defined in the present context as the injured athlete's perceived comfort, caring, assistance, and information received from others. Coaches and mental skills coaches are interested in the role of social support in influencing any targeted goal such as exercise rehabilitation, sport, and other physical activity behaviors. Injured athletes require considerable social support as an integral part of the rehabilitation process.

The five types of social support, each of which a coach should consider implementing for a successful return to competition, include (a) *instrumental support* (i.e., providing tangible, practical assistance that will assist the injured athlete to achieve goals during and following rehabilitation); (b) *emotional support*, offered in the form of expressing encouragement, empathy, and concern toward the injured athlete; (c) *informational support*, including giving directions, advice, or suggestions about the most effective ways to recover from injury and to experience a successful return to competition; and (4) *companionship support*, which entails the availability of others to be company and to distract the injured athlete from the frustration and anxiety of (albeit temporarily) losing the opportunity to compete and contribute to the team. Companion support should include those with whom the athlete prefers spending time relaxing (e.g., friends, teammates, family, social partners). (5) Finally, *validation support* involves comparing the injured athlete's situation and status with other, previously injured athletes who successfully completed their rehabilitation program and continued to perform at a high level and maintain their athletic career. Validation support is a source of valuable information that offers hope, optimism, and confidence to the injured player ("If he/she can do it, so can I"). Social support is an enormously important component of full adherence to the rehabilitation program.

Provide athlete with team-related tasks to feel an integral part of the team. I have observed repeatedly injured athletes who attend practice during the week and may be allowed to join their teammates on the sidelines during the game. However, too often the injured athlete is given no other team responsibilities. Recording game statistics, ensuring that equipment is in sufficient supply, sitting in team meetings, engaging with coaches, observing video and other forms of information as part of the team preparation are only a few examples of keeping the injured athlete engaged during (and between) seasons. The injured athletes need to feel a sense of inclusion as a relevant team member who will one day return to action.

Only the team doctor (not the team's athletic trainer) should diagnose an injury. Only licensed medical staff are ethically allowed to diagnose an injury. I witnessed an inappropriate abuse of power in which a college football lineman suffered a knee injury. The athlete was "examined" by the team's head athletic trainer, who made a quick diagnosis after a brief evaluation by announcing, "It looks like torn cartilage." The lineman was understandably upset to learn that his football career may be over. Then the team physician arrived and diagnosed the injury as a "likely" sprain, but would await a clinical diagnosis after further tests at the medical center were completed. The physician's less severe diagnosis turned out to be accurate; no surgery was needed. Sadly, the athlete was exposed to premature and unnecessary diagnosis from a person, the AT, who was inaccurate and premature in announcing a far more damaging assessment. I urge all coaches to avoid clinical assessments from unqualified team personnel.

Allow athletes a chance to vent feelings. Injuries are very upsetting to most athletes. Coaches would be providing valuable support to all injured players if they "allowed" athletes to express feelings about relieving their anxiety about the future. "Will I still be on the team?" "Will my injury cause me to lose my scholarship (or lose my team status)?" Athletes need reassurance and emotional support from their coach after experiencing this traumatic event.

Avoid discounting athletes' feelings. Discounting is a way to reduce the importance and seriousness of a person's feelings or behavior. If your family member has a temper tantrum, you might "discount" his or her actions by concluding "Oh, he's always like that around dinner time," or "I just don't pay attention to her when she's upset." Discounting an athlete's feelings says to the athlete "I don't take you seriously" or "What you say or think is not important." It is wrong to minimize the importance of an athlete's pain, fear, anxiety, and doubts about the future. Statements such as "Oh, you're alright, it's nothing"; "No big deal"; or "You'll be fine" deny the athlete's fears and feelings about the source of pain, inability to be mobile, or anxiety about performing at pre-injury levels. Coaches need to give the athlete time and attention when they have something to say. It's a sign of emotional maturity and integrity to disclose feelings, not a sign of immaturity and oversensitivity. Showing athletes that they are being heard also communicates to athletes they are important and respected. It also clears the air about their perceptions—or misperceptions—about future expectations and goals.

Beware of athletes who "play through" an injury. For some reason, continuing to perform in sport while feeling considerable pain—the Superman complex—and even masking an injury is supposed to be honorable and a sign of determination. Since when is sacrificing one's physical health desirable and encouraged, despite evidence of severe injury, pain, and long-term or even permanent disability? Is continued participation in the competition while ignoring the signals of a dangerous condition meant to impress the coach or meet the coach's expectations? Coaches should view their athletes' health as a long-term investment and inform them that there is no shame in taking a time out from competition if pain or impairment is evident. Athletes should never be encouraged to play through their pain and injury.

Use mental practice (MP) to improve learning and performance. MP is defined as the covert (mental) representation of overt (physical) practice. Numerous studies concur that learning sport skills occurs with—and requires—overt active physical practice. Other past studies have also clearly shown that mental practice is very effective in enhancing learning and performing motor (sport) skills. The benefit is even greater when mental and physical practice are used alternatively in combination, particularly as a component of sports injury rehabilitation. MP, also called *visualization* and *mental imagery*, can be delivered to the injured athlete in any venue that is quiet and void of interfering noise and visual stimuli. There are guidelines for experiencing MP, which will be discussed later.

Beware of the "malingering" athlete. Malingering is defined as a person who intentionally lies about an injury to avoid practice or competition. Insight into the malingering athlete is that the malingerer will derive some benefit as a consequence of having a "problem" that requires medical attention. The greatest need of a malingering athlete is to obtain attention and pity from others. The athlete's greatest fear is "getting caught." For a thorough review of the malingering literature, including a description of coach's reactions to the malingerer, see Rotella, Ogilvie, and Perrin (1999). If a coach notices continued and repeated injuries by an athlete, that the injured athlete is not healing or not adhering to the prescribed rehabilitation program, or that the athlete spends considerable time in the athletic training facility waiting for or experiencing treatment, the coach should alert a mental health professional and schedule a private and confidential session between the athlete and therapist. Malingering is a psychopathological (mental health) condition that has been learned and effectively executed. To understand the source and treatment of this condition requires professional counseling.

Mental Strategies for Full Recovery

Athletic injuries are always unpleasant and often painful. While researchers and practitioners have examined the effects of various physical treatments to expedite recovery from injury and reduce the athlete's discomfort level, less research has addressed the effectiveness of psychological (mental) strategies as part of the package of post-injury treatments. Listed here are a few of the cognitive strategies that have been shown to be effective in assisting athletes in overcoming the deleterious effects of their sport injury, each of which can be carried out by coaches, ATs, or the athletes themselves. A licensed psychologist, also called a mental health professional, may be involved as a member of the rehabilitation team and participate in the athlete's overall treatment. None of the following strategies, however, require licensure.

Goal setting. There is extensive literature in sport and performance psychology related to the guidelines for effective goal setting. Goals should reflect performance change, not outcome, and be measurable, challenging but realistic, positively (not negatively) stated (i.e., what the injured athlete will be able to do), and motivating to the athlete. Ironically, not every person/athlete finds goal setting desirable. Some individuals, especially based on a rehabilitation protocol, find goal setting stressful and not motivational. If an athlete finds a task rewarding and pleasant, adding a goal to the procedure removes the fun component. The goal changes the source and type of motivation from intrinsic (i.e., fun, enjoyable, meaningful) to extrinsic (i.e., based on some tangible reward). Athletes should be consulted about the desirability of setting a rehabilitation goal rather than imposing it on the athlete as part of the program for every participant. Here's a sample goal: "I will increase the resistance on "x" strength exercise by 10 pounds in 4 weeks;" "I will improve my performance on the 50-yard sprint by 1 second after 4 weeks of training."

Relaxation training. Because many injuries tighten muscle groups, numerous studies have shown that various forms of muscular relaxation will improve the athlete's flexibility. There are several forms of exercise for this purpose, including progressive relaxation, yoga, and mindfulness.

Mental imagery (MI). A very popular technique, also called mental practice and visualization, MI requires the athlete to create a mental representation of the rehabilitation task and of replicating sport skills. There are published guidelines for performing this technique.

Positive self-talk (PST). This is a highly motivational strategy that requires the injured athlete to provide optimal exertion just prior to executing the task. Examples include "I can do this" and "Stay with it; go, go, go!"

Attentional focusing. Athletes typically concentrate on external stimuli or events while ignoring internal feelings and sensations. In a rehabilitation program, it is best to focus externally on the task at hand, while ignoring internal processes such as exertion and physical fatigue. One approach in using this strategy is to focus externally, starting 5 seconds before play begins, while ignoring pain and specific body parts that can distract the athlete.

Social support groups. Exercising in a small group or with a partner often improves exercise program adherence. Partners can psych up each other. If the athlete prefers to exercise alone, that wish should be respected.

Coach and team support. Coaches should keep in contact with the injured team member, with some athletes and conditions requiring more contact than others. The athlete has the right to know he or she remains part of the team and that his or her return to action is anticipated.

In conclusion, it is important for coaches to recognize the potential value of an injured athlete to the team. Every team member is only one injury away from needing the recognition and services of coaches, ATs, a mental skills coach (or licensed psychologist), and medical staff. National organizations identify a 1-day limit on participation for an athlete to be considered injured, while others use a 3-day period as activity cessation to be considered a sports injury. Still others define a sports injury as debilitation resulting in the inability to function as competently as before the occurrence of physical trauma during sport participation. Sports injuries are often devastating to the athlete and to the team. Coaches have enormous influence to make the sad experience of sustaining a sports injury less traumatic and potentially more constructive. The coach is an integral and powerful resource of the injury rehabilitation process. This chapter provides coaches with guidelines for using their influence in helping the injured athlete to achieve a full recovery and to continue contributing to team success.

chapter eight

Building Team Cohesion

Sports teams are groups in which individuals interact with and influence the thoughts, emotions, and behaviors of each other. Coaches and sport psychologists agree that developing strong player loyalty toward each team member and increasing a sense of team identity contributes to group unity, player loyalty toward team goals, and, ultimately, team performance. This requires that team members have a similar mission and that the team's success in meeting group goals is their ultimate vision. This requires the ability to "stick together" a characteristic called *group (team) cohesion* (Carron, 1984). The feeling of togetherness is considered important in satisfying player needs, deriving and making the effort to meet team goals, enhancing each player's loyalty to the team and coach, and gaining support among teammates.

The purposes of this chapter are (a) to determine the factors that contribute to team cohesion and team climate, (b) to examine the extent to which team cohesion and the development of healthy player relationships contribute to group member satisfaction and performance outcomes, and (c) to suggest ways in which coaches can promote a supportive and constructive social and task team cohesion and team climate.

For years, coaches have assumed that positive feelings among team members result in better sport performance. Coaches contend that team unity is essential for success, and, consequently, they have used techniques to help ensure an "esprit de corps" among the players. The pregame meal, physical conditioning programs, meetings, study hall (in which team members engage in academic learning together), and pregame preparation traditionally occur as a group. Ostensibly, when the players interact and share team-related experiences, they develop closer interpersonal relationships and feelings of mutual support and trust. Although this outcome is intuitively appealing, researchers aren't certain that it is true.

For example, several studies have shown that highly cohesive teams also achieved superior performance outcomes, but other studies have indicated a low relationship between cohesion and team performance. In an older study, Fiedler (1967) showed that poor team cohesion interfered with team success. Fielder found that basketball teammates who were very close friends chose to pass the ball to one another rather than to players in better shooting positions. In this case, team success was not a priority. Thus, coaches who try to promote cohesion might, under some circumstances, do more harm than good.

An example is the common strategy in team sports of requiring all athletes to be together and to follow the same protocol up to 24 hours before the competition. I found that collegiate and high school football players were annoyed at following this procedure (Anshel, 1989). My more recent consultation with professional athletes supports this finding. Many players preferred to be alone with their thoughts or to have the option of attending team activities that did not relate directly to game preparation, such as viewing a commercial film, engaging in mental imagery, spending their free time with their position (assistant) coaches, spending the night before competition in a local hotel (and being assigned their roommate), or being with personal friends. Still, many coaches believe, perhaps based on their experiences as athletes with a former coach, that this "we" feeling improves the level of interpersonal attraction and feelings among team members.

What Is Team Cohesion?

Cohesion is a term used to describe feelings of interpersonal attraction and the sense of belonging to the group by its members. It also signifies the members' desire to remain in the group. Two different types of cohesion have been identified by researchers: *social cohesion* and *task cohesion*. Social cohesion is the degree of interpersonal attraction among group members, the extent to which the group allows a person to reach a desired goal. Task cohesion refers to the athletes' objective appraisal of their group's level of coordinated effort or teamwork. In other words, it is the degree to which the team and team members reach their respective goals. Acknowledging the differences between social and task cohesion is imperative in determining how each might affect a person's level of group satisfaction. For example, Carron (1994) concluded that "athletes on teams perceived to be high in task cohesiveness readily accept more responsibility for team failure than athletes on teams perceived to be low in task cohesiveness" (pp. 94-95).

Qualities of Team Cohesion

A plethora of information exists—books, research articles, media stories—describing the characteristics of "effective" groups that reach their goals consistently and efficiently while maintaining high member satisfaction and loyalty. Let's discuss the most critical of these characteristics in relation to the coach's role on sports teams.

Leadership skills. As indicated in chapter 3, effective coaches use a variety of leadership styles to promote consistent and optimal athletic performance. Effective coaches also know when *not* to lead. For instance, team personnel other than the head coach (e.g., assistant coach, team captain) should be occasionally assigned leadership tasks. For example, perhaps have an assistant coach address the team before the competition, during time-outs, at halftime or between periods, or even after the competition The head coach traditionally takes center stage during these times, but there are times when athletes become "coach deaf" and stop listening and responding to the same voice during a season. Some athletes will "perk up" and be more attentive and responsive to a different voice—and a message that varies from the past. Sometimes less is more when it comes to a coach's decision to share the stage with his or her assistants.

Another reason to change the source of information is to give other coaches a chance to show their own competence (e.g., "Coach really makes a lot of sense") and to demonstrate their commitment to the team. Other coaches use their own way to demonstrate their loyalty to team goals and support the head coach's message(s). This strategy promotes a sense of togetherness—team cohesion for players and their coaches—for *all* team members.

A sense of belonging. Coaches require specific strategies that facilitate the athletes' feelings of belonging on the team. For instance, the coach may place photos of outstanding former team members in highly observable places. The team's trophy case, reminders of past successes, should be placed in prominent areas for spectators and team members to observe year round. This reminds current team participants of the team's elite history and the importance of maintaining the team's traditions. Being a team member should be bigger than any one individual. To compete on "this" team should be viewed as playing a part of this organization's legacy, with a sense of honor and pride. Effective teams consist of athletes who are proud of their team affiliation and believe that their role will contribute in some way, large or small, to the team's success.

Commitment of the team. In sport, commitment means that each athlete makes the effort to learn skills and strategies, to mentally and physically prepare for each competition, and to support other team members. Members of effective teams feel a strong sense of belonging to the group and are proud to represent the team outside of the sport arena. Ideally, each team member should find pleasure in the success of other teammates.

Setting and achieving goals. Successful teams include athletes who are both *aware* of and in complete agreement with their goals. Individual athletes—starters and nonstarters—should have had a role in establishing their goals. Defining team standards is important so that performance levels and expectations can be set *realistically* and yet be as *challenging* as possible. Team goals must take precedence over individual goals and achievements, but both are important. The role that the athlete is asked to play in optimizing team success sometimes requires the modification of individual goals. For instance, the team's strategy that prioritizes defense may supersede a player's desire to score a given, predetermined number of points. When goal setting is a joint effort, teammates are more likely to support each other. Group cohesion grows.

Problem-solving and planning skills. The team should develop a systematic and effective way of solving problems and planning future programs and strategies jointly between coach and athletes. Soliciting player input into the planning of team strategies and activities promotes a sense of personal commitment in each team member. One way to do this is to broaden the base for making decisions that affect team members. While it is more efficient for coaches to make decisions that affect team members, there are advantages to making team members responsible for decision making when possible.

Well-organized team procedures. Effective teams have clearly defined player roles and well-developed communication patterns and administrative procedures. At appropriate times (e.g., when there is sufficient time, promoting self-reliance and independence), players might be consulted before group goals are developed. This could be one role of the team captain(s) or an assistant coach, though ultimately it is the coach's responsibility to make final decisions firmly and without equivocation. Another advantage of player input is it can help coaches examine alternatives and, perhaps, change a coach's initial decision.

Critique without rancor. An effective team consists of secure members. This means players and coaches agree on the need for feedback as part of the learning process. Players, therefore, must be receptive to feedback for improved performance. Team and individual errors and weaknesses—I prefer to use the words, "areas for future growth and improvement"—should be examined objectively without attacking a player's character or personality (e.g., "Joe that was a stupid mistake"). The correct policy is to learn from past mistakes to improve future performance and to take responsibility for one's own actions.

Positive intergroup relations. Players should be aware of the benefits of personal contact with other team members. Sometimes assignments and strategies can be learned and remembered better under conditions of peer teaching (where the environment may be more relaxed) than if the coach provides the instruction. It is not uncommon for higher-skilled athletes to interact on the sidelines, sharing information about what they have experienced during the competition or acknowledging a teammate's effort or success.

Factors That Influence Team Cohesion

There are several factors that contribute to developing and maintaining group cohesion.

Group size. The larger the group, the less chance there is for task and social forms of group cohesion. The number of group members that most strongly affects cohesion differs because it depends on the type of task being performed. Results of studies have shown that group member enjoyment and cohesion decrease as group size increases.

Interaction among group members. Some sports require more interaction among team members than others. In team sports, such as basketball, football, and soccer, performance success is directly linked to the ability to coordinate various roles and functions and interact with one another simultaneously. Other team sports such as rowing, tennis doubles, and, to some extent, baseball, in which performers are co-acting rather than interacting directly, do not require the same degree of group cohesion for team success. For instance, Lenk (1969) found that *low* group cohesion contributed to the success of his Olympic German rowing team (which won a silver medal). According to interviews conducted by author George Will (1990), professional athletes consider sport their job and perform it to the best of their ability, often with little regard for the success or friendship of team members. Finally, individual sports, even when performed on a team basis, such as swimming and track, require far less group cohesion for performance success.

Clarity of group goals. Teams that are highly focused on meeting team and individual goals perceive a greater task orientation than teams whose goals have not been stated or are unclear. The term clarity is important here because it represents two factors: (a) setting goals that are challenging and agreed on by team members, and (b) the ability to measure (and hopefully observe) if goals have been met successfully. Under these conditions, the group's direction and focus for performance effectiveness strengthen its cohesiveness.

Acceptance of group goals. Goals are only as effective as the group's agreement with them. In 1987, the first-year head coach of a college (U.S.) football team made the grave mistake of informing the media before the team's first game that his team would go undefeated during the season, a virtually impossible goal, considering the team's losing record over the previous several seasons. Sure enough, the team lost its first three games of the season, drastically reducing the team's preseason cohesion level. Closer team cohesion is far more likely if all or at least most group members accept its goals. With greater participation in team goal setting, team cohesion is greater, and when cohesion is high, athletes are more satisfied with their team's goals for practice and competition.

Warmth of group atmosphere. A hostile, authoritarian coaching style is less likely to foster team cohesion than a leadership style that balances the need for authority with a more humanistic, respectful approach. Results of past studies have showed that a warm, supportive team climate not only heightens group member satisfaction, but also increases player motivation to improve performance.

Clarity of members' roles. Researchers have found that group members who understand their position and role in the group will be more likely support its goals. This is not to say that the individual should perceive his or her role as unimportant for group success. For groups to function properly, some members must play a more prominent role than others in initiating and completing tasks that directly lead to meeting group goals; not everyone can be the team captain. The clarification of roles within the group fosters cohesion by increasing group identity, focusing on necessary tasks, and mutually enjoying the benefits of group success.

Geographical factors. Group cohesiveness also reflects the physical proximity of group members. Athletes will bond more closely due to more opportunity to interact and communicate about sport-related issues. Examples include playing positions that require frequent interaction (e.g., the shortstop and second baseman or pitcher and catcher in baseball), or locker location in the locker room.

Personal sacrifice/overcoming adversity. Giving up something of personal value for the group's benefit, or overcoming barriers in meeting a group goal, tend to improve cohesion and facilitate bonding among group members. Spending considerable time and energy in training, practice, and travel, often at the expense of one's personal life, or experiencing the loss of a team member (temporarily or permanently) tend to improve group member bonding.

Leaders' appreciation of members' performances. Recognition is a basic and normal social need. Group leaders and, to a lesser extent, other group members, would improve social group cohesion measurably by providing positive feedback and, if needed, instructional input on some aspect of the members' performance (e.g., a positive attitude, good effort, skilled performance).

Factors That Inhibit Cohesion

Several factors have been identified that can hurt team togetherness. These include the following:

- Disagreement among team members about the group's goals (e.g., "Are we here to win by playing as a team or to help individuals score more points?")
- Rapid or frequent changes in group members
- A struggle for decision-making power within the group
- Poor communication among group members
- Unclear task or social roles among team members (e.g., which player will tell the coach that early morning exercise is at an undesirable time of day)
- Role conflict (e.g., when members usurp the team captain's authority)
- Lack of a clear vision by the team leader (e.g., what does the team want to accomplish and how will it get there?)
- Ongoing criticism of team members by the coach; blaming individuals for poor team performance
- A clash of personalities among team members (e.g., outgoing, loud, and talkative versus more inhibited and quiet, especially during times that require concentration)

Does Team Cohesion Matter?

Cohesion and Player Satisfaction

How important is it for athletes to like one another or to be close friends to win consistently? Can teams be successful if some (or even most) of the players do not get along or if they compete among themselves for playing status? With the vast array of coaching responsibilities, does the coach need to be concerned about the players' social interactions in addition to other coaching responsibilities?

Feeling "satisfaction" as a team member is in the eyes of the beholder. Each individual athlete must define what he or she finds satisfying as a team member. Many coaches contend that one important component of player satisfaction is being recognized for effort and talent. One strategy used by many coaches to facilitate player satisfaction is to encourage the press to interview the players rather than speaking only with the coaching staff. Some coaches mount press clippings on the team bulletin board and continually update them. Whereas cohesion is a group construct, satisfaction is an individual one; there is a strong positive relationship between cohesion and satisfaction.

If satisfied athletes feel closer to one another, does this mean that their level of satisfaction will also enhance performance success? There is little evidence that team member satisfaction leads to an increase in performance success. However, successful performance may be related to improved satisfaction. The combination of performance success and cohesiveness leads to greater team member satisfaction, but satisfaction, in turn, does not lead to anything. Being a satisfied team member may inhibit dropping out and improve team morale, but this does not necessarily influence performance outcome. Athletes who perceive their team as successful will more likely feel closer and happier as team members than athletes who do not view their team as successful. Effective leaders do well in building group cohesion because being in a cohesive group is satisfying, reduces the dropout rate, and may enhance performance.

Cohesion and Team Performance

Intuitively, we assume that cohesive teams win more games or, inversely, that teams lacking in cohesiveness (with more dissension and conflict) fail to live up to their potential. Some investigators have found that cohesion is related to team success—that there is a high relationship between team cohesion and winning. Others have found that team success is not related to whether the players like one another, but rather to the extent to which they can interact constructively during the competition to use proper skills and strategies. In other words, the concept of task cohesion—strong team interactions—is a better predictor of team success than social cohesion—whether the players like each other.

Making any definite conclusions about cohesion and performance is difficult because researchers have studied different types of sport populations. Generalizations about the results of these studies for all teams and different sports would be unsound since most of the research on team cohesion has centered on university intramural teams.

The results of past studies have shown that highly cohesive teams win significantly more games than do low cohesive teams. Similar advantages for cohesive teams are found in examining team success on postseason performance; high cohesive groups win more games. High team cohesiveness is positively related to team success (i.e., close teams win more games). In addition, low cohesive teams have less satisfied team members than their high cohesive counterparts.

Researchers have found that "commitment to task" was the most critical component of group cohesion that best predicted team success. Interpersonal attraction among group members and group pride, however, were not related to team success. It would appear, then, that task cohesion is of greater importance to desirable performance outcomes than social cohesion.

One possible reason for the lack of clarity between group cohesion and performance is that different sports place various types of physical and mental demands and interactions on their participants. Researchers classify sports as interacting teams (e.g., basketball, field hockey, soccer), co-acting teams (e.g., archery, bowling, golf), and mixed co-acting-interacting teams (e.g., American football, baseball/softball, rowing, swimming, track and field). Interactive sports require that players work together and coordinate their actions to reach team goals and be successful. Co-active sports, on the other hand, do not require similar levels of team interaction to be successful. A mixed co-acting and interacting sport includes segments that require both co-acting (e.g., kicking the ball) and interacting (e.g., passing the ball). Cohesion may be more closely associated with team success for (interactive) sports that require ongoing interaction and coordination among players. Cohesion would be less related to team success among (co-active) sports that require no such extensive engagement among teammates.

In summary, high team cohesion is improved by team success. While coaches may not need to be concerned with building cohesiveness to enhance the chance of winning, cohesiveness still may be important since participation on cohesive teams appears to be more satisfying than participation on less cohesive teams. Highly satisfied players are more motivated to give optimal effort and to support team goals than players who are dissatisfied.

When Low Cohesion Is Better

Is it possible that sometimes low team cohesion is more effective and results in better performance than high team cohesion? German sport scientist Hans Lenk (1969) studied two high-caliber rowing teams over 4 years (1960–1964). One team (1960) represented its country in the Olympics. The second team (1962) became a world champion. Lenk studied the interactions and interpersonal relationships and attractions among team members. His data were derived by directly observing the behaviors of the athletes and through self-report techniques. In his 1960 study, Lenk observed sharp conflicts among racing team members, especially between two unfriendly subgroups. He reported that the internal strife was so bad that the team was almost abandoned. Nevertheless, a performance deficit was not found as a result of group tension. Ironically, performance slightly improved as team members became increasingly combative toward one another over the 2 years of the team's existence. In fact, the team became an unbeaten Olympic champion. Lenk concluded that teams in sport are capable of achieving maximal performance outcomes despite strong internal conflicts.

How can Lenk's findings be explained? The world champion rowers of 1962 were from a club team rather than a racing team. Lenk noticed a subgroup of four rowers that set itself apart from the others. The subgroup formed due to the mutual attraction of the team's four strongest rowers, leaving the remaining four members to affiliate among themselves. Moreover, the cliques resented each other for different reasons. Members of one subgroup thought of themselves as physically superior to the others, while the second subgroup resented the "second-class" treatment and one-upmanship attitude of their teammates. This led to infighting for team leadership. The intra-team rivalry intensified with time. Despite this lack of cohesion, the eight teammates won the European championship during the second year, the time at which intra-team rivalry was strongest. The level of performance had not suffered from the conflicts over the players' status.

Consider two important and unique circumstances that surrounded Lenk's studies. First, these were world-class athletes, not exactly players from the local high school or club. These men were highly skilled; had a history of past success; were self-confident about their ability; and were less reliant on teammates for recognition, support, and affiliation than less-skilled competitors might have been. Further, the team's relatively short life span—about 2 years—in which to train and compete, combined with the unified purpose of representing its country successfully in international competition, were likely more important in the team becoming successful than were team members' establishing close relationships.

The second circumstance is that rowing is a co-acting sport requiring less interdependence for team success than other types of sports. Other examples of co-acting sports are team (or doubles) versions of tennis, bowling, and golf. As Lenk readily admitted, co-acting group members can successfully meet their goals without extensively affiliating with others. On the other hand, interacting sports, such as baseball, basketball, or soccer, require far more interdependence and therefore higher social cohesion. Further,

Lenk never claimed that low cohesion in teams was desirable. He contended only that his study found no decrease in performance.

Supportive (warm) team climate. When the team atmosphere is relaxed and nonthreatening, athletes feel more comfortable engaging in direct, honest communication with others. They are more likely to feel secure and unthreatened in taking logical risks in their planned strategy performance, and they trust a teammate's or coach's motive in providing constructive feedback. Should there have been an attempted steal of second base under the circumstances? Talk it over. This sets up the ultimate goal, discussed next, in developing the proper team climate.

Developing an Effective Team Climate

Team climate is a psychosocial construct (i.e., the influence of environmental factors on the performer's thoughts and emotions) and reflects the relationship between external conditions (e.g., tasks are well structured, precontent warm-up routines are conducted without confusion, team tasks are organized) and the interrelationships among group members (e.g., supportive, friendly, resilient in response to challenges and stress; no choking in pressure situations). The key issue in understanding group climate is the group (team) members' perceptions; it is not the coach who evaluates and determines the team's climate, but rather the players. Athletes make an assessment, or a value judgment, based on their own needs and priorities in identifying and categorizing the team's atmosphere. What is so important about these perceptions is that they have a significant impact on each athlete's attitude about being a team member and, ultimately, influence player motivation and performance. Researchers refer to this feeling as *team member satisfaction*.

The coach, the person in the most powerful position on the team, has the greatest influence on establishing team climate and ensuring a healthy psychological environment. "Healthy" in this context means that the relationship between coach and team members is generally positive, respectful, constructive, and trusting. Effective coaches, whose teams win and whose players have high group member satisfaction, follow certain guidelines that create a positive team climate. Much research has focused on determining these guidelines and strategies.

Factors That Affect Team Climate

Team climate is more likely in response to the following factors.

Autonomy. *Autonomy* is the opportunity to function independently of the group leader. Autonomous athletes might feel more satisfied if they were allowed to make decisions on their own—at least occasionally. For instance, many collegiate and professional athletes would prefer to plan and implement at least *some* of the plays themselves, without the coach making all the decisions. While it is understandable that coaches feel they are always in a better position to call the plays (in most sports that allows for play-calling), there are several factors that work against this strategy.

One of the negative outcomes of always having the coach call the play is players' not taking responsibility for the failed play. Instead, players blame the coach for performance failure (e.g., "He called the wrong play. If only he had called 'this' play, we could have scored"). The players may not accept responsibility for the outcome. Second, occasionally allowing athletes to make their own decisions or, perhaps making a joint decision in which coach and athlete consult, can promote coach loyalty ("The coach trusts me and respects my opinion"). A third reason for sharing decision-making responsibilities is to prepare athletes for this role during the competition when a planned play must be abandoned and the players must quickly react to a new, unplanned situation. Many athletes over the years have expressed frustration due to the coach's refusal to include the athlete's opinion about calling a certain play or using a particular strategy, especially when the coach's play calling lead to team failure.

Emotional support. Perhaps no greater need exists for the athlete than emotional support from coaches and teammates, especially when the athlete's optimal effort in competition does not lead to success. This sense of "caring and sharing" provides participants with fundamental psychological needs such as recognition for a good effort and psychological comfort to help reduce the stress of nonsuccess. Negative, inappropriate responses from group members, such as harsh criticism, sarcasm, lack of recognition of effort (ignoring the performer), and, in extreme cases, wishing physical harm or failure to a team member, can result in a cold, disloyal, nonsupportive team climate. The coach is the one agent in the group who makes a major impact on whether the atmosphere of a team is positive and supportive.

Pressure to succeed. Meeting the coach's expectations and reaching predetermined goals is an integral aspect of competition. Tension and stress are often inevitable, perhaps leading to a "tight" team environment in which the athletes are afraid to make a mistake. Or, the climate may be threatening and, due to perceived excessive pressure, prevents performers from reaching their full potential. The athlete's perception of pressure inevitably heightens anxiety and pressure, antecedents to what is known as *choking*. Two ways to reduce these undesirable emotions and build confidence are to help athletes to feel more competent and to focus on the athlete's performance improvement (e.g., "You are getting better at that") rather than only on between-player comparisons. Studies have shown that elite competitors define success as improving on or at least matching previous attempts.

Recognition and approval. Psychologists claim that all humans have a natural need for recognition and approval, so athletes need the coach's recognition of their efforts, improvements, and successes. The results of coach recognition and approval include heightened self-confidence, feelings of responsibility for one's performance, and establishing and maintaining close personal friendships with peers. The relationship between recognition and team climate is that more secure athletes tend to be more supportive of their teammates.

Trust. One of the most important components of team climate is trust. Each athlete on the team should feel that performing certain, perhaps risky, actions during competition is allowed, even encouraged, to help the team. The performer should not fear being emotionally and physically abandoned by teammates or losing group identity. The feeling of "You can count on me," "We're in this together," "It's okay to take a chance," or "You gave it your best" is very motivating and reassuring for most athletes. It creates a sense of fairness and stability among teammates. Good athletes—and successful teams—take risks, and without mutual trust, no one is about to risk failure.

Fairness. Most of the time, we get what we deserve in life. But other times, we experience life in unfair ways. Fairness is in the eye of the beholder; it's based on the athlete's perceptions of the situation. Being blamed for a situation that was not the athlete's fault or out of his or her control (e.g., a teammate misses his or her assignment, the sun prevented tracking the fly ball) lacks fairness. This perception may be different from the coach's interpretation—and even different from reality. Coaches must do what they can to create an atmosphere of fairness. Perceived fairness promotes team loyalty.

An athlete's interpretation of fairness is partly based on three issues:

1. The degree of compatibility between the coach's and the player's respective assessments of the performer's skills and contributions—or potential contributions—to the team. Why, for example, does the player not start or not receive more playing time?
2. The coach's manner in communicating—or not communicating—his or her views to the athlete.
3. Evidence of the coach's attempt to help the athlete to improve skills and feel like an important part of the team.

The athlete's personal view of being treated fairly by the coach will have a strong and direct impact on the athlete's level of commitment, motivation, and satisfaction as a team member. This issue is capable of bringing a team very close together or driving its members far apart. An effective team climate must be based on the *athlete's view* of fair treatment. If this view differs from that of the coach, these two individuals must communicate directly to work it out. Why was the athlete not starting or taken out of the game? What does the player need to do to become a starter or see more game action? These issues should not be a secret.

Innovation. One relevant issue in fostering innovation, or creativity, on the team is the group's and coach's willingness to tolerate—even to facilitate change. Occasionally, athletes should have a chance to be creative in planning and executing strategies. The effective coach need not feel compelled to give directives and be "in charge" every minute. When possible, athletes and assistant coaches should be allowed to take risks in planning and carrying out strategy.

For instance, instead of the coach being responsible for calling all the plays, the players can be allowed to react to game situations independent of coach directives. The dynamics of sport competition sometimes mandate impulsive changes in behavior, a bit of risk taking, and reacting quickly to sudden events. Offering new and exciting alternatives to practice schedules and drills and teaching new skills and strategies during practice are other ways to improve team innovation. A positive, effective team climate is one in which change, creativity, input from athletes, and some risk taking are encouraged. In this way, the participants are cognitively involved in all aspects of the team's performance, feel accountable for the outcome, and are mutually supportive—all key aspects of group cohesion.

Team Climate Checklist for Athletes

The best way coaches can assess their team climate is by asking the athletes using a team climate checklist. The checklist concerns ascertaining the players' feelings about being members of the team and their perceptions of the coach's behaviors and attitudes. Its usefulness is dependent on the coach's willingness to read, reflect on, and react to these opinions in a positive and serious manner. See Appendix D for this checklist.

There are three guidelines for generating and using the checklist. First, the checklist is without norms; no scale defines a "warm" or "cold" team climate or a satisfied or dissatisfied competitor. Everything is relative, so coaches should be interested in changes in scores over time. Thus, the checklist should be administered periodically, preferably before and during the season, so that coaches can ascertain team climate and use the information. Second, the players should be told that the checklist is not a test, which means there are no "right" or "wrong" answers. The items are based on the athletes' perceptions. And third, anonymity is essential! Athletes need to feel that they can respond to each question with complete honesty and without fear of repercussions from the coach. To avoid such fears, the coach might want to ask a player—perhaps the team captain—to distribute and collect the checklist to/from the athletes, whose identities would be coded—perhaps by using the birthday of a parent or by selecting a number from a hat. The coach can compare scores based on the coded number on the different administrations of the checklist.

Collective Efficacy: The Group's Beliefs About Member Competence

Team cohesion and climate can be enhanced under a condition called *collective efficacy*. Success in sport is closely tied to the performer's belief that he or she is capable of achieving certain short-term and long-term goals. The strength of this belief is called *self-efficacy*. This concept is similar to confidence; however, whereas confidence refers to a *general* feeling about performing well in many types of situations (i.e., the "confident athlete"), efficacy is *situation specific*. Thus, an athlete can feel certain of his or her capability during sports competition (i.e., high self-efficacy), but feel less certain about being successful in non-sport settings. The concept of self-efficacy can be transferred to group situations and develop the concept of collective efficacy.

Interactions among each group member to complete numerous functions in a timely, planned manner that meets group needs and leads to successful outcomes is called coordinative capabilities. A basketball player would strongly consider passing the ball to the "open" teammate rather than take a longer, riskier shot. Bunting in baseball is another example, in which the player sacrifices personal statistics (e.g., raising one's batting average) to move the runner into scoring position. Of course, in contemporary baseball, try asking a major league ballplayer making millions a year for his batting skills to bunt. Indeed, bunting is very rare in professional baseball, perhaps a partial reflection of low collective efficacy (e.g., "My statistics are more important than helping the team win"). When collective efficacy is very low, a new condition called self-handicapping can emerge.

Self-Handicapping (SH): The Anticipation of Losing

Self-handicapping (SH) in competitive sport is defined as athletes' strategies that protect their self-esteem by providing excuses before events occur and explaining reasons for the anticipated lack of team or individual success. Self-handicappers externalize or excuse failure and internalize (accept credit for) success. These athletes do not link failure due to their low ability following failed performance, thereby protecting their self-esteem.

Group cohesion is influenced by SH if any individual team member feels, before the competition, that he or she will not be at fault for group failure, yet takes full responsibility for group success. Researchers have found that high social cohesion (i.e., the extent to which team members interacted positively away from the sport venue) was related to *less* SH. In addition, low task cohesion (i.e., the degree of team harmony and effective interactions while executing performance skills during the game) was associated with *high* SH. Thus, SH enhances group cohesion because it improves members' sense of acceptance and support from others, increases the sharing of responsibility for team failure, and results in more acceptance by and support for other team members.

While an SH disposition may improve group cohesion, the problem is that it ensures low to moderate expectancies. Remember, SH is a proactive explanation of not being responsible for possible future team failure. Thus, athletes may use excuses, such as injury (imagined or real), lack of practice time, fatigue from travel, or lack of practice as possible (and plausible) reasons to attribute the reason(s) for losing the competition or not performing well. Conversely, if the athlete is successful, his or her self-esteem is enhanced because the victory was obtained despite the presence of an injury and lack of practice. However, many coaches like the idea of each team member feeling responsible for both individual and team performance. As the old saying goes, "There is no 'I' in TEAM." The use of SH strategies should be less necessary in cohesive groups. Responsibility for perceived failure is usually shared equally in cohesive groups, in which group support is readily available and there are fewer threats to self-esteem.

Social Loafing: Going Along for the Ride

Social loafing (SL) is a decrease in individual effort and performance due to the physical presence of other persons as opposed to performing the task alone. SL is evident only under conditions in which more than one person is performing *the same task simultaneously*. Examples include blocking by the offensive line in (U.S.) football, group tackling in contact sports, and rowing. Usually social loafing in competitive sport occurs when the athletes perceive the to-be-performed task as unimportant, meaningless, not motivating, and often performed under noncompetitive conditions. SL has been explained as a motivational loss, because individuals are less likely to feel accountable for the quality of their performance if they are held collectively responsible for task success. An example would be a team who celebrates a victory due to the recognized successful, high-quality performance of individual players. Studies have shown that social loafing may be strongly related to task duration; athletes are more likely to loaf under conditions of fatigue, boredom, or prolonged repetition of tasks.

In summary, researchers have concluded that the tendency to engage in SL *increases* when the following occur:

1. The performer's effort cannot be assessed independently of the group
2. The task is perceived by the performer as not meaningful
3. The performer views his or her contribution to the outcome as redundant
4. The performer's personal involvement in the task is low
5. The performer questions the relevance of his or her contributions to the outcome
6. The individual's coworkers/teammates are highly skilled and expected to perform well
7. A comparison against group standards is not available

There are several strategies for overcoming or preventing social loafing in sport:

1. Identifying the performer's efforts (the coach would likely be the most powerful source of incentive, here)
2. Helping the individual form perceptions that he or she is making a unique and important contribution to the group's effort
3. Recognizing that the task being performed is difficult
4. Performing the task with friends as opposed to strangers or performing as a group high in social cohesion
5. Ensuring that the task personally involves the performer (i.e., that the individual has a personal stake in the task's outcome)

6. Making each athlete's task unique to increase a sense of control over his or her efforts and personal responsibility for performance outcomes.

Tips for Improving Team Cohesion

If having a cohesive team is important to the coach, several strategies can help to make it happen. Researchers suggest the following:

1. *Acquaint players with the responsibilities of their teammates.* This will help to develop support and empathy among the players. This can be facilitated by having players observe and record the efforts of other athletes at their positions. If subunits naturally exist on the team, which is common in many team sports, coaches will want to develop pride within each of these subunits. Players need the support of their peers, especially of the same positions and in team sports where the interaction among athletes is required for success.
2. *Use effective communication strategies.* The appropriate use of humor and praise in verbal and nonverbal forms is advantageous in generating feelings of mutual satisfaction and enjoyment. Athletes are especially responsive to recognition for special contributions.
3. *Know your players.* Coaches should be "in touch" with their players and should know something personal about each one. If a competitor has a problem that affects his or her play quality or, conversely, is celebrating some joyful event (e.g., a birthday or receiving a good grade in class), the coach can acknowledge it and perhaps respond to the athlete appropriately. How do the players feel about the team? What changes would they like to see? What explanations do they need that will help them understand better the reasons for certain approaches to game preparation? How can they receive better coaching? What do they need to get to the next level of performance?

4. *Look for and communicate something positive after each game.* Playing effectively, yet losing, does not have to result in a hostile, negative response from other players and coaches. There should always be something to feel good about after the competition regardless of the final outcome. Was there improved performance? Are they progressing? Was the loss a matter of bad luck?
5. *Provide feedback to players.* To promote motivation and team loyalty, players should be informed about their status on the team, given an explanation for this status, and told what they can do to upgrade or maintain it. Each athlete should feel that he or she has an important role with the team. Further, the value of every role should be expressed by the coach. Coaches need to ensure that every team member feels he or she is contributing to the team and is receiving the coach's attention and feedback.
6. *Teach and require interpersonal player support.* Players should not be allowed to hurt the feelings of teammates, although there is nothing wrong with friendly teasing and maintaining a sense of humor, as long as the verbal exchanges are delivered with friendly and positive intentions. The coach has an obligation to the players to promote group support. Unhappy athletes are unproductive and demotivated. Scapegoating, blaming, and chronic teasing must be stopped quickly, or cohesion will dissipate.
7. *Be consistent when setting limits.* Discipline of players should be consistent for all team members. Starters (or "stars") should not be treated differently from others with respect to setting limits.
8. *Try to inhibit player dropouts.* Excessive turnover of personnel does not promote cohesion. Establishing close rapport with a group is difficult when its members are unfamiliar with one another, are uncertain as to the longevity of their group, and have not established trust. Individuals avoid risking being close to teammates when they perceive the relationship to be short term. So, when a new member joins the team or a player

appears to be isolated from other team members, established players should interact with that individual and attempt to establish friendships. In addition, required tasks and expectations should be clear. At least one team member should be given the responsibility of establishing good rapport with the new arrival.

9. *Elect and work with player representatives.* Group cohesion means, in part, open communication between coach and athlete. Therefore, it is wise to have player-selected team representatives (even from each subunit, if necessary) meet with the coach on a regular, prescheduled basis—perhaps weekly or biweekly—to discuss various issues.

10. *Leadership should be developed among team members.* Coaches are mistaken in assuming that they are (and should be) the only team leader. Athletes respond favorably to peer leaders, sometimes better than they respond to coaches. Perhaps player leaders can lead discussions among themselves about developing or maintaining good team cohesion.

Taken together, it may be concluded that team cohesion is an important and desirable component of team success—but not essential. Certainly, a positive team climate and establishing friendships among team members is especially important in youth sports, since having fun and meeting new friends form some of the reasons young athletes engage in sport competition. Team success is not 100% dependent on the level of cohesion for success. This is especially true for social cohesion, which consists of team member social interaction, friendships, personal support, and favorable attitudes toward each other. Task cohesion, on the other hand, is central to performance quality, especially on highly interactive sports such as soccer, basketball, ice and field hockey, among others. It is better to coach a team of athletes who feel they have the opportunity to demonstrate and improve their skills. It is also important to remember that coaches have a role in promoting team cohesion and the idea that "there is no 'I' in "TEAM."

chapter nine

Coach Communication Beyond Athletic Performance

Many fine coaches are geniuses at planning team strategy, teaching performance techniques, and knowing the detailed rules of their sport. Sadly, many coaches are unable to effectively communicate their knowledge either due to the inability to establish an open and trusting relationship with players and/or due to the lack of knowledge of proper teaching skills. The purposes of this chapter are to provide insights into ways to establish high-quality coach-athlete relationships and to suggest specific communication techniques that will improve the coach's ability to share his or her knowledge, which will benefit the athlete's skills and performance.

Unless a coach first masters the basic skills of communication, all his or her knowledge about improving an athlete's sport skills will not be translated into improved performance. In addition, the coach's ability to influence the team's thoughts, emotions, and behavior will be less effective and less influential. No matter how brilliant a coach might be in planning strategy and knowing the technical aspects of his or her game, success depends on the coach's ability to communicate effectively with the athletes. Communication may be the essential skill without which the coach's efforts are doomed to failure. Very little has been written in sport literature about effective communication and counseling techniques. It is little wonder that coaches develop their style of addressing athletes through modeling—often imitating the mannerisms and styles of their own coaches from the past.

We will review some of the most common situations in which communication becomes an integral part of coaching—and athlete—responsibilities. The examples we will review illustrate the need for dialogue in developing an effective communication style.

Who the Coach Communicates With

Consider all the people with whom coaches must interact if they are to be successful: players, assistant coaches, coaches from other teams, parents of the athletes (i.e., in youth sports), referees, teachers of the athletes (i.e., in secondary school and college sports), the media, and the coach's own supervisor (i.e., the athletic director, organization administrator) or employer.

Players. Coaches must maintain an open dialogue with each team member, including coach assistants and athletic trainers. Examples, in addition to "regular" (managerial) coaching duties, include providing instruction, reviewing team rules and policies, making decisions about the starting status of each player, determining short-term and long-term performance goals, and soliciting player feedback about changes in the team's current routines and future directions. In addition, coaches should consider using nonverbal communication techniques such as smiling, patting players on the back, and thumbs up—all examples of positive communication with athletes. Coaches who maintain an impersonal, distant relationship with players cannot expect to have the same level of influence, trust, and loyalty as the coach who frequently interacts with the players and creates a warm and supportive team climate.

Assistant coaches. Soliciting information from assistants, including the team's sport psychology consultant, about the performance of various players on the team, as well as on opposing teams, developing game strategy, receiving feedback from assistants about how to improve the team's—and the head coach's—performance, providing updated information on the condition and future prognosis of injured athletes, helping to plan game strategy, allowing assistant coaches to address the team (perhaps without the head coach's presence), offering input to assistant coaches about their performances, and engaging in informal verbal exchanges in a social context off the field or court all require effective communication by the head coach.

Parents. Coaches are accountable only to their supervisors —professionally and legally, that is. But if the coach wants to gain the loyalty of the athletes and, in many instances, keep the athletes playing on the team, especially for child and adolescent-aged competitors, then communication with parents is inevitable, appropriate, and sensible. Discussion topics include providing a "report card" on their athlete's current performance level, areas the athlete needs to improve, explanation for the athlete's current playing status (e.g., a timetable for improving the athlete's playing status (i.e., going from nonstarter to starter), status on rehabilitation from injury, and plans for the athlete's future team roles.

Game officials. Constructive dialogue with the sports official is often necessary and desirable, before, during, and sometimes following the competition. Coaches are models to their athletes of appropriate and ethical behavior and therefore are responsible for conducting themselves in a manner that demonstrates maturity and integrity. Contrary to the view of many coaches, evidence suggests that it is not an effective strategy to argue with the game official to excite and motivate the team. Conflict between the coach and game official raises the athlete's level of mental discomfort, anxiety, and reduced concentration. In addition, the athlete's sense of self-control about the game's outcome is diminished; feelings of helplessness emerge.

Educators. For sports competitors who participate through their educational institution, eligibility to play depends on maintaining academic standards. It is imperative, sometimes required, that coaches interact with the athlete's teachers or professors to monitor the athlete's academic progress and to respond quickly to concerns about his or her academic performance. There are stories of coaches who interact with the athlete's teachers only after the athlete has received a poor grade. Educators have been asked either to change the grade or to allow the athlete to "earn" an improved grade by completing additional work—or being allowed to submit or resubmit assignments or to retake exams so that additional points may be earned. This is irresponsible, of course, and may be contrary to the rules of the school's or sport's governing body. The athlete's academic eligibility may be at risk. The ethical coach understands that the athlete's education is a priority and helps the athlete feel responsible for, and commit to, the education process to reach long-term goals.

The best, most ethical coaches ensure that their players attend class, apply good study habits, and that they have high graduation rates. Coaches should ensure that they keep in touch with each player's teachers throughout the school year, even in the offseason, to ensure that studying and a commitment to their education is maintained and perceived by athletes as an integral part of sport participation.

The media. Newspapers, television, and radio form the link between the team's fans and players. Proper communication with the media is crucial because athletes are very sensitive about how they are perceived by others. Players typically read and hear about their coach's remarks concerning members of the team. Derogatory statements by the coach are usually demotivating and embarrassing to athletes, whereas complimentary remarks improve self-confidence, coach loyalty, and effort. We turn, now, to a list of must-have communication skills if the coach is to have the credibility and respect of his or her athletes

It's no secret that many, sometimes most, players do not receive an opportunity to play in the competition, particularly at more advanced levels of competition. Nor can everyone have an opportunity to play in every game, with youth sport teams the possible exception. Due to the extensive time required to teach and practice skills and strategies to athletes who will compete, some coaches will neglect the nonstarter. This is a terrible mistake that need not be committed.

It is wrong to ignore or dismiss the importance of nonstarters on sports teams for several reasons. First, the nonstarter is only one injury away from becoming a starter. How many athletes enter a game and play as effectively as the starters? Not too many. Yet skill differences between starters and nonstarters are often relatively minimal, especially among elite performers. One possible reason why nonstarters do not perform at levels similar to starters may partly be due to differences in the time and effort coaches offer starting players relative to players who are not scheduled to play or start. The high relationship between the coach's expectations of player performance and actual performance outcome is a phenomenon known as the *self-fulfilling prophecy* (also known as the *Pygmalion effect*). This phenomenon is partly dependent on the lack of attention and practice given to nonstarters for whom the coach expects—and gets—relatively lower skill execution than from starting players (Martinek & Karper, 1984).

Other reasons the nonstarter should receive attention, respect, and consistent communication from the coach include (a) to avoid the appearance of a double standard between starters and nonstarters that, if perceived by the players, would divide the team, reduce team loyalty, and lead to feelings of helplessness about future game participation by nonstarters; (b) to allow the coach to observe and provide feedback on improvements in skill and performance of a given athlete; and (c) to prevent the deterioration of team morale—a devastating psychological state that leads to the low self-image of participants, a lack or absence of motivation to learn and perform at optimal levels, and a conscious or unconscious desire by players to see their coach and, perhaps, their teammates fail. It is important to remember that members of sport teams are often friends in addition to teammates. Such friendships are not often composed of nor dictated by similar status on the team. If nonstarters are perceived by team participants as being treated unfairly, all team members are affected, with only rare exceptions. The coach must treat the team as a unit of individuals who jointly serve the common purpose of performing all the necessary tasks to win.

These 10 guidelines of effective communication, if applied consistently, will vastly improve the coach's ability to help each athlete find greater enjoyment in sport and help them more closely approach their performance potential. Communication, however, is a two-way street. In the next section, we look at what athletes can do to foster the coach-athlete interaction.

Soliciting Feedback

Learning and improving a sport skill requires instructional feedback from a coach (or physical education teacher in a school setting). This form of feedback consists of information about the quality of the athlete's movements, more specifically, the ways in which the current performance state and the desired state deviates from each other. My throwing or ball kicking accuracy will not result in perfection (i.e., hitting the center of the target bulls-eye) without knowing the location and extent of this deviation. Learning cannot occur in the absence of information feedback, also called informative, instructional, augmented, external feedback, or knowledge of results. These terms, reflecting the learner's observations, differ from another category of feedback that occurs naturally during performance execution: internal, neural, proprioceptive, tactual, knowledge of performance movement forms of feedback, which are part of the performer's neurological processing. Extrinsic forms of feedback are imperative for learning and improving sport performance and serve several purposes. For example, feedback serves a motivational function by providing learners with the incentive to reach their goals. Athletes have a strong need to achieve as part of their personality. Receiving information that reflects improved performance meets this achievement need. Similarly, external feedback reinforces successful performance and encourages athletes to maintain their performance quality. When athletes are praised, either verbally or visually (electronically), on the high quality of their performance, they are more likely to replicate these performance skills.

I have observed considerable time devoted to practice either in the absence of feedback or feedback that is wrongly provided. Before feedback is provided, coaches may want to consider the following issues:

a. Is feedback even needed? Perhaps the athlete already knows what he or she must do to improve and providing additional input from the coach may create information overload.

b. Coaches need to determine what type of feedback to provide and in what form. Feedback can be verbal or visual, reflect what was performed (i.e., descriptive feedback) or what to do about it (i.e., prescriptive feedback). In addition, feedback can consist of the quality of the movements (i.e., knowledge of performance) or be presented in term of the results produced by the athlete's movements (i.e., knowledge of results).

c. How much information feedback should be provided? Less-skilled and younger learners have a limited ability to process information. Therefore, coaches might consider providing their athletes with limited amounts of information, especially if the skills are complex, not well rehearsed in the competition, and provided at the early stages of learning.

d. How precise should the feedback be? In the earlier learning stages, feedback might be more general and reflect "getting the general idea" or "the hang of it," especially if the coach can attach new (i.e., more recently learned skills or skill components) to old (previously learned) skills. The mechanics of swinging a tennis racquet and hitting a tennis ball has both similarities and distinct differences from swinging a badminton racquet and striking a birdie. Athletes, especially novices, need to apply what they already know—previously learned skills—with what they don't—new skills.

e. The frequency and timing of feedback is a further consideration, often reflecting the athlete's level of maturity, skill level, past experience, and ability to incorporate complex and sophisticated content into present competitive conditions. To prevent information overload, feedback should not be given after every attempt in practice settings. One style of feedback that if often neglected in sport settings is the written word.

Role of Team Captains

Some coaches are not knowledgeable about the role of team captains, even having doubts that captains have a valuable role to play, at least in team sports. One college football coach (with 10 years of experience as a high school coach) told me that "To this day, I don't know what a team captain should do beyond leading team exercises and working the coin toss before the game." Another college football coach disclosed that he designates a different set of team captains on the team each week, which changes the captain's intended role. One very important role for a team captain is to lead team (or partial team) meetings—either in the presence of, or perhaps more comfortably, in the absence of team coaches. Captains might lead small group sessions that partially determine the team meeting agenda. For example, the coach might designate two team co-captains to hold small group meetings to make recommendations to the coach on team policy (e.g., the value of scheduling workout sessions early in the morning versus after regular practice late afternoon, or planning the menu for team meals).

Often, players are more apt to disclose feelings with their peers than in the presence of the coach. And they may more comfortably decide issues or determine policies that the coach has delegated to the team. For instance, should there be a team party after the season, during the holiday, or to commemorate some other event? If so, where will it be held and should personal friends be invited? Of the list of videos the coach has provided, which one would the players like to see on the night before the game? Coaches should be cautious in living up to these agreements. Giving responsibility to and supporting the team and team captain's decisions on selected issues is critical. Preplanning is essential to effective control and content of team meetings. Coaches should not have the team meet without goals and an agenda that is well thought out. The next step is implementation.

Team Meetings

It is the coach's role to schedule team meetings—for any one of several reasons, not just to meet. Meetings should have special meaning to each team member—players, assistant coaches, athletic trainers, administrators, and so on—so that this activity is perceived as important, even necessary, to maintain and improve the team's operation. Here are some advantages of team meetings that have psychological benefits for team members.

1. *To gauge group feelings.* In team meetings, coaches can spot problems before they have a chance to spread among the players and undermine morale. Ultimately, the honesty and openness that develops between coach and athlete can be transformed into a highly effective tool to enhance player loyalty to the coach and the team.
2. *To provide information and insight.* From group counseling sessions, the coach can obtain information on the thoughts, feelings, needs, motives, and problems of the team members. The coach, therefore, becomes more effective because he or she understands what's happening behind the scenes.
3. *To humanize player-coach relationships.* Coaches should welcome the opportunity to interact with the players on an informal,

nonthreatening basis rather than only in a sport-related context. Athletes are markedly more loyal to coaches who relate to them in ways beyond the role of player. Many athletes have loyal feelings toward a coach who treats them as mature, thinking human beings (Anshel 1989a). Group counseling is a process that allows a coach to be human or say "I don't know, but I'll find out." The players have a chance to disclose their insecurities, questions, fears, and feelings on a variety of issues.

Planning the Team Meeting

Surgeons don't walk into the operating room before examining the patient's medical history and gathering as much information about his or her medical condition as possible. Lawyers never enter a courtroom without prior extensive preparation about the client and the situation they are representing. And, just as effective coaches would never approach a competition without a game plan, neither should they approach a team meeting unprepared.

Several questions should be addressed. What is the meeting's purpose? Who will lead the meeting? Does a specific topic need attention, or is this a gathering with an open agenda? What outcomes need to be derived from the meeting, or is this exclusively a "kick back" social gathering? Is there a time limitation on completing the agenda? What will be the roles of the players, coach, team captains, and assistant coaches? Is someone dictating information, or is the item open for discussion? Will this be a passive audience (listening only) or will they take a more active role (discuss, debate, decide)? If a follow-up session is necessary, will the coach be able to indicate the time and place before the meeting is adjourned?

Implementing the Meeting

One way to avoid having a meeting that no one wants or that elicits virtually no active participation by the players is to be clear and honest with the group at the start. Remember that the purpose of the meeting may be to address a need, either of the team, an individual player, a group of players, or the coach. As the players enter the meeting area, allow a brief time for "chitchat" among them. Informal interaction among group members before a meeting often serves to relax participants. Serving refreshments may improve the players' moods and relax the atmosphere of the meeting. Perhaps the coach can also speak informally with a few players or with other team personnel. This is a time to loosen up. Anxious group members do not talk; relaxed, secure members do. The coach is now ready to open the session, one in which an exchange of feelings is planned. See Anshel (1992b) for additional guidelines in conducting group and individual meetings for coaches and other supervisors.

The meeting's purpose. Inform the players at the start about why you've gathered. Stating the meeting's purpose helps the participants to stay on track rather than trying to cover too much ground or discussing extraneous issues. For example, "The purpose of getting together is to review the strengths and weaknesses of our weekly practice schedule and to try to meet the needs of many of you who claim to need more time to study. If this meeting is going to be successful, it will require that the people in this room feel comfortable voicing their opinions. That means each of you."

Expectations of the meeting. What are reasonable expectations of the meeting? Can players and coaches expect to reach decisions on at least certain issues at the end of the gathering? Or is it more probable that the coaches will take the athletes' feelings (those generated in the meeting) into consideration and decide on a plan of action in the near future? To keep expectations about the meeting's outcome realistic and conservative is important. In most cases, change takes time, and deciding to make changes from previous habits or policies takes even longer. Rarely should the coach promise a change or decision before the meeting ends unless the meeting's primary objective was to resolve an issue. Then a decision is imperative.

Establishing the ground rules. If full participation is to take place, the players need to feel secure about several items. For instance, they should be made to feel that everything said in the meeting will remain confidential. To gain trust and credibility, the coach may need to promise not to tell parents that their son or daughter engages in some behavior of which they would not approve. If it is learned that a player broke the law, the promise of confidentiality means that the coach will not consult the school principal or law officers unless school policy dictates otherwise. Of course, it is also against the law to hide information about a past crime, and the coach does have an obligation to convince the athlete to approach school or legal authorities under extreme conditions. In extreme cases (e.g., assault, robbery, taking or selling drugs), the coach has a moral and legal obligation to consult the proper authorities.

Another ground rule is a promise not to use the athlete's words against him or her in future encounters. What would a player's perception be if he or she said something at the meeting that may have offended the coach and never or rarely played thereafter, especially if that player received more playing time in competitions before the meeting? Could the coach keep the team's loyalty and trust? Could the coach again be viewed as credible? Unlikely! So, it might be prudent to tell the players, "This is the time to get those feelings off your chest" or "I will respect all points of view at this meeting without feeling insulted or upset, as long as we talk to one another in a mature manner and with respect." For many athletes, a preferable tactic would be to have the team captain or an assistant coach run the meeting rather than the head coach.

A third ground rule concerns the choice of topics under discussion. The coach may feel that it would be more productive to center the discussion on one or two issues at a given session and then discuss other issues at another meeting on a later date. The coach might suggest, "Let's keep the discussion limited to your feelings about practice time and game preparation. In this way, there's a better chance of reaching an agreement sooner than if we were to go off in different directions. At the next meeting, we can discuss other issues."

Another rule is to encourage the participation of *all* team members present, but not to force participation. Players can be invited

Coach Communication Beyond Athletic Performance | 245

to send an anonymous note about their feelings at some future time if so desired. Also, participants should agree that one or more players may not dominate the conversation unless the players announce that one player is acting as the spokesperson for the group. However, the participation of relatively few players may defeat the purpose of a team meeting. Further, team counseling (expressing feelings, changing behavior, and so on) requires massive participation. Only in this way will each athlete feel responsible for fulfilling the agreement of the meeting.

Respecting the feelings of each participant is another ground rule. Before the meeting, members should agree that none of them will be insulted, teased, ridiculed, abused, laughed at, or threatened. Everyone should be entitled to and respected for his or her point of view.

Finally, the time limitation of the meeting should be announced before beginning, for example, "We will adjourn in one hour"; "We need to conclude this meeting no later than 6 p.m. I will tell you when we have 10 minutes left"; or, "In another five minutes, we will bring the discussion to a halt, and I'll summarize where the group stands and then review our options."

Grayson (1978) makes the following additional suggestions to keep the session moving:

1. Guard against going on unrelated tangents. Stick with the agenda and the meeting's goal(s).
2. Give credit to individuals for all contributions, however small (e.g., "That's a valid point, Marcy. I appreciate your honesty").
3. Take time out at appropriate points in the session to summarize what has been said up to that point, being fair to each point of view. Writing key words or issues on the board might be helpful to provide organization to the ideas or feelings being expressed.
4. Point out related areas or issues that the group might explore. If the subject is lack of team harmony or poor teammate support, the coach might want to explore the underlying reasons

for that perception and for that "truth" (if most players agree the perception matches the reality).
5. Encourage the expression of different points of view. Know the difference between inaccurate information and personal opinions. The latter should always be encouraged unconditionally (no right and wrong reaction), whereas the expression of misperceived or wrong information needs correction. Coaches must never appear defensive and unwilling to listen to an athlete's perspective. If the coach solicits input, then athletes should be encouraged to reveal their feelings.
6. Tactfully discourage "soap box" oration, including that of the group leader. This is especially harmful to a positive meeting environment if someone has a gripe that is unrelated to the matter under discussion.
7. Patiently help members to express themselves if they are floundering in the attempt. Without appearing rude and interrupting the speaker, the meeting's leader (i.e., chairperson or coach) can help the speaker formulate the main point (e.g., "Joe, let me be sure I am hearing you correctly; you feel that coaches should consider doing. . . . Is that right?").
8. Never criticize, demean, or embarrass a speaker for expressing a point of view. Hostile exchanges will threaten the meeting's integrity and most, if not all, players will stop talking. The meeting's goal(s) will less likely be met.

Closing the session. As indicated earlier, the length of the meeting and ending time should be determined and communicated to all group members at the start. The coach should remember several points about terminating the session:

- *Be prompt when ending the meeting.* If one hour is set aside for the meeting, stick with the schedule.
- *Summarize.* At the time of termination, review the highlights of the session with the group. The summary should include a brief restatement of all points of view expressed by team

members. Were there any particularly interesting issues raised or statements made during the session that are deserving of further comment? Group participants will feel a sense of closure, purpose, and accomplishment if the numerous comments and issues are crystallized into meaningful units. In this way, the meeting's contents and decisions will be better remembered and the basis for the decisions better understood. This means more support for carrying out these decisions.

- *Suggest further exploration.* Certain points may need additional discussion at subsequent meetings. Perhaps more information must be gathered or more exploration of established policies is needed before a decision can be made. The coach, in his or her concluding comments, can point out these needs, which will be the basis for further discussion. Perhaps a committee can be formed whose responsibility it is to generate recommendations or obtain information about an issue. Name the committee members at the meeting and provide their objectives, task(s), and a deadline by which to provide their findings.

- *Express gratitude.* Thank participants for their attendance, contribution, and willingness to speak. Perhaps offer special recognition to individuals who were instrumental in the meeting's outcome. In addition, the coach might want to suggest that certain positive outcomes were derived from the meeting. These may include (a) a sense of fulfillment and accomplishment in expressing feelings and making decisions, (b) feelings of team togetherness, (c) improved team morale, (d) an optimistic view of the team's future, (e) better team member satisfaction, (f) learning and sharing new ideas that might improve team or individual performance, and, perhaps most important of all, (g) the coach's sense of appreciation for the players' candor and honesty in expressing their sentiments. If possible, the coach should inform the group when the next session will be held and provide some information about the possible agenda for that session. Better yet, it makes sense to establish a regular (possibly weekly) meeting time so that meetings are not only about negative issues or emergencies, but are also used to keep communication open and regular among team members and coaches. A regularly scheduled meeting allows the players' time to think about the issues, to plan their responses, and to begin to make observations and notations that may serve as topics or ideas for further discussion.

After the session. When the meeting has concluded, the session leader should remain in the meeting area to discuss any personal or follow-up issues with group members. Unless previously arranged and announced, the coach should *not* socialize with the players at a club or restaurant after the meeting. Players need the opportunity and the "mental space" to share their feelings about meeting content and to discuss ideas about future directions of the team without the presence of an authority figure. After all, the coach is not the players' "buddy" or best friend.

The coach's job at this point is to ensure the proper follow-through on issues and decisions that were discussed. It is crucial that decisions from the session be carried out as soon as possible (or when agreed on) to support the coach's credibility. In some cases, a written summary of the meeting's points and decisions might be distributed to the players within a few days after the meeting.

Finally, on occasion, participants can evaluate the session by having players complete an anonymous form in response to specific questions about the session (with room for additional comments). Alternatively, the team captain can get verbal feedback from several players. Perhaps the captain can offer the coach a summary. In this way, confidentiality and anonymity are ensured.

chapter ten

Coaching Youth Sports

Organized sports programs are characterized by an arranged schedule of competitions for children in a competitive environment using prescribed rules. Competitions may be held within or outside a school. Pick-up games and other free-play situations are not considered youth sport; instead, they are recreational sport. The primary mission of youth sports is to teach children sport skills and to develop enjoyment and a positive attitude toward future and continued involvement in competitive sport. If we can promote enjoyment for child athletes, it is likely they will want to continue to participate in sport and remain active for the rest of their lives.

Other desirable outcomes of sport competition include learning to deal with stress and adversity, making new friends, sacrificing personal gain for the sake of team success, and building self-esteem. Child athletes have different needs and priorities, as compared with older, better-skilled, more "mature," sports competitors. Kids are not miniature adults.

The primary purposes of this chapter are to highlight the unique needs of child athletes, typically defined as under age 14 years. How can being a sports competitor meet these needs? Why do children participate in sport and why they drop out? Finally, how can coaches and parents of young performers help the young athletes enjoy the experience of competitive sport and avoid quitting?

There is nothing wrong with wanting to win and executing sport skills successfully. Performing sport skills efficiently is difficult, especially for the younger athlete who has limited physical capacity and a very limited history of success. Sadly, some parents and coaches have unrealistic expectations of the younger athlete's current level of talent; it's called *perfectionism*. Adults have to be very careful about making harsh assessments of children's performance level, and avoid using the term "failure" in describing the younger athlete's performance level (Anshel, 2016). The problem for child athletes is the level of unrealistically high standards, expectations, and reactions to less-then-perfect sports performance that coaches and parents direct toward children. Since when is striking out considered "performance failure," especially if baseball batting is a complex skill? And why would parents and coaches express anger and disappointment toward a young athlete who is giving 100% and, in fact, is demonstrating improved skilled performance over time and with practice? Adult behaviors in competitive sport are leading to an alarming sport dropout rate, which results in a sedentary lifestyle and missing out on some of the wonderful memories that youth sports can provide (Anshel, 2016).

Sport Socialization

The interest in developing sport skills and maintaining athletic participation begins in childhood, but *participation should not be restricted to one sport, unless this is the child's own wish*. Specializing in some sports (e.g., tennis, swimming) need not occur until the adolescent years, whereas other sports (e.g., gymnastics) require childhood participation. The child athlete should possess reasonably high expectations of success in any chosen sport; expectations should be positive and achievable. Perceived ability and expectancies not only influence performance, but also influence the child athlete's interpretation of success or failure. That is, persons who expect to succeed tend to feel good about their ability and effort in response to their success if they actually achieve it. This leads to the next factor that influences sport participation, explaining the causes of performance outcomes.

After the performance outcome is derived, the competitor searches for an explanation for the outcome. This is important because this explanation for success or failure strongly influences the motivation to maintain sport involvement. Here are the guidelines for increasing sport motivation.

Explaining Causes of Success That Increase Sport Motivation

- Success was due to high ability
- Success was due to good effort
- Success was achieved despite a highly skilled opponent or due to a challenging task
- Good luck had nothing to do with success

Explaining Causes of Success that Decrease Sport Motivation

- Failure was due to low ability
- Failure was due to poor effort
- Failure was due to an easy task ("We should have won; we were the better team")
- Success occurred by competing against a poorly skilled opponent
- Success was due to our good luck ("We were lucky")

Thus, how an athlete reacts to particular situations and performance outcomes strongly influences the motivation to remain a participant and to find pleasure from the situation. Child athletes would be unlikely to experience and maintain their interest in sport if they did not receive the approval and reward (through positive feedback, successful performance, or both) from a parent, peer, spectator, or instructor.

Personal Factors That Explain Youth Sport Participation

The skills and dispositions that athletes bring to the sport milieu are a function of abilities and other genetically based physical attributes, in addition to early childhood experiences in which personal attributes, values, and attitudes are learned. The level at which abilities are demonstrated in performing sport skills is at least partially inherited. This means that all people have their own unique capacity or optimal level of sport performance. The skill level that athletes demonstrate is partially guided by 11 motor abilities.

An *ability* is something that is enduring and general; it's a trait affected by both learning and heredity. A *skill*, on the other hand, is specific to given tasks and is attained with experience. Thus, hand-eye coordination and visual tracking are abilities, whereas baseball batting or throwing for accuracy are skills. Other examples of motor abilities include speed of movement, reaction time, and hand-eye coordination. Abilities, which are different from skills, are enduring and at least partially genetic.

Skills are susceptible to short-term conditions such as fatigue, mood, and drugs (e.g., alcohol, caffeine, or tobacco intake). Early childhood experiences include opportunities to engage in motor activities and an activity-oriented environment. Abilities and social environment are important contributors to a person's success and enjoyment as a sport participant. The important point to remember, here, is that *elite-level athletes have certain high abilities that allow them to learn and perform motor skills at a superior level.*

Why Children Play Sports and Why They Drop Out

Youth sport involvement is becoming more and more popular around the world, especially in North America. Unfortunately, equally common is the degree to which children drop out of sport. The pattern of involvement indicates an increase in youth sport participation up to the age of 13 years, with a marked decline after that. If we can identify the reasons for participation, then adult leaders of teams and organizations can more adequately meet the needs of child participants and significantly lower the dropout rate.

Many studies have examined the reasons for sport participation. The age of subjects in these investigations ranged from 6 to 18 years; there is a lack of full agreement among researchers concerning the age range of youth sport involvement. Some studies label "youth sport" up to age 13 years, while others refer to young athletes at age 16 years and younger. Nevertheless, there is widespread agreement among age groups as to why younger athletes join sports teams and the reasons they quit them.

The young athletes tended to rank their reasons for playing in the following order: (a) to have fun, (b) to learn and improve skills, (c) to be with friends and make new ones, (d) for excitement, (e) to succeed or win, and (f) to exercise and become physically fit. Other researchers, in athletes ranging from 7 to 14 years, found that pleasing others, receiving rewards, and even winning the game—contrary to popular opinion—were consistently rated *least* important. Of far greater importance was the excitement of the sport, personal accomplishment, improving one's skills, and testing skills against others.

Of great interest when reviewing children's reasons for participating in sport is the dichotomy between what adults *think* children want and what the children really want. The use of rewards, the importance of winning, the benefits of competition, and pleasing others (parents, for example) are viewed by adult leaders in youth sport programs as imperative for success. Program leaders insist on providing elaborate rewards to participants (sometimes only to athletes on winning teams), stress the importance of being in first place or winning the championship, called *outcome goals (performance goals* are preferred), and convince parents of the need for children to "build character" through competitive sport.

"Getting rewards" and "pleasing others" often rank very low in importance as reasons for enjoying sport. Instead, "fun," "improvement of skills," and "personal accomplishment" tend to be rated high. Of more moderate ranking are "excitement" and "to compete." "Getting rewards" and "being on a team" are considerably more important for the enjoyment of younger participants but become less significant with age.

Apparently, young children react more strongly to material reinforcers (i.e., rewards and recognition from "important" adults) than older players who, with age and maturity, find these reinforcers less crucial. Further, younger players identify with being part of a team—for many their first organized team experience—more strongly than do their older counterparts. Researchers have found that winning and receiving rewards for playing sport, which appear to be very important to parents, coaches, and the media, are of secondary importance to the participants' enjoyment and accordingly should not be heavily emphasized. So why do children drop out of sports that they at one time considered fun and enjoyable?

Why Children Drop Out of Sport

Children approach the sport environment for different reasons and to meet various needs. These reasons are dependent on psychological factors (e.g., experiencing success), emotional factors (e.g., feeling competent), and social factors (e.g., affiliating with and meeting new friends). Regardless of the factors that underlie their involvement in sport, for some reason child athletes do not tend to "stick with it." The dropout rate in youth sport is soaring. Between the ages of 10 and 17 years, about 80% of all children in the United States who are enrolled in organized sport drop out. Why?

The primary reason for quitting is an overemphasis on winning. A lack of success, not playing, involvement in other activities, and "other interests" are also rated highly. Other reasons for dropping out include boredom, little skill improvement, and excessive competitive stress. Typical examples of reasons included in some studies were "The coach yelled at me when I made a mistake," "I never got to play," and "I wasn't good enough."

Researchers have written extensively about the needs of young competitors and the factors that appear to be most responsible for quitting sport. The causes of quitting sport fall into three areas: (a) comparative appraisal, (b) perceived lack of proper sport skills, and (c) low intrinsic motivation (i.e., playing sport for fun and enjoyment). The athletes' coaches and parents need to understand the reasons for dropping out so they can institute strategies that prevent it, which is covered later.

Comparative Appraisal

Comparative appraisal concerns a self-assessment of one's competence as compared to others with similar characteristics (e.g., boys comparing their skills with other boys of similar age, position, size, motor ability, and so on). Children begin comparing themselves with others to determine their own relative status on motor ability starting around ages 4 to 5 years. This process increases in importance through the elementary years. During grades four, five, and six, both appraisal and the number of children engaged in youth sports interact optimally; young athletes are comparing themselves with others more often at this time than at any other. The reason for this is that children have relatively little past experience on which to base accurate self-appraisals. Consequently, they become dependent on others for information about their own adequacy. The input comes in verbal and nonverbal forms—both positive and negative.

Positive verbal statements reflect pleasure, recognition, and praise, while negative verbal communication includes ridicule, reprimand, and rejection. Nonverbal cues, both intentional and unintentional, are emitted continuously. Parents telegraph pride and approval, or embarrassment and annoyance, by facial expressions, body language, eye contact, or ignoring the child. For example, I observed a young athlete's father throw his baseball cap against a fence after his son struck out (looking, not swinging, at the pitch). That's a flagrant example of how adults send messages of approval or disapproval based on the appraisal of their child athlete. It is easy to see how comparative appraisal, at first externally derived from others, then internally defined by the athlete, can lead to the athlete's persistence or withdrawal from the competitive sport experience.

The primary objective of coaching child athletes should be to provide them with information that promotes a feeling of success or improvement at performing sport skills. When this happens, other needs are also met (e.g., enhancing self-concept, the feeling of mastering one's environment, receiving recognition for effort and improvement, and gaining a sense of competence and achievement). The following suggestions indicate how coaches and parents can help young participants deal constructively with the process of comparative appraisal.

1. *Avoid comparing children.* Every child has his or her own skill level, strengths, and weaknesses. The role of the adult is to inform participants about their adequacies and to help them learn skills and improve performance. Statements such as "If Jimmy can do it, why can't you?" are unfair at best and destructive to a child's character at worst. Children excel at different sports and skills. Coaches and parents need to give them the credit they deserve so that they stay involved in sport.
2. *Help children realize that "different" doesn't mean "better."* Because of the social pressures exerted by parents, children will compare their performances to those of others. However, when a child believes that love and recognition from "significant others" (i.e., persons whose opinions are valued) depend on

favorable performance outcomes, such as getting a hit, catching a pass, or scoring a point, the child is apt to be more intense in the comparative appraisal process. Consequently, he or she will be more critical and will manifest insecure behaviors. One child might possess a set of skills different from that of another child. The important issue is that each young competitor should have something to feel good about.
3. *Adults should be positive models for children.* If we expect our children to avoid criticizing peers, coaches and parents must do likewise. Children's performances should be critiqued, particularly during practice and in private, not in public. The desirable outcomes of sport, such as skill learning and fun, become nonexistent under the umbrella of too much criticism.
4. Finally, *help to prevent sport-related stress.* Adults can help children make more positive appraisals of their sport experiences and overcome stress in sport. The sport environment is filled with evaluative messages of approval and disapproval. Coaches and parents can help children deal with the unpleasant messages given by fans, opponents, and others. A pat on the back with a few kind words of support go a long way toward preventing depression—especially after the player has made an error or in some way contributed to an unfavorable team outcome (missing a shot, for instance).

Perceived Lack of Ability

The best advice for leaders of youth sport programs is to focus on the young athlete's improvement of skills and making the effort. The lack of ability should not even be mentioned. As indicated earlier, the primary reason children drop out of sport is that they attribute failure (poor performance) to their lack of ability. Early in a child's athletic experience, successful performance is based on merely completing the task—just getting to the finish line in a 50-yard dash, for example. Later, however, social approval becomes an important goal. If the athlete is to maintain participation in sport, he or she needs the approval of significant others such as the coach, teammates, friends, spectators, and parents. The young player soon realizes that the approval of the coach is dependent on effort. "If I try hard, the coach will like and accept me," he or she feels. Therefore, trying hard becomes the main criterion of success and failure.

Starting at about 11 and 12 years (and sometimes younger), "perceived ability" becomes of paramount importance as the motivating factor for playing sport. Instead of completing a task (the goal of the 6-, 7-, and 8-year-olds) or vying for social approval (common at the ages of 8, 9, and 10), youths' primary source of motivation in sport becomes feeling competent. For example, an 8-year-old feels successful after completing a 50-yard dash. A 10-year-old may reflect success if a coach, parent, or peer praises the runner's effort. An adolescent, on the other hand, is pleased if he or she is a first-place finisher. The outcome of winning takes on an increasing importance with age. The lack of competence is now attributed to low ability (poor skills), instead of to a lack of effort or to task difficulty. Most kids who drop out of sport (as many as two-thirds, in some studies) think that they are "not good enough."

Low Intrinsic Motivation

Individuals have a need to feel competent. Researchers agree that an athlete's perception of competence or incompetence are the most critical factors that influence performance and persistence as a sport participant. Young athletes constantly strive to demonstrate high ability and minimize low ability in making judgments about their competence. Thus, an athlete's perception of success is based on his or her interpretation of demonstrating high competence; an athlete's perception of failure is based on his or her interpretation of demonstrating low competence. It is important to point out that the athlete's *actual* success or failure (e.g., winning or losing, making an error, or demonstrating skill mastery) is not the important issue, here. Rather, it is the individual's *perception*, or *interpretation*, of success or failure that determines the influence of competence on motivation and persistence. This interpretation is a crucial factor in making decisions about maintaining sport participation or dropping out. When a child perceives his or her competence as low, he or she realizes there is only so much "trying hard" can do before giving up. To maintain motivation and task persistence in any achievement situation such as sport, it is important that athletes perceive their participation as generally successful and attribute this success to high ability. However, the athlete's conclusion that he or she is deficient in both will likely lead to termination of the activity, that is, becoming a sport dropout.

Coaches in particular can directly affect a child's feelings of competence in sport by helping the child interpret the causes of performance outcomes. Missing a shot or making an error can be interpreted as a lack of ability ("You don't have a good eye for hitting") or lack of effort ("With more practice, performance will improve; keep trying"). Coaches and parents need to offer feedback to young players that indicates three things:

1. That doing the best they can—making the effort—is very important for success
2. That their performance (any aspect of it that can be observed and identified) is, in fact, improving
3. That lack of ability has nothing to do with poor performance outcome because they are capable of improving with practice and instruction: "Don't quit!"

The game outcome is not an end in itself but merely a result of learning, performance improvement, and higher self-confidence. *Once a player feels that he or she lacks the ability to be successful, the probability of dropping out of sport increases dramatically.*

When are Children Ready to Compete?

The word "readiness" implies that a person has reached a certain point of maturity and skill development that allows for the opportunity to succeed. A match should exist between a child's level of growth, development, and maturation and the demands of the task. The use of a batting tee to replace a live pitcher in baseball, lowering the height of baskets in basketball, and lead-up games that make fewer complex physical and psychological demands on the players are three popular examples that facilitate this developmental match.

How do physical education teachers, coaches, and parents know when that point has been reached? Specialists depend more on tradition than on developmental progressions. We depend on the performer to tell us when the state of readiness exists. For many years, researchers have attempted to identify the primary factors that underlie a child's state of readiness (i.e., the abilities that allow for sport involvement) and to recognize the initial signs of readiness to learn and perform sport skills. This process occurs when a minimal degree of competence in entry behaviors, or "must-have" skills that allow for successful participation, are demonstrated.

Primary Factors of Readiness

Maturation, the most important determinant of readiness, is one of three primary considerations indicating a young participant is ready for skill introduction. The child's *prior experiences* through learning is the second consideration. Learning occurs with greater efficiency during some periods in life than in others. According to Magill (1990), the so-called critical period for learning sport skills is when sensory (mental) processing and motor responses are functioning at optimal levels. The child must be able to understand and to identify the demands of a task—the speed and trajectory of a ball in flight, for example—and respond accordingly for a successful outcome. The third consideration is *motivation*. Learning theorists agree that skill acquisition is impossible unless the learner has the incentive to learn.

Thus, the child's greatest potential for achieving in sport is dependent on his or her maturation level, prior experiences through learning, and motivation. These factors, however, do not necessarily function independently of one another. For example, a child might have the incentive to play a competitive sport—perhaps to please parents or to emulate older athletes—but not have the mastery of skills or the experience to perform effectively. The result of premature participation could be inefficient performance and failure, with the subsequent dropping out of sport. Children who do possess the proper skills might be afraid to fail, feel "burned out" from too much participation and too much pressure to succeed, or for some reason not to have the motivation to continue. All the readiness factors must be present if sport skills are to be learned and performed successfully and consistently.

There are two important issues concerning readiness in sport: (a) children are not likely to be ready to compete in sport until they have acquired the necessary skills to become successful, and (b) the likelihood of skill learning and performance is dependent on the individual's level of cognitive (perceptual and sensory) and physical (movement coordination) maturation.

Meeting the needs and limitations of children as sport participants requires instruction and adaptations in the environment that will lead to successful experiences. Wise choices need to be made about the type of sport in which a particular child should engage, about changes in rules and equipment, and even about the dimensions of the playing surface that will accommodate the child. Examples of the "smaller is better" approach include fewer players per team, smaller fields, reduced equipment size (e.g., lower basketball goals, smaller and lighter balls), and less emphasis on competition outcomes and more emphasis on skill development and player achievement. Finally, for young children, in particular, equipment should be altered to promote fundamental motor skills such as climbing and throwing. Climbing equipment should accommodate children with limbs of all sizes; balls should not be too large, heavy, or hard to control. Striking movements should be aimed at stationary targets (bowling pins or a ball dangling from a string, for instance) rather than at balls in flight at high rates of speed.

Signs of Readiness for Learning Sports Skills

For a child to be ready to participate in sport, he or she must have the ability to learn and demonstrate competence in requisite skills. Before enrolling their child in a sports program, parents should determine if their child has the subordinate or prerequisite sport skills and cognitive maturity (e.g., coping with failure and other sources of stress, handling pressure and the expectations of others) to successfully engage in competitive sport.

There are several factors that accompany psychological development through competitive sport, usually starting at 8 to 10 years of age. These include empathy (i.e., sensitivity toward the feelings of others), understanding one's role and the responsibilities of each team member (i.e., valuing cooperation and sacrifice rather than competition), and placing one's needs and interests above those of other team members. The appreciation of other perspectives is essential for cooperation and is especially important in team-related sport activities, in which each individual must understand the importance of cooperation for the good of the team.

Another approach parents and coaches can use to ensure that children are ready to participate in a sports program is to encourage youth to experience and develop a variety of sports skills and to compete in more than one sport, at least during childhood. Researchers have found it unwise to restrict a child's repertoire of skill development. Children who start early in one sport and rarely engage in others tend to burn out by the time they are adolescents. Stories abound of famous athletes who quit or took a prolonged "breather" from sport competition, particularly in individual sports such as tennis and swimming. As young competitors, they either were bored or were under too much pressure to be successful in the activity.

In addition, growth and maturation may dictate that the child is better suited for a sport other than the one that he or she experienced in earlier years. For instance, a boy who matures early in junior high school may actually be too small to play contact sports by the time he reaches high school or college. Another suggestion is that children should be allowed to participate in sports that they enjoy and not compete in sports to satisfy parents, coaches, or others; otherwise, they may not persist very long at the activity. How are children to know whether they enjoy badminton or some other sport until they try it? A final suggestion is that children, like individuals of all ages, tend to maintain interest and incentive to participate in activities in which they succeed. Each person should be allowed to willingly experience as many different sports as possible to increase the probability of success in many sports.

Perhaps the most important factor that underlies acknowledging a child's readiness to play competitive sport (aside from physical or anatomical limitations) is that of *competence*. How well can the young participant perform the fundamental skills of the sport? Is he or she able to catch a hard baseball without fear? Can a rapidly pitched baseball be visually tracked and the bat swung at sufficient speed to contact the ball? Can the ball be thrown at the proper speed or distance to ensure a successful outcome? How many children are playing basketball who lack the physical maturity to shoot the ball into a hoop their shot cannot reach, perhaps resulting in using improper shooting technique? And what about the young athlete's ability to learn and apply cognitive and performance strategies in competitive situations?

The acquisition of primary skills associated with the particular sport, which often takes years rather than weeks or months, is imperative, but often lacking. This is the first step before children are involved in competition. When children are able to perform the necessary tasks successfully, then parents can consider enrolling them in a low-pressure, competitive sports program—given, of course, the child's wish to become involved in such a program. They may prefer to play the game in a recreational setting, but not participate in an organized league, which emphasizes the pressure to win. In addition, learning is enhanced in a low-pressure, less win-oriented setting.

Talent Identification Programs

Talent identification (TD) programs are planned processes for predicting sport performance over time. This is accomplished using information obtained from selected measures of the athlete's' physical, physiological, and psychological measures. The primary purpose of TD programs is to screen younger athletes to determine those most likely to eventually succeed in sport. A second purpose is to direct them toward the types of sports to which they are most suited. Individuals who appear to possess the characteristics important for success in a particular sport are matched with various performer characteristics and the task demands of a given sport. Thus, TD programs recognize which individuals currently involved in competitive sports programs have the potential to become elite-level athletes.

Two related programs that are intended to locate and nurture athletes with the potential to currently or eventually demonstrate high-quality sports performance are called *talent selection* (TS) and *talent development* (TDV). TS programs identify athletes at various stages of the training program, while TDV implies that the athletes are being provided with the appropriate learning/practice conditions to promote and realize their potential.

There are several advantages of TD programs, such as assisting coaches, athletes, and their parents to identify the type(s) of sport(s) that is most compatible with the performer's physical and mental attributes, which reduces the likelihood of an athlete dropping out of a sport, a costly and time-consuming outcome. Determining the sport and position that best represents a young athlete's skills might prove more efficient than traditional trial-and-error approaches.

TD programs provide athletes with relevant feedback so that they can effectively monitor their progress throughout the entire training program. Ostensibly, TD programs can maximize the number of children who have positive sport experiences and a greater likelihood of success, thereby reducing the rate of sport dropout.

If researchers can identify psychological characteristics that are unique to elite-level athletes representing specific sports, perhaps valid measures that detect these characteristics among younger competitors might encourage parents and coaches of athletes to commit time and resources for future skill development.

Coaches, sport psychologists, and parents have to be aware of numerous limitations for using psychological tests to assess psychological skills and predict the athlete's future skill level, sport type, or sport position. The most compelling case *against* the use of psychological measures in TD programs is research evidence, reflecting what is called *poor predictive validity*. This means that the inventory does not predict an athlete's future sport success. Numerous studies have attempted to identify certain psychological factors as predictors of talent in various sports. These studies have a very low prediction rate.

In summary, psychological tests do not take into account common factors in sport such as availability of high-quality coaching; opportunity for practice; availability of proper equipment and facilities; and the athlete's own growth, maturation, and development over time. The extent to which psychological inventory scores can contribute to the selection and training of future elite athletes remains questionable.

Perhaps the final word about whether coaches, athletes, or their parents can accurately describe the characteristics of elite-level athletes and predict their future success ignores the fundamental issue of providing athletes of all ages the opportunity to excel. Providing young athletes with (a) high-quality coaching and skill instruction, (b) first rate equipment, (c) opportunities to learn and practice skills, (d) incorporate mental skills into their training regimen, (e) safe transportation to the sport venue, (f) a safe physical environment (including proper maintenance of sport equipment and facilities), and perhaps most important (g) ensuring that the each participant is enjoying the sport experience. All these factors supersede the results of paper and pencil inventories in predicting future sport performance and to optimize the benefits of school and community resources.

The Role of Parents in Promoting Youth Sports

No one has a more powerful influence on whether a child decides to participate in youth sport—and remain committed to it—than the athlete's parents. Fred Engh (1999), former president of the National Alliance for Youth Sports, has generated a "parents code of ethics" that requires parents to pledge their cooperation in youth sports environments. Some sample items for this code are as follows:

1. I will encourage good sportsmanship by demonstrating positive support for all players, coaches, and officials at every game, practice, or other youth sports event.
2. I will place the physical and emotional well-being of my child ahead of my personal desire to win.
3. I will insist that my child play in a safe and healthy environment.
4. I will support coaches and officials working with my child to encourage a positive and enjoyable experience for all.
5. I will do my best to make youth sports fun for my child.
6. I promise to help my child enjoy the youth sport experience by doing whatever I can, such as being a respectful fan, assisting with coaching, helping improve my child's sport skills through practice, or providing transportation.
7. I will remember that the game is for youth, not for adults.
8. I will ask my child to treat other players, coaches, fans, and officials with respect, regardless of race, sex, creed, or ability.

9. Finally, I will demand a sports environment for my child that is free of drugs, alcohol, and tobacco, and will refrain from their use at all youth sporting events.

Parents and coaches can help prevent youth sport dropout by doing the following:

1. *Make within-individual (not between) comparisons.* Help to focus the child's attention on how he or she is performing in relation to previous performances and away from comparing himself or herself with other children. To do this, orient the child to the use of performance goals within the sport rather than to the outcome of winning or losing.
2. *Focus on the athlete's strengths.* If assessing one's own ability is inherent in older children (about 10 years and up), then coaches can encourage a positive perception of ability through sport mastery. Reinforce the specific skills that each athlete can perform competently while emphasizing improvement on weaker skills.
3. *Set performance (rather than outcome) goals.* Children might view themselves as skilled in some areas and unskilled in others. To help children develop accurate and stable views of their abilities, set performance goals for each individual that he or she is capable of achieving. Use performance (e.g., number of catches, tackles, or weight lifted in strength training) as the standard for success and failure rather than winning or losing outcomes. Children will be less apt to fail if goals are set realistically.
4. *Encourage children after failure.* Children tend to have global perceptions of their abilities after success or failure—particularly after the latter. Making an error translates to "I'm a terrible player." Children need to be reminded that a quality athlete can also experience performance failure. They need to be reminded of their competence.

5. *Stress individual differences.* Children, parents, and coaches need to know that children and adolescents grow and mature at different rates. Comparing one child's physical characteristics with bigger, stronger peers may promote feelings of inadequacy and low self-esteem. In young males, low testosterone levels prior to puberty will minimize marked increases in strength and other physical development. This is why physical conditioning in youth sport should be secondary to building skills. Coaches should communicate to young athletes about what is happening to their bodies and assure them that they will grow, become stronger, and improve their performance. The message should be "Be patient."
6. *Don't predict the child's future.* An additional issue is that parents and coaches should never attempt to predict the young athlete's future in sport, what may be called "playing God." Statements such as "You'll never do well at 'X' sport (or perform 'X' skill effectively)" are likely inaccurate and extremely demotivating. On the other hand, "You should make the pros" is equally detrimental to participation satisfaction. If given proper instruction and the opportunity to practice skills, the potential of any sport competitor is unknown.
7. *Talk to each other.* Parents and their child's coach should interact—in private if possible—to discuss the young athlete's progress, development, and future needs. What skills need improvement and what should the young athlete be practicing between scheduled games? Should the younger attempt to play another sport, and if so, which one would suit his or her skills? How can the athlete be coached at home—perhaps after school or on certain preplanned days (and hours) of the week. Schedule it.

Young athletes drop out of sport because they feel incompetent. Quitting helps them avoid further anguish and saves face in front of others. One way to help these children deal with the stress of athletic competition is to teach them how to ask the right questions.

Asking "How can I improve?" or "How can I improve this skill?" is a far more constructive strategy than "Can we win?" or "Am I good enough?" Children should be concerned with sport mastery and not with ego-involving outcome assessments.

Children should never be "pushed" into sports prematurely. This means judging a child's skills objectively and avoiding sports for which the child is unenthusiastic about participating or physically ill-suited. Instead of pressuring a child into certain sports, perhaps they should introduced to a variety of other sports they find attractive and enjoyable . Parents and coaches should help a child find one or more sports which will allow him or her to enjoy the experience most.

Why is a child participating in a particular sport? The reason(s) should never include "to make my mom/dad happy." It should be "for the fun of it." If children a in sport for the wrong reason, then the parents and, perhaps, a coach, should help their child find another another (perhaps noncompetitive) recreational activity. Inflicting feelings of guilt (e.g., "Make us proud of you") is inappropriate (Ginott, 1965). Knowing when their child is physically and mentally ready to engage in competitive sport challenges most parents in their wish to "do what's best for their child." Parents should consider a contingency plan if the sport experience is not working out: "Try it, and if you don't like it after (insert time frame here) you can try another sport or come back to this sport at a later time."

Low Intrinsic Motivation: Reexamining the Value of Trophies

As discussed earlier, the main reason children want to participate in sport is to have fun. Perhaps, not surprisingly, the most common reason they offer for dropping out is "It's not fun." This fun component underlies the concept of *intrinsic motivation*. Motivation is having the desire and drive to move toward some goal. Intrinsic motivation is the desire to do something because it's enjoyable; the experience itself is enough to feel good about performing some task. Outside rewards and ultimate goals are not necessary (with one exception, as discussed later in this section). *Low intrinsic motivation plays a significant role in withdrawal from sport.* Parents and coaches, often unknowingly, contribute to this predicament.

Adult leaders in sport typically claim that children want and need a reward system (trophies, for instance) to maintain interest in, and derive pleasure from, playing competitive sport. Researchers have not found this to be the case. Reliance on rewards, a form of *extrinsic* motivation, turns play into work. Activity that is intrinsically motivating is often play activity.

Adults should be asking (a) "What can I do to maintain or increase intrinsic motivation in child athletes and reduce or prevent the onset of extrinsic motivation?" (b) "Does the use of all rewards undermine intrinsic motivation?" and (c) "Do kids want and enjoy receiving rewards?" The good news is that the selective use of rewards in sport has been shown to benefit young athletes; rewarding play activity can increase intrinsic motivation under certain circumstances but can decrease it in others.

The effect of an award on intrinsic and extrinsic motivation is directly related to how the child perceives the reason for the award. Sometimes a child's motivation for engaging in an activity goes from internal (e.g., fun) to external (e.g., a trophy). This process has been termed the *overjustification effect* (Lepper et al., 1973), and it persists today. This occurs when the child receives an award that is expected and highly recognized—not just a pat on the back but a highly visible reward such as a trophy.

The overjustification effect is based on adult assumptions that the child can't possibly want to participate in an activity simply for its enjoyment. "Doesn't every kid want a trophy?" they seem to ask. "Won't most-valuable-player awards and all-star team recognition motivate them to play better and have more fun?" The answer is an emphatic no. Sport leaders and parents of many child athletes "overjustify" the child's reasons for engaging in the activity by making an erroneous assumption: that kids can't possibly have the incentive to play sports in the absence of some tangible reward. Awards can increase intrinsic motivation, but only under certain conditions.

To increase intrinsic motivation through the use of rewards, coaches and parents should consider the following suggestions:

1. *Rewards should reflect skill level and competence.* Remember that children seek information about personal ability through high-quality sport performance. Therefore, rewards should reflect some aspect of "successful" performance, however "success" is defined. If parents and coaches do not perceive the athlete's performance as high quality or as "successful," than praise the athlete's good effort and/or performance improvement. A trophy, ribbon, certificate, or positive verbal remark should recognize some accomplishment, at least improvement or effort. In this way, all team members can be recognized and praised. This avoids team members from collecting multiple post-season awards while other team members receive nothing.
2. *Don't coerce participation.* Let the motive for playing be self-determined by the athlete. The motive should not be to gain their parents' love or succumb to peer pressure, but should be because they *want* to play.
3. *Teach skills.* Children can improve only if they are taught sport skills. It's unfair to expect better performance simply as the result of repetition in practice—or, worse, no practice at all.
4. *Promote social support.* Help the team members cheer for each other. Point out to the team a well-performed skill shown by any given athlete. Encourage mutual support by team members, especially after an unpleasant sport experience, such as making an error or some other undesirable performance.
5. *Remember the modeling effect.* Often, coaches are the models for desirable behaviors. As such, their statements and behaviors of positive verbal and nonverbal communication, support, and

approval of others will facilitate similar responses by team members.

6. *Allow for team decisions.* Whenever possible, give players an opportunity to make decisions that affect their play or the game. The coach need not make all decisions before and during the competition. For example, have the players vote for a cocaptain, while the coach selects the second cocaptain. Other examples of shared decision making include choosing one's position and developing team strategy. Shared decision making can build intrinsic motivation through self-determination.

7. *"Ensure" success.* Try to have each child experience some degree of success as soon as possible during the sport season. The need for competence is most salient at the early stages of involvement when children have the most doubts about their skills and make rapid judgments about further participation.

8. *Awards should be unexpected.* Researchers have found that children who receive rewards unexpectedly maintain a stable level of intrinsic interest. Avoid promising rewards if they win (called conditional reward) because *not* winning will be perceived by the athletes as failure. After a well-played game or practice session surprise them with a treat or social outing. The effect will be much longer lasting. The participant will receive the reward as an outcome of competence rather than playing for the treat; although the reward is external, it is noncontrolling.

9. *Set goals jointly.* Establish individual goals jointly between coach and athlete based on realistic expectations of the athlete's future performance.

10. *Keep practices and games fun, yet productive.* Fun is the top-ranked reason most children give for playing sport. Highly regimented practices, lack of playing time, and verbal abuse destroy their primary motive for participating. Kids are not miniature adults, so adults—coaches and parents—should try to keep the environment light.

The comparative-appraisal process, the lack of perceived ability, and lower intrinsic motivation are each—and in combination—primary causes why kids drop out of sport. But the single condition that underlies each of these perceptual processes leading to withdrawal from competition is stress.

Competitive Stress in Youth Sports

If competitive sport is a game, and kids participate in sport to have fun, why do so many children find the sport experience unpleasant and even stressful? The negative emotional reaction of a child when his or her self-esteem is threatened is referred to as competitive stress. Competitive stress among child athletes reflects two factors: (a) children's perceptions of inadequacy in meeting performance demands, and (b) their perceptions of the consequences of failure. It is the child's own appraisal of the situation that determines whether his or her self-esteem is threatened. If the child predicts that not scoring a point will result in negative consequences (e.g., being ignored by peers, reprimanded by parents or the coach, booed by spectators), then competitive stress is heightened. If the child feels comfortable that doing his or her best is all that's expected to gain the approval of others, the perception of threat (i.e., competitive stress) is greatly reduced.

Competitive stress can occur at any time: (a) *before* the competition in anticipation of poor performance or a superior opponent, or if game preparation is considered inadequate; (b) *during* the competition if performance is viewed as inadequate, the opponent shows superior performance, spectators offer negative input, there is a "bad" call by the referee or umpire, equipment or facilities are poor, or the athlete is experiencing pain or injury; or (c) *after* the competition if the child has concluded that the completed performance or game outcome did not meet expectations. The most common cause of competitive stress is the threat of failure, a source of state (situational) anxiety. State anxiety increases with age and is most prevalent at age 12 and during adolescence, the time when dropping out of sport is highest. Children in sport fear failure because of the importance adults place on success and a successful game outcome.

What is apparent is that (a) child competitors are often being placed under great pressure to succeed, not just to do their best, but to win, and (b) adults (i.e., coaches and parents) need to help young athletes improve their pre-competition mental preparation. Helping child athletes cope with the pressure of winning may include using *cognitive strategies*, such as positive self-talk and mental imagery, *behavioral techniques*, such as emphasizing effort ("Just do your best and don't worry about winning and losing"), goal setting, and positive reinforcement ("Nice work; good job of hustling on that play"). Taken together, these mental skills can reduce the unpleasant effects of competitive stress.

Combating competitive stress in youth sports may include placing less emphasis on three factors: meeting performance expectations, winning the competition, and comparing athletes' abilities. At the same time, more attention should be given to teaching skills, emphasizing effort and performance improvement, training coaches to communicate with young athletes in a mature, nonthreatening manner, and deemphasizing championships and trophies that reward relatively few children and generate feelings of failure and inadequacy in a far greater number of child participants.

If trophies or some other form of reward are included in a youth sports program, it's best to link the trophy to a competency such as "best hustling athlete," "most extra base hits," "most tackles," and so on so that every player is recognized for some form of competence, skill, or improved play. A greater perception of fun on the part of the young athlete is strongly related to lower stress levels, both before and after the competition.

Young athletes experience excessive stress in the following situations:

1. They feel and show little confidence
2. They make negative self-statements ("I am terrible at . . .")

3. They feel ill the night or immediately before competing (called "little league syndrome")
4. They have trouble sleeping the night before the event
5. They consistently perform better in practice than in games (have a tendency to "choke")
6. There are observable changes in personality before the competition
7. They urinate frequently the day of the competition

Although some degree of stress is inherent, even necessary, in sport, a chronically stressed child is an unhappy participant and will soon withdraw from further competition.

Coaching Children: Positive Approaches to Avoiding Dropout

One way that coaches can provide effective leadership to children is to understand the children's reasons for dropping out of sport and to address concerns on an individual basis.

Reason 1: Not getting to play. Given the choice, more children in sport would rather play on a losing team than remain on the bench of a winning team. Playing is valued much more than winning among child athletes. Therefore, coaches should be sure that skills are taught so that all players on the team can participate successfully. If arranging for game participation is difficult, then coaches should ensure that all players receive plenty of attention and positive feedback during practice.

Reason 2: Negative reinforcement. Errors, for children and adults, are a normal part of learning, particularly with less-skilled performers. Children are especially vulnerable to negative feedback and ridicule because it's so difficult for them to put the situation in perspective. Kids have poor coping skills. Eventually, if insults don't stop, self-esteem plummets, and the kids will drop out. Coaches should focus their comments (even critical comments) on performance ("Watch the ball into your hands"), not character ("You look terrible out there"; "Don't you know better than that?"). Also, keep errors in perspective; it's part of the learning process. Again, kids are not miniature adults.

Reason 3: Mismatching. When kids are mismatched in size and skills, the underdog finds little about which to feel successful and motivated. Boys of the same chronological age may differ by as much as 5 years anatomically. Try to provide a safe and enjoyable environment for each child. Each player should enter a program and be assigned a team that is compatible with his or her physical maturity and approximate skill level.

Reason 4: Psychological stress. Kids should not feel anxious (i.e., worried) before games. The competitive process should be challenging but also rewarding and fun. The more closely practice situations simulate actual games, the more easily athletes will be able to adjust to game conditions. Also, coaches should avoid telling the players about the importance of winning or reminding them of who's watching them—both tactics raise anxiety and pressure needlessly and contribute to poor performance and high dropout rates.

Reason 5: Failure. An error can be interpreted as failing, making a good attempt, improving, bad luck, or just being human. The positive aspects of performance should be emphasized. Errors can be minimized by teaching skills and engaging in efficient practice sessions.

Reason 6: Overorganization. When practice is boring and physically inactive, the fun component has been effectively removed. Coaches should follow the principles of effective skill instruction: talk less and do more and keep the kids moving. Be creative; simulate game conditions; have competitions among team members during practice that utilize game-related skills, promote fitness, but don't overwork them. Child athletes need skill development more than bigger muscles and aerobic fitness.

Success is not necessarily the same as winning. Kids should not be overly dependent on the outcome to conclude that they benefited from playing sports. Success and failure are not related to winning and losing. The athletes are reminded that success is related to commitment and effort—the energy that goes into doing one's best and striving for a desirable outcome. If athletes try hard and give 100%, they have every right to feel positive about their sport experience.

Gender Differences: Implications for Coaching Females

What do the physical differences between males and females tell the coach about coaching female athletes? Before puberty, girls are similar and in many instances superior to boys anatomically, physiologically, and in their motor coordination. Thus, before this time, coaches, teachers, and parents should feel comfortable in coaching girls and boys in a similar manner and in encouraging co-ed sport competition in which boys and girls can engage jointly. Researchers contend, however, that children should not engage in contact sports before puberty. No evidence supports the use of a double standard in sport where girls are automatically assigned substitute roles or asked to play positions of less importance, or worse, not given the same opportunities as boys to learn and improve their sport skills.

Parents, teachers, and coaches should promote sport involvement for females, particularly at relatively young ages when women are less conscious of culturally based gender-role stereotyping and engage in sport because it's fun. This is when they possess sport skills similar or superior to those of boys. Attitudes about sport involvement are developed and nurtured early in life. There's little doubt that the development of skills and relatively limited participation in sport by women is a cultural, rather than a genetic, outcome. Coaches, educators, and parents have an obligation to develop healthy attitudes, mental well-being, and physical stature for both genders. It makes good sense to give both genders the opportunities to reach these objectives. To do so makes winners of all sport participants.

Coaching philosophy and values in youth sports. The coach's and the program's goals should be articulated to parents and to child and adolescent athletes. Is winning the most important thing? If having fun and learning skills take priority, it is crucial that parents realize that winning and losing are mere by-products of the child's involvement. Other rules concerning who starts; who plays; discipline; expectations about showing up—or not showing up—for practice; and the rationale for, or existence of, awards and other forms of recognition should be discussed.

1. *Re-examine the need for awards banquets and trophies.* I was the guest speaker at a high school's sports banquet one year, and noticed something very sad: Just a few athletes (out of about 50–60 in attendance representing all of the teams) were receiving *all* the trophies—some athletes were awarded 8 or 9 trophies—in contrast to 90% of the other athletes who received none—zero! This was a tragic mistake fueled by adult thinking that only the "best" athletes who deserve "most valuable this" and "best that" be recognized for their talent. I wonder if these adults—I presume they were the coaching staff from all school sports—realized they were embarrassing some of the recipients of these awards, while missing opportunity after opportunity to give recognition and gratitude to the multitude of athletes who also worked hard all season to show up and train and who played a supportive role in helping their teammates excel and achieve. In fact, the recipients of these trophies were more than embarrassed; they were humiliated.

The child's responsibilities. If children are to mature due to their sport experiences, they must assume certain responsibilities. These include (a) reporting promptly to practice and games, (b) cooperating with coaches and teammates, (c) wearing the proper uniform and equipment at games and practices, (d) following team rules, (e) making the proper effort to condition their bodies, (f) making a commitment to learn sport skills, and (g) conducting themselves in a mature manner before, during, and after team-related functions—to be "good sports" and not harass, criticize, embarrass, or attempt to injure an opponent. Parents should be asked to support these behavior expectations at home.

The parents of youth sport competitors' responsibilities.

1. Learn what their children want from the sport and why they are participating in the first place. If the child does not want to participate, especially after meeting the coach and team members, parents should not force it. Maybe after observing a few games or maybe even next year, the hesitant child will feel more comfortable participating. Perhaps he or she prefers to play a different sport. If children are playing only to please their parents rather than to enjoy themselves, they should be allowed the freedom to say "no thanks," at least for now.
2. Children should feel accepted and loved by their parent(s) and respected by their coach whether their team wins or loses, whether they have scored many points and played well, or whether they committed two errors and struck out with the bases loaded. Avoid *conditional love* (i.e., "I'll love when only when you improve your performance"; "We'll go to your favorite fast food restaurant after the game only if we win").
3. Solicit information from the coach about the child's progress or offer to assist the coach at practice or after the competition but do not interfere with the coach during the competition. Parents should be role models to these young athletes. Here is a real-life example of a hostile youth sport environment. During a baseball game of 13- to 14-year-olds, an angry father of one baseball player called the umpire a derogatory name after disagreeing with a "strike-three" call. This was followed by the umpire's derogatory reply, which then escalated into a physical wrestling match between the two adult males. Fortunately, no one was hurt and no arrests were made. After the father departed the grounds, the game was completed, but what kind of role modeling is that for kids to observe?
4. Parents should conduct themselves in a mature, supportive manner at games and practices. Let the coach do his or her

job and stay clear of coaching decisions. Sit back and applaud your child.

Recommendations for providing a healthy and effective youth sports environment.

1. *Develop a mission statement.* A mission statement reflects the primary plan of action—where you want the organization or league to go and how you intend to get there—in reaching the organization's goals. Youth sports administrators need to build a mission statement into their philosophy of operation. Is winning most important to the league's mission? How relevant is playing the team's best players while the other team players sit and watch the games without being given an opportunity to learn and practice sport skills?
2. *Establish expectations and policy for appropriate adult behaviors at competitions.* Poorly chosen words directed at players and game officials can create a hostile environment among spectators and upset young participants. Parents who attend their children's games and, in fact, all spectators of any age, should be informed of the regulations of appropriate behavior prior to, during, and following these events. And a policy should be established and communicated that abolishes alcohol, smoking, and other undesirable behaviors at the competition.
3. *Teach sports skills (and include mental skills).* Good coaches are good teachers! Youth sports organizations should include at least one practice session per week in addition to game competition, and coaches should either learn the necessary sport skills or bring in an older, better-skilled person—perhaps an older former or current athlete—to teach these skills. Mental skills can be acquired by obtaining reading materials or working with a local sport psychology consultant.
4. *Establish guidelines for trophies and other awards.* Trophies (or any other form of award) are fine *if* the intention is to recognize the athlete's competence or team contribution and

the athlete perceives the trophy as a concrete indicator of a desirable outcome (e.g., performance outcomes) or role (e.g., team player, relief pitcher, co-captain). The aim of trophies or other forms of reward is to recognize the athlete's competence and to build intrinsic motivation.

5. *Establish a proper coach-parent relationship.* There is only one coach, and that role should not belong to the athlete's parents. This means two things. First, parents should not coach their own children. It's a direct conflict of interest. Second, the athlete's coach and parents have different roles. However, it is perfectly appropriate if coaches and the player's parents (or guardian) communicate on various matters about the athlete. Examples include player progress, the player's role on the team, areas—both physical and mental—in which the player needs to improve, understanding the player's role on the team, and resolving possible conflicts or misunderstandings between all parties. These interactions should always be held in a mature, supportive, and informative manner.

6. *Establish guidelines for proper conditioning.* Sports performance is partially dependent on good physical conditioning. Overtraining and exercising as a form of punishment are inappropriate and destroy a young athlete's enthusiasm for preparing properly for competition. Youth sports experts advocate skill development rather than improved fitness as a priority in this age group. This is partly due to the lack of hormones during prepuberty stages of the athlete's development that have not "kicked in" as yet.

7. *Use proper communication skills compatible for children.* Children do not handle harsh language and reprimands very well, nor should they have to. Children require relatively more praise and messages that build self-esteem and emotional support than their older counterparts.

8. *Set strict limits on inappropriate player behavior.* Cheating, overaggressive play, hostile actions, unpleasant forms of communication, lack of emotional control, being disrespectful

toward others (e.g., coaches, game officials, spectators, teammates, opponents), wearing improper attire, and not following coach instructions are valid reasons for warning and, eventually, dismissing players.

9. *Have proper medical care readily available.* Be sure there are proper medical procedures and personnel in place if an athlete is injured, especially if a physician's care and hospitalization is needed. A person should be designated to render first aid, if needed, and a person should also be prepared to call for an ambulance, if needed. Proper protocol to respond to a head injury or concussion should be firmly established. Sports organizations should have insurance—or require that all participants be insured—for immediate medical care, if needed.

Young athletes are especially in need of effective leadership. Most often the coaches in youth sports are volunteer moms and dads who often know relatively little about the sport, its rules, and how to teach its skills to team members. It is far preferred to have coaches attend seminars on how to teach the needed sport skills and how to use effective coaching skills before being allowed to take on the responsibilities of team coaching. There are several books and programs that provide guidelines for coaching youth sports. Here's a reminder worth repeating: Children are not miniature adults. A high-quality sports program means that every child is a winner!

chapter eleven

Coaching with Diversity in Mind

This chapter addresses the use of coaching psychology as a function of individual differences, that is, recognizing the uniqueness of coaching athletes with different needs, characteristics, and skills. How should the application of coaching psychology differ based on the athlete's age, skill level, race, gender, sport type, and culture? Are all athletes the same with respect to their psychological needs and what it takes to perform at an optimal level? Do the athlete's personal characteristics—individual differences—translate into different coaching strategies? In what areas of coaching do the athletes' personal characteristics require an adjustment and sensitivity changes in coaching techniques? How, for instance, would coaching sports be a function of differences in culture, gender, skill level, and so on? In what ways are coaching skills similar for all athletes irrespective of individual differences?

Effective sport leadership can be complicated, with coaches trying to influence the thoughts, emotions, and behavior of competitive athletes. One hidden challenge of coaching is to meet the individual needs of athletes who bring to the competition their own unique personal characteristics, which often requires changes in coaching strategy. These unique characteristics often require the coach's awareness. Athlete characteristics that may require the coach's attention include gender, age group, race, skill level, sport type, and the less obvious but highly influential characteristic culture. The focus of this chapter is to recognize how these unique characteristics (i.e., individual differences) can benefit performance and the implications this has for coaches. To use a common metaphor, one size does not fit all. The primary areas of differences in sport psychology are culture, gender, race, culture, age, skill level and sport type. The first area that coaches need to monitor is the role of cultural differences in sport.

Culture

Culture is usually defined as the customary practices and language associated with a particular racial or ethnic group. To others, culture refers to widely shared ideals, values, assumptions about life, and goal-directed activities that become accepted as correct by people who identify themselves as members of a society. The sport environment, therefore, consists of events and situations perceived differently by athletes who represent various cultures and whose reactions to these events and situations differ.

Perhaps one reason the role of culture in sport has not received more attention by scholars is the failure to consider the cultural context in which a particular sport is experienced. Coach awareness of cultural differences among team members is highly relevant, even predictive, of the athlete's responses to sport situations. Culture is entrenched within an individual's emotional system to make certain decisions and reactions in preparing for and competing in the competition.

It is well known, for example, that words and nonverbal cues differ between cultures (Hoedaya & Anshel, 2003). In addition, numerous studies have shown that culture strongly influences, predicts, and explains events that are experienced during the competition and how athletes react to certain coach decisions and behavioral tendencies. Individual differences have yet to be addressed adequately by researchers and practitioners when it comes to sports leadership.

Cultural differences. One culturally sensitive area in competitive sport concerns experiencing and coping with sport stress. The influence of culture on coping with stress is pervasive, and yet researchers, practitioners and coaches have failed to recognize the striking individual differences between how performers deal differently with sport stress, both chronic (i.e., ongoing; long term) and acute (sudden; short term). Examining cultural differences in the sport stress literature has been surprisingly rare.

Culture influences exist on the coping process in response to acute stress among competitive athletes. In one study, Puente-Diaz and Anshel (2005) compared U.S. and Mexican highly skilled male and female tennis players on1their respective sources of sudden stress and their use of coping strategies. They found that Mexican athletes cited receiving negative comments and injuring themselves during the match as the two most stressful sources. U.S. players, on the other hand, cited the opponent cheating as the most stressful event. Cultural differences in coping were also found, with U.S. players who used active (i.e., more emotional and confrontational) coping strategies, whereas the Mexican players were more likely to avoid high emotional intensity and argumentative coping. Results of this study serves as only one example how culture can play a role in the athlete's thoughts, emotions, and actions, in this case, how they perceive and react to stress during the match.

In another stress study, Hoedaya and Anshel (2003) compared Indonesian and Australian team sport athletes on experiencing sudden stress prior to and during the game. In response to *pregame* stress, Indonesians were more likely than Australians to use a coping strategy called "emotional social support" (i.e., interacting with and supporting teammates) and "denial" (i.e., dismissing the stressful experience as a normal part of the competition) following the stressors "seeing significant others," "being ignored by a teammate," "opponent's quality of play," "importance of a particular game," "doubting own performance," and "thinking about family problems." Cultural differences were also found for stress experienced *during* the game. Indonesians used denial, restraint, and confrontational coping more so than their Australian counterparts.

The results in the Hoedaya and Anshel study are particularly insightful into why it is important for coaches to be aware of cultural differences in sport. Results of studies clearly indicate that culture markedly influences an athlete's perception of the sport environment, including evidence of experiencing stress and evidence of unique ways of coping with it. For instance, Passchier and colleagues (1991) found that Indonesian culture, more than Western culture, is likely to value cooperation and consensus than independence to obtain individual goals. Thus, Indonesian athletes are more likely to value and feel motivated by setting and meeting team than individual goals. In addition, according to Triandis (1994), Indonesians are more likely to express courtesy and are more "subtle" in expressing disagreement or objection, respectively, than other cultures. Each of these personal characteristics has important implications for understanding individual differences, particularly in coping with sport stress.

Researchers have also examined cultural differences in coping with stress among sports officials. Anshel and Weinberg (1996) examined the coping strategies of highly skilled Australian and U.S. basketball referees using the approach and avoidance framework. While the researchers found more similarities than differences between cultures on their respective use of coping strategies, some stark differences surfaced as well. For instance, in response to an abusive coach who questioned the official's call, U.S. referees were more likely to speak calmly to the coach than were Australians. In response to abusive player comments, however, U.S. referees were more likely to use a more confrontational coping style (e.g., giving a technical foul) and showing relatively little tolerance for player misconduct than Australian referees, who considered player comments as part of the game and were less likely to be stressed and more likely to move on to the next play.

Differences in the coping process in sport has also been studied in Asian countries. For instance, Anshel and Si (2008) examined the coping responses of Chinese athletes and found that elite Asian athletes are more likely to adopt an avoidance rather than an approach coping style. Examples of avoidance coping are turning one's attention to the next task at hand, learning from the experience, and perceiving the stressor as a normal part of the competition. Avoidance coping was especially prevalent in situations of low perceived control (e.g., coach reprimand). The researchers point out that the coach is highly respected in the People's Republic of China, perhaps more so than in Western countries. The Chinese athletes expect, understand, and even appreciate coach criticism as a reflection of the coach's desire to improve their athlete's performance and success.

Thus, the coach is viewed very differently between Asian and Western cultures. For example, coach behavior that is considered "harsh," such as reprimanding or even corporal punishment (i.e., striking the athlete), or any other form of critical feedback, is more often expected and even appreciated by the Asian athlete, as compared to his or her counterparts from Western countries. Corporal punishment would not be tolerated in most Western countries, but this is the norm in Asian sport, especially at advanced levels. The results of these studies strongly suggest that culture strongly influences the coping process in sport, in particular thoughts, perceptual processes, emotion, and behavior, as indicated in numerous reviews of this literature (Wong & Wong, 2006).

Gender

The sport climate in recent years has seen an emergence of independence and opportunity for females—girls and women—to compete, particularly among highly skilled athletes. The question is whether female athletes require special needs and different coaching strategies as compared to their male peers. Differences between genders would have implications for coaches in their leadership styles and strategies toward male and female athletes. For example, in one study, highly skilled male athletes, as compared to female athletes, used more confrontational and assertive coping strategies (Anshel & Kaissidas, 1997). Female athletes, particularly those less skilled, applied more avoidance (e.g., not taking the stressful event too seriously or refusing to become more stressed than males). Gender differences have also been found for 11- and 12-year-old male and female field hockey players (Anshel & Delany, 2001). Specifically, girls used more confidence-building self-talk considerably more than boys, while boys more often used resignation (e.g., "I reminded myself that things could be much worse") than girls.

Results of other related studies indicated that (a) no gender differences were found on coping with failure and changes in confidence between male and female tennis players; (b) ineffective coping (e.g., self-blame, ignoring) was associated with low self-esteem for both genders; and (c) female athletes perceived less control over environmental threats than male athletes and used venting emotions, positive reinterpretation, dissociation, and emotional social support more often than males did.

These examples are important for acknowledging individual differences in providing coaches with insights about the unique needs of female athletes. Coaches and sport psychologists who practice in various Olympic team facilities agree that highly skilled male and female athletes are psychologically similar in virtually all attitudes, emotions, and the use of mental skills. The demands of elite sport do not allow for athletes of either gender to exhibit "weak" personal characteristics under challenging competitive environmental conditions. But does this mean that male and female athletes should be coached exactly the same way? Not necessarily.

The first issue that needs to be recognized when discussing differences in coaching males and females differently is related to an area called *sport socialization*. That is, coaching techniques and styles differ as a function of the athletes' child rearing and upbringing. Specifically, males, beginning in youth sport, are socialized to view sport participation as a "right of passage" to becoming a skilled competitor. It's expected by various sources of information that "encourage" us to take certain paths in life. There are multiple intersecting cultural identities that influence males and females in various age groups to be attracted to sport participation, in general, and for certain types of sports, in particular. Results of studies in sport sociology, for instance, indicate that competing in sports is viewed as more important for males than for females. Sport sociologists contend that females who choose to participate in sport step outside recognized social boundaries and confront a dilemma. There are social and emotional limitations placed on young girls who desire to engage in sport, particularly after reaching puberty. These females are more likely to overcome barriers to becoming an athlete—or at least attempting to learn and perform sport skills in organized competition. While a discussion on parents role in a young female athlete's decision to participate in organized sport goes beyond the limitations of this chapter, researchers are clear that the female's parent(s) have an active and significant role in supporting their daughter's attraction toward sport.

How does this issue—the socialization of females in sport—affect coaching of female athletes? It would be helpful to describe and summarize the factors that help explain the factors that have influences female athletic participation.

First, sports competitors are more likely to come from families that are active in or support participation in sport.

Second, while interest in developing sport skills begins in childhood, participation should not be restricted to one sport unless this is the child's own wish. Some sports can wait until adolescent years (e.g., tennis, soccer), while other sports require childhood participation (e.g., gymnastics, swimming).

Third, children of both sexes are more likely to persist in sport if they are exposed to the "proper" models with whom they can identify. To increase competition for females it is preferable that both mothers and fathers encourage their daughters to play and develop their skills. Parental game attendance would be enormously helpful, and so would practicing skills between games. Sons rely more on their father's than their mother's encouragement to remain a sport participation. For single-parent families, the presence and encouragement of either parent will be helpful to maintain sport participation and meet his or her child's need for parental support and recognition.

Coaching the female athlete. When it comes to possessing psychological characteristics (e.g., confidence, attentional focusing, concentration, competitiveness, mental toughness) and possessing various psychological characteristics (e.g., mental toughness, resilience, ability to cope effectively with stress, being goal driven), higher-skilled female athletes are more similar to their male peers than their less-skilled, younger counterparts. Coaching male and female athletes is far more similar than different from a mental perspective. Are there no areas that the coach of female athletes should address that recognize the unique needs of female athletes? It depends on the athletes' specific characteristics. Here are a few suggestions as reflected in the sport psychology literature.

First, competing in sport for both sexes is highly desirable toward promoting an active lifestyle, particularly exercise and other forms of physical activity, learning new (sport) skills, the opportunity to achieve success (which builds confidence and other desirable personal characteristics), and helps younger individuals deal with stress, anxiety, and other unpleasant thoughts and emotions. This is especially true with females whose socialization experiences typically follow gender roles and deemphasize these highly desirable qualities. Therefore, in addition to building sport skills, coaches need to build a bond of trust, encouragement, and confidence. Female competitors, more than males, have to overcome the stigma of engaging in a segment of society that does not strongly encourage participation.

A second issue concerning effective coaching of female athletes is helping the female athlete find a peer group and/or models that will promote, encourage, support, and motivate the female athlete's desire to experience competitive sport. Female athletes should feel that sport competition is a normal, enjoyable, fun, fulfilling, and rewarding experience. Examples include highly skilled athletes, friends, parents, and other family members, who attend games and drive their athletic children to practices, and receiving positive feedback from others.

A third issue, based on the results of related studies, suggest that sex differences between male and female athletes are far more likely to occur at younger ages and lower skill levels. In particular, male and female athletes are far more alike than different at more advanced levels of competition. Among lower-skilled and younger performers, however, psychological differences abound. This means that coaching style and strategies are more similar than different. This does not mean that coaching female athletes requires a strictly humanistic, emotionally sensitive, "soft" approach. Rather, it means that the level of sensitivity, compassion, performance feedback, praise, and clear and honest communication style be similarly applied to both males and females. At younger, lower-skill levels, coaches should show patience, respect, and never reprimand or embarrass athletes of both sexes.

Along these lines, females are, indeed, more emotional and expressive than males, and that's a good thing. Females cope with stress differently, but more effectively, than males. Female athletes are less stressed than male athletes due, in part, to their propensity to perceive and react to stress more productively. Tears are fine; they represent a normal biological habit and should not be discouraged for both sexes.

> **Case study on gender differences in sport**
>
> A study from the University of North Carolina, Asheville by Keathley, Heimlein, and Strigley (2013) entitled "Youth Soccer Participation and Withdrawal: Gender Similarities and Differences" explored the reason for differences in sports attrition between males and females. Why do high-level male and female soccer athletes (average age: 16 years) continue versus quit soccer? Results indicated that athletes' perceived time demand was the primary reason for quitting, with significant challenges being the second reason. Girls were more likely than boys to leave soccer due to negative coaching experiences, whereas girls maintained their participation due to the social rewards of playing soccer (i.e., a stronger relationship orientation among the female adolescent players. Fulfilling social needs was a primary outcome for girls' participation more so than male players. Implications for this study are that female adolescent needs and development warrant greater attention to team interpersonal dynamics; friendships and social interactions matter. For the male athletes, results suggest reevaluating the intense time and pressure demands. Perhaps more time and energy can be devoted to building friendships and social support among the males.

Race

One area of sport and coaching psychology that has received virtually no attention by scholars, coaches, and practitioners, at least in the professional literature, is the effect of race—racial differences—on coaching behavior. This is surprising given the extent to which sport includes such a large percentage of African American (AA) athletes. There are psycho-behavioral differences between genders, cultures, skill levels, and age (e.g., youth sport versus adolescent and adult performers), so why not examine racial differences as well to draw conclusions and generalizations about approaches to coaching athletes from different races (e.g., AA, Asians, Latinos, and so on.

In some cultures and communities, sport is a primary vehicle to demonstrate competence, achievement, and recognition. These values are inherent in the AA community, in which sport has been widely institutionalized as the only path to success, especially among males (Kochman, 1981). AA male youths indicate that excellence in sports is what drives their culture, despite receiving traditional exposure to reading, language, and the arts by their parents. To AA males, in particular, sport participation is an important resource for achieving respect (Messner, 1992), perhaps more so than among other racial groups.

It is not surprising, then, that AA athletes consider sport to be relevant to their self-identity, and threats to success in sport will be perceived as stressful. While numerous studies have been published in the general psychology literature comparing African American characteristics with other racial and ethnic groups (see McCreary, Cunningham, Ingram, & Fife, 2006, for a review), many sport psychology researchers have failed to study these comparisons.

In a rare study comparing racial groups, Anshel and Sutarso (2007) examined sources of stress and coping styles between competitive Caucasian and African American athletes. Caucasians reported more intense perceived stress than African Americans for two categories of stress: stress generated by the performer and stress related to the athlete's coach. With respect to coping style, they also found that Caucasian athletes were more likely than AAs to use what is called approach coping (i.e., confrontation, arguing, expression of anger, complaining, seeking information). Sample coping strategies were "I complained to a friend or another objective party," "I discussed the problem with others," and "I asked other people to give me their opinion." On the other hand, AA athletes were more likely to apply an avoidance-cognitive coping style than their Caucasian counterparts (i.e., non-confrontational, moving on, discounting the stressor's importance). Examples of avoidance-cognitive coping include "I prayed to help me deal with the problem or situation," "I believed the situation was in God's hands," and "I thought to myself that things could be worse."

Athletes use avoidance coping by reducing the stressor's importance (e.g., "I'll get better next time"), explaining or rationalizing the stressor (e.g., "I know I can play better than that," "That was a difficult task"), or perceiving the stressor objectively (e.g., "The coach must do what he or she has to do"). It appears, then, that stress intensity is associated with the athlete's approach or avoidance coping style, and that sources of and coping with stress is influenced by racial differences.

The use of avoidance coping as a function of race is understandable, according to Belgrave and Allison (2006). The authors reviewed numerous studies indicating the importance of spirituality "to be an influential factor in helping African Americans cope with problems and stressful life events" (p. 195). The belief that "one's final destiny is in God's hands provides hope and inspiration" and is more likely in the AA community than among other racial groups (p. 195). Boyd-Franklin (2003) found from her review of related literature that "many African Americans will talk about their use of prayer to cope with life's challenges" (p. 127). It is possible that AA athletes may adopt a similar coping style during the sports competition. Spiritual beliefs reflect an avoidance-cognitive coping style.

Similar to any group, racial differences are evident because individuals—including athletes—are born and socialized in different cultures that teach acceptable ways to think and act. Kochman (1981) explains, "black and white cultural differences are generally ignored when attempts are made to understand how and why black and white communication fails. One reason for this is that cultural differences play a covert role in the communication process" (p. 7). "The chief reason cultural differences are ignored is that blacks and whites assume they are operating according to identical speech and cultural conventions. . . . This assumption (fails) to recognize that black norms and conventions in these areas differ from those of whites" (p. 8). For example, one way the AA athlete often copes with stress, both in life and in sport, is prayer, reflecting the use of spiritual beliefs—a cognitive-avoidance coping strategy (Boyd-Franklin, 2003).

It is thought that AA athletes adopt a similar coping strategy following stressful experiences before or during the sport competition. An athlete who exhibits avoidance coping might *appear* to be low key and lacking in excitement and energy. Perhaps the (Caucasian) coach's and teammate's perception might be that the AA athlete is not taking the situation seriously or even acting lazy when, in fact, the AA athlete is coping quite actively through spiritual self-talk. This perception by the coach, however, would be mistaken, a situation that warrants better understanding about ways to interpret the cultural and racial norms of team members.

To use a cliché, one size does not fit all. Certain leadership styles and coaching techniques might be effective for one athlete but not work for another. Researchers, teachers, and clinicians must modify their models of stress and coping to reflect the unique cultural and social circumstances of different ethnic groups. Similar racial modifications are needed in other areas of sport psychology. Coaches, in particular, need to be race sensitive during processes associated with coaching and teaching sport skills and strategies. Effective coaching of the AA athlete consists, in large part, of understanding the athlete's foundations and cultural characteristics, which will enhance communication, build trust, and nurture relationships with all team members. The AA athlete seeks from his or her coach what all athletes want: respect, the opportunity to learn and improve sport skills, and the chance to perform at an elite level. So, how does a coach make this happen?

Schroeder (2010) conducted a study that has direct implications for coaching athletes with unique characteristics. Ten highly successful head coaches from Division 1 (elite-level) sports programs were interviewed. Coaches of sports represented included softball, football, men's and women's basketball, and men's volleyball. The study focused on four issues: (a) what is required to develop and maintain the proper *team culture*, that is, a team's psychological and social environment; (b) to what degree team improvement includes a change in team culture; (c) to develop ways to reward and punish athletes who either demonstrate support or fail to comply with the team's core values; and (d) the leadership behaviors used by coaches to change team culture.

The first step in developing a team culture was to determine the team's core values. Core values established early in the program were categorized as relationship, strategic, and behavioral. Results indicated that (a) team culture was a function of the values that each team developed and that athletes embraced the team's values within the first year of team participation; and (b) coaches established relationship values, which reflected the way that coaches interacted with players, and the way that players interacted with each other. These values were established early in their program due to the lack of trust between coaches and players and among the players, themselves. The coaches were challenged to assure each athlete that they (coaches) really did care about them as people and students, as well as athletes.

For instance, some coaches held from two to four individual player meetings during the year to establish the proper rapport and trust. Some coaches held team forums so that players could communicate with each other on various topics to gain trust and to establish a "family feel." Different coaches from the same team sometimes alternated on leading the forum. Sometimes "team talk" devoted 30 minutes of a practice session discussing topics unrelated to the team's sport. Another value was to provide an enriched environment to improve player learning and improve sport skills. Criteria for desirable performance outcomes were determined, monitored, and recognized by coaches and players.

Results of this study confirmed that changes in team culture are a function of determining team and player values and linked those values to player beliefs, behaviors, and performance without increases in financial resources. According to Schroeder (2010), "By simply reframing the meaning of team membership, the coaches in this study created championship-level teams in less than five years" (p. 84). Establishing and providing the forum for discussing and carrying out the team's core values reflected the importance of establishing and improving team culture irrespective of the player's race, gender, skill level, and cultural background.

Age and Skill Level

These two factors, the athlete's age and skill level, present some unique challenges for coaches that warrant different approaches and considerations. Age (e.g., youth sport under age 14, adolescents, adults) and skill level (e.g., low, moderate, and high) are combined because their psycho-behavioral characteristics, needs, and coaching techniques are similar. While the athlete's age and skill level can be mutually exclusive, there are strong similarities in providing these athletes with a safe, secure, and fulfilling environment in which to enjoy their sport experiences. Certainly a case can be made for coaching novices as compared to moderate- and high-skilled performers. Here are some considerations for coaching different age groups and skill levels.

1. *Establish a positive, non-threatening rapport with each athlete.* Coaching less-skilled sports participants, particularly in younger age groups, begins with *building trust* with each individual athlete. Learning new, often complex sport skills is very threatening to many competitors. As described earlier, Fitts and Posner's (1967) three-stage model of learning motor skills, still relevant today, explicitly describes the first *cognitive* stage that requires learners to plan and slowly execute a skilled movement. This takes time, however, and time is the one factor that sport competition often does not allow. The sports community can be very cruel to learners of sport skills, who need time to process instruction. Too often, the sport culture demands instant skilled (error-free) performance, often without opportunities for practice. Thus, building trust

begins with establishing a warm and supportive sport environment and providing time and opportunity for instruction and practice.
2. *Provide regular information feedback.* Results of studies have repeatedly indicated that learning motor (sport) skills must include either verbal or visual—preferably both—information feedback on performance. This procedure is especially important for less-skilled and younger (child) athletes, but, in fact, is helpful at all levels of sport. After all, just look at the number of coaches per team in professional sport. Feedback on proper technique, movement mechanics, and performance outcome is persistent and continual. However, athletes of different age groups and skill levels differ regarding the *content* of that feedback. Lower-skilled and child competitors can be overwhelmed by too much information or input that is too detailed. Higher-skilled and older performers can integrate information in greater amounts and in more detail. Remember that early learning is highly cognitive, in which a great deal of thinking occurs. Therefore, it is easy to have a condition of *information overload* in which the learner/performer is unable to consciously process information in a coherent manner. Coaches should provide information on a regular—consistent but not constant—schedule, but keep the type of information highly visual (e.g., a technique called modeling) as well as verbal.
3. *Practice, practice, practice.* The only way that athletic performance will improve is by providing the players with meaningful practice that includes stoppage of play, provision of information feedback, and the opportunity to apply that feedback. As indicated earlier, to prevent information overload, feedback should be "regular" but not constant. Athletes need time to integrate and carry out performance that reflects the arrival of new information.

Practice differs from game play based on the session's objectives. There should be a big difference in protocol between practice and games, the latter of which is, by definition, competition. Practice, on the other hand, focuses on skill development and improved skill retention. The only element of competition in practice should be game simulation, in which practice includes segments of actual competitions but serves an instructional purpose, not recording or reflecting winning or losing outcomes.

Here is a highly debatable issue: Should all team members be required to participate in the game irrespective of skill level, even if this decision risks a team loss? Good question, and one without a definite answer. The response to this question ranges from "definitely not" to "absolutely yes." Some sport organizations include a policy that "everyone—all team members—must play in every game." Other organizations take a far more competitive approach, leave playing status of players to the coach's decision, and they "play to win." This is certainly more common in organized sport, such as school teams and at the professional level.

There are obvious advantages to both league/team policies. Yes, playing the "better" players is more likely to result in a winning outcome. The less-skilled players will sit throughout the game and watch; perhaps learning a few skills by observing others—the modeling effect. The advantage of best players play is that winning enhances game enjoyment. But what if the team that allows only the "better" players to participate and the team does not win?

Another issue concerning who plays and who sits is that the nonstarters will feel unmotivated by putting on their uniform, attending games and practices, but feeling left out. They are more likely to ask, "Is it worth it?" Child athletes want to have fun, but having fun is far less likely if they are watching and not playing—game after game.

Some sport organizations take a middle position that promotes participation in games and practices of all team members without the expectancy of making repeated errors, playing the game poorly, and losing. This middle-ground position requires all team members to participate in the game under the condition that they show mastery of the requisite sport skills (e.g., demonstrating proper form and skill mastery they will be expected to perform in a game situation). This criterion will greatly reduce the likelihood of being ostracized and rejected by their teammates—and perhaps the coach—for not meeting the necessary skills that demonstrate competence. Skills would be mastered and demonstrated in practice settings, after which time they could meet the performance standards expected in an actual game. Important: The criteria for the athlete's game participation should be communicated sooner than later. Will participation be likely after 2 weeks of instruction? What will the athlete have to demonstrate to play? Who is making this judgment and decision about meeting the minimum skills?

> Finally, coaches should be available to the athlete's parents. Yes, it's true that some parents have a reputation for getting too emotional during the game, which reduces the enjoyment of attending games. An open communication style between the athlete's parents and their child's coach would clarify the player's strengths, areas for improvement (I purposely avoid the term "weaknesses"), and provides parents with what skills they can practice with their child athlete between games. Some coaches have used an assessment form in which they write a brief report and refer to this written document for signs of improvement during the season, and also to refer to these assessments when determining the allocation of awards for distribution at the team's post-season or end-of-school banquet.

It is apparent that many characteristics of athletes differ as a function of age and skill level. After all, as indicated earlier, child athletes are not miniature adults. Skills must be taught, probably the coach's primary responsibility, and learning sport skills takes time. Researchers have confirmed that the athlete's growth and development requires four factors, without which learning sport skills cannot occur. These factors are (a) goals (i.e., the outcome that informs coaches that learning has been achieved), (b) motivation (i.e., the athlete must want to achieve a certain outcome, otherwise learning cannot occur), (c) practice (i.e., meaningful repetition of intentional behavior is a necessary component of skill development), and (d) information feedback, which provides athletes with a sense of competence and improvement.

Sport Type

This section will review the psychological factors that are relevant in coaching athletes who compete on individual versus team sports. Are there different factors that influence performance based on coaching different types of sports? Yes, there are different psychological dynamics when coaching team sports, as opposed to individual sports (Dosil, 2006). Perhaps the primary psychological factor that is present in team sports is group dynamics and team cohesion. Teams are groups, and within a group there are roles called *group dynamics*. Group dynamics concern the roles and interactions of different members of a group or team. Another factor that is unique to team sports is the concept of *cohesion*, or a sense of togetherness and mutual team member support. We will explore the coach's role in addressing both these factors to achieve optimal performance.

Group dynamics. A group becomes a more cohesive sports team when seeking the answers to the following questions.

1. What is our goal? Learn skills? Improve performance? Win in a competitive environment? Have fun? Some of each?
2. How do we determine the position of each team member and formulate team leadership (e.g., team captain?), team rules, team decisions, and team policies?
3. What are the roles of the coach, coaching assistants, team captains, and other team members?
4. Who are our team supporters? To whom are we accountable? Members of the community? School officials? Parents of the athletes? The coach?

5. How do we work through problems and challenges? Is the coach open to the contributions of all team members, and is there an open communication style for team members to interact with captains, coaches, medical staff, and the sport psychologist? Are team meetings held, and if so, how frequently and for what purpose?
6. How should we work together to perform successfully as a team? Should we separate starters and nonstarters in how we develop our skills and fulfill team goals, or should there be a supportive team climate in which all team members are encouraged to make their respective contributions? In other words, should there be a within-team rivalry?
7. What are the benefits of being a team member? Establishing new friendships? Affiliation with the sports organization? Recognizing player competence? Learning new skills? Having fun? Becoming more fit?
8. How, and under what conditions, should the team be included in determining team policies and regulating team members' behavior?

Team climate. Team climate is a psychosocial construct in which environmental factors influence the performer's thoughts and emotions and reflects the interrelationships between external conditions and group members. The key issue in understanding team climate is the team members' perceptions; it is not the coach who evaluates and determines the players' climate but the players themselves. Athletes make an assessment or a value judgment based on their own needs and priorities in identifying and categorizing the team's atmosphere. These perceptions are important because they have a significant impact on each athlete's attitude about being a team member and, ultimately, influences player motivation, group member identity (i.e., I wish to support my teammates), and performance. Researchers refer to this feeling as *team member satisfaction*.

Team climate consists of the following components: autonomy (an athlete's feeling of independence), emotional support (assisting with coping with stressful events, helping a teammate overcome a bad situation), pressure to succeed (managing anxiety), recognition ("My team contributions are recognized), trust ("I believe what my coach tells me"), fairness ("My coach will continue to improve my performance so I can eventually participate in games"), innovation ("It's ok to take risks or try something new"), and cohesion (discussed next).

Group cohesion. In sport, this concept is a measure of an athlete's attraction to, sense of belonging to, and desire to become and maintain a member of the team. A warm and enduring team climate reflects high *social cohesion*, in that participants develop and maintain an atmosphere that members find attractive and desirable. Team members support each other. In a high social cohesive team climate, members are communicating, and the athletes' collective personality is compatible with that of the coach. High *task cohesion*, on the other hand, includes team goals that reflect those of the individual members, and all participants clarify, understand, and agree on the roles of each member. Teams with the proper team climate provide players with the incentive to invest energy in meeting group (team) goals.

One role that often gets overlooked by coaches is the team captain—or co-captains. I have consulted with and heard numerous coaches claim very little understanding about how to include a team captain. Some coaches designate one team member—perhaps who plays a key role on the team—as captain in name only, but with no "official" role (other than dealing with coin tosses or being the team representative to interact with game officials). This is a lost opportunity to work with team captains in very important and constructive ways. Briefly, captains can support the coach's team policies and rules, act as a liaison between the coach and team members, seek clarification from game officials in response to a questionable call, talk to a struggling teammate and try to enhance the athlete's positive state of mind, communicate with the coach about an issue that concerns one or more players, or deal with team conflicts. What is the process of becoming a team captain? Try to divide the role into two co-captains, one of who is voted by the team and the second designated by the coach. Make sure both individuals have precise roles and are given specific tasks to perform at any given moment. To paraphrase famous UCLA basketball coach, John Wooden (1988), "[F]ailing to prepare is preparing to fail."

The main objective of this chapter is to alert coaches about the individual differences that each athlete brings to the competition that require different approaches to coaching. Effective coaches maintain self-awareness about how they incorporate the athletes' age, race, gender, and sport type into their arsenal of strategies and communication styles to help athletes reach and maintain their ideal performance state.

It is apparent that effective sport leadership requires being sensitive to individual needs, with specific reference to an athlete's cultural background, gender, race, age, skill level, and sport type. All athletes do not respond to a coach's leadership style in the same manner. The coach who ignores these normal individual differences may be undermining an athlete's potential talent and contribution to the team. Based on a review of related literature, coaches should demonstrate greater awareness of an athlete's background, perhaps as a function of the level of competition.

Epilogue

The primary purpose for writing this book is to share with sports coaches the accumulating body of knowledge in sport psychology, an area that has been relatively ignored by the coaching profession. While there are thousands of studies, published in over 25 scholarly journals, on the effectiveness of applying sport psychology concepts to improve sport performance, many coaches remain distant from this literature. This book attempts to familiarize coaches, athletes, sport psychologists, and athletic trainers on ways to promote and apply this emerging literature. Sport psychology is a field that consists of researchers/scholars in one domain, and a growing group of practitioners (i.e., mental health professionals) and coaches who will benefit from applying these concepts on the other.

Despite strong advances in the field, it is apparent that the coaching profession still relies on the mentoring of former coaches and contemporary colleagues in applying sport psychology techniques. In addition to using this book's information first hand, an additional purpose of this book is to consider including a mental skills coach, also called a sport psychologist, as a team consultant who will deliver this specialization to athletes. This specialization, however, has gone relatively unrecognized as an integral part of the coaching staff. Strategies from the sport psychology literature clearly influence athletic performance, leadership effectiveness, coach-athlete communication, recovery from athletic injury, and other desirable outcomes. Promoting the transfer of theory to practice in sport psychology is a desirable outcome of this book.

Improving Coach Awareness of Sport Psychology

The intention of the book is to increased awareness and the use of sport psychology for coaches. Sport psychology is flourishing in the United States and internationally, as shown by the increased availability of educational programs, updated certification programs (proper courses, instruction, and credentials to become a sport psychologist), professional conferences, intercollegiate sports programs, professional sports teams, and research journals that contain thousands of articles, some more applied (hands-on) than others. The field, therefore, is growing and becoming more integrated into the training of athletes. Surprisingly, and sadly, however, the field still has to convince many sports coaches of the ways in which the literature and the practitioners who apply it can make a difference in coaching and performing skills.

For example, many coaches are still using the same militaristic tactics used by their coaches (e.g., exercising as a form of punishment, motivating athletes through threats and high emotional intensity, not allowing athletes to have input on most decisions, proper use of mental skills). The application of mental skills to manage stress and anxiety both before and during the competition is often nonexistent. Even at the professional level, many coaches see no reason to change the way athletes and teams mentally prepare for the competition and use the same coaching tactics used by their own coaches. One exception to this behavior patterns is at the elite level. For example, the U.S. Olympic Center program employs several clinical sport psychologists at its headquarters in Colorado Springs, Colorado (USA).

Another possible reason for full recognition of sport psychology services by the coaching profession is the absence of applied material that is accessible and understandable in real-world settings. As one coach remarked to me, "I can't understand the stuff in journals." This feeling is easy to understand. Many sport psychology practitioners complain that the quality of research journals with their academic jargon is usually judged by the scientific community according to the sophistication of the research design and statistical analyses. Many of these scholarly articles are challenging for the nonresearcher/coach to comprehend; the language of scholarly research not only lacks application, it's written in a language most nonresearchers would consider foreign. More hands-on books for coaches and athletes are needed to overcome this problem. There has been an evolution in sport psychology has been the improved credibility of psychological and behavioral techniques based on published research.

More research is needed in examining the effects of various psychological techniques and interventions on desirable changes in emotion and performance. Many newer approaches to sport and exercise performance have replaced the earlier techniques and recommendations. As more professionals in the field receive the proper educational training, the use of sport psychology will gain an increasing foothold among sport leaders.

Future Directions

Sports coaches and administrators who seriously consider including sport psychology service for any team member need to know what skills and credentials are required in the process of soliciting and hiring the person who meets a team's particular needs. The following issues must be considered:

Titles and qualifications. Most professions require recognition of specific skills and areas of expertise. The term used for establishing and recognizing these skills, usually controlled by state, national, or professional organizations, is called *credentialing*.

Titles in the world of consulting and credentialing are important for several reasons. Not unlike using the prefix, "Dr.," for a person who has been awarded a doctorate from a reputable and recognized university program; the title "psychologist" is legally protected. Thus, there is a difference between a person who can legally use the title "sport psychologist" and a person who may not use that title. Psychologists should have met the criteria as outlined by two governing bodies that publish these guidelines, the American Psychological Association (in the United States) and the organization from the state in which the person intends to practice. Each state has a board that governs these standards.

Nonpsychologists who provide sport psychology services, that is, professionals who work with athletes and coaches on improving athletes' "mental game," have options for proper titles. These titles include, but are not restricted to, mental skills coach, performance coach, sports counselor, mental health professional, and sport psychologist for use by individuals who have met the criteria for this credential. The one exception to the proper use of the title "psychologist" occurs when the individual did not meet the criteria for this credential; however, the psychologist title is allowed on a university/college campus. A person may use the title sport psychologist or any other title if services are rendered strictly to a member of the academic community, including athletes, coaches, college faculty, graduate students, or anyone who the athletic department designates with a title with the approval of the athletic director, the team's head coach, and ultimately, the university administration. Titles, such as sport psychologist, however, may not be used and promoted off campus.

Organizational memberships and conference attendance. Most professionals choose to become members of their respective sport organizations. However, the enlightened coach who wants to learn and apply new state-of-the-art knowledge and information in sport psychology as part of his or her (the coaches') repertoire of expertise may want to consider affiliating with and becoming a member of organizations that promote the mental aspects of sports. Examples of organizations, each of which sponsors an annual conference, includes the American Psychological Association (Division 47), Association for Applied Sport Psychology, and the American College of Sports Medicine, among many others, particularly in other countries.

The need to establish trust and confidentiality. If a coach and sport psychology professional agree to provide service, such an agreement must include the understanding that all sessions—with coaches and athletes—are held in strict confidence, and that meeting content may not be shared without the client's permission. If it becomes known that the mental skills coach cannot be trusted due to sharing private meeting content, then the service will be rendered mute and irrelevant.

Coach consultations. There are different models for delivering psychological services. One model concerns providing service through the team's coaches instead of dealing directly with the athletes. During the sport season, regular meetings can be scheduled—weekly, for instance—in which issues that are relevant to the coach can be discussed. Handling a "difficult" situation, improving communication channels, ways the coach can build an athlete's mental preparation or ability to cope with stress, proper ways to set performance goals, or ways to improve player relationships are sample topics.

Working with nonstarters and injured athletes (a low-risk starting point). If the team's coaching staff is hesitant to include a mental skills coach/sport psychologist for various reasons, then a less "risky" approach to begin this type of service would be to work with team members who are often neglected—injured athletes in rehabilitation settings and nonstarters who are challenged to maintain their enthusiasm and self-motivation to provide 100% effort throughout the season. Players who fit the criteria for obtaining this service can be required to attend one session only and, if they wish, to continue meeting with the mental skills coach on a regular basis.

Providing service to different populations. Dancers, theatrical performers, professional or college-level athletes, musicians, exercisers/team workouts, youth sports organizations, injury rehabilitation, students (e.g., test anxiety, high stress, depression), and corporate clients who are stressed or burned out are examples of different populations who would benefit from this type of service. If a person living or working in the community or employed by a university has the skills and interests in providing sport and performance psychology services, perhaps the opportunities can be expanded to include other groups and populations. This can result in providing the community (or education system) with adequate income that would warrant a full-time position. The opportunities to provide psychological services beyond sports teams are endless.

Youth sports outlet. One additional market to gain credibility in sport psychology consulting is community youth sports programs. Parents often provide more resources in time and money toward their children than themselves. It is likely, therefore, that sport psychology consultants have become increasingly involved with younger athletes and their parents, both independent of the community sports program and through community sports organizations by advising and developing sport programs. Consultants will gain far more credibility and recognition through community sports, as child athletes have a more fulfilling and rewarding experience.

National and international recognition. In recent years, there has been extensive recognition of professional services rendered by the sport psychology consultants (among other titles), especially at the elite level (e.g., college, Olympics, professional athletes). For instance, the United State Olympic Center employs at least four full-time sport psychologists, an accurate title because each of these individuals have attained a credential in psychology. These individuals, and others, provide counsel to athletes, coaches, and athletic trainers, often present their work at professional conferences and publish in reputable scientific journals. Sport psychology services are not restricted to the United States. Other countries, such as the United Kingdom, Australia, China, Israel, Russia, Poland, Korea, among many others, employ sport psychologists. The working arrangement of these professionals includes full-time employment or shares services with a university student counseling service, academic counseling, or other community involvement that involves human performance (e.g., the arts, law enforcement, community recreation programs, physical or mental rehabilitation centers, medical settings). This illustrates the increased importance placed on providing psychological services for athletes and coaches. In addition, national psychology organizations in several countries have recently recognized sport psychology as an area of academic credibility.

Using psychological assessment techniques. Numerous psychological inventories, interviews, and behavioral (observational) assessments have been used for the purpose of selecting, screening, and counseling athletes. The ability to predict the quality of an athlete's performance or the likelihood of becoming successful in sport has had only limited success. Assessment tools are best used to describe behavior or emotion, not predict them, nor should psychological inventories be used to screen athletes who aspire to compete in sport.

There are limitations to using inventories. While sport psychology researchers, scholars, and practitioners have conducted sophisticated research over the years, the field has also seen more than its share of charlatanism. The history of sport psychology is strewn with "corpses" of false claims of making accurate predictions about an athlete's future success in sport through the media, conference presentations, and marketing of published materials, not, however, through scholarly research articles. Although, there have been improved methodological and statistical procedures in recent years, in which inventories have accurately (revealing good validity and reliability) described psychological characteristics and behavioral tendencies of targeted sports and populations. To their credit, authors of these inventories, often published in scholarly journals, have not contended that the inventory predicts future success in sport, only that selected items best describe the construct (e.g., confidence, anxiety, perfectionism, commitment). Perhaps the preferred delivery model of sport psychology services is working through team coaches.

In sport settings, working with athletes through their coach has its advantages and disadvantages. On the plus side, the sport psychology consultant may be more helpful to the team when advising coaches on the use of certain techniques. In most situations, coaches have already established the necessary credibility and trust with athletes to suggest the use of certain mental strategies. On the minus side, the sport psychologist often needs direct contact with participants to determine individual needs, to suggest alternative approaches in meeting those needs, or to provide an opportunity for the player to disclose personal information that he or she might otherwise withhold from the coach. In the final analysis, sport psychology consultants must function in the athlete's world and have hands-on experience in working directly with players and coaches if they are to understand the role of sport psychology in competitive athletics and to identify common problems and issues that are experienced by competitors and coaches.

Separating the consultant from the mental health professional. The title sport psychology consultant, has been used extensively in this book rather than the title *sport psychologist*. The reason is that consultants carry a title that does not infer licensure by a state psychological association, whereas certain titles related to the use of mental health interventions are legally protected (e.g., psychologist, therapist, counselor, social worker). As indicated earlier, the title of psychologist is reserved only a person who has earned a PhD from a program certified by the American Psychological Association and has met other criteria, such as completing a certain number of hours of clinical supervision, passing two national examinations, and other criteria that are required by a particular state in which the person wants to practice.

The distinction between titles is important, not only for proper professional identification, but to deliver a particular service at the expected level of expertise: possess the proper knowledge and skills in meeting the client's expectations. Thus, a sport psychologist, but not a consultant, might be asked to provide clinical rather than educational services. The types of clinical services go beyond the scope of this chapter, but include areas of psychopathology (i.e., mental illness or areas in which the individual is unable to properly and normally function).

The best-known and recognized certification program that ensures the appropriate knowledge and skills in sport psychology, sponsored by the Association for Applied Sport Psychology (AASP), suggests that sport psychology consultants who are not necessarily (but may be) licensed psychologists, should learn how to detect psychopathological problems (e.g., chronic anxiety, eating disorders, depression, neurotic perfectionism) so they may refer their client to a qualified clinician. Not to do so is unethical.

To put sport psychology in perspective, much research and trial-and-error experience lie ahead before established, functional techniques are effectively employed on a regular basis. The field must avoid the "Eureka" complex, the need to declare that "the answer" is at hand. It's this rush to make superlative, hyperbolic statements about linking mental techniques and interventions to positive performance outcomes, and to draw final conclusions based on relatively minuscule evidence, that has drawn the ire of researchers, coaches, and even a few practicing sport psychology consultants. See the extensive critiques of current practices, shortcomings, and concerns in the practice of applied sport psychology (e.g., lack of proven intervention effectiveness, poor measurement and evaluation tools and methods, lack of proper training by practitioners) located in most sport psychology journals such as *Journal of Sport and Exercise Psychology, Journal of Clinical Sport Psychology, Psychology and Exercise*, and *The Sport Psychologist*.

Suggestions for Moving Forward

Based on the advice of some of our most respected and well-published sport psychology researchers and practitioners, here are a few recommendations about how sport psychology consultants and coaches can work together in this growing field in a constructive and productive manner.

Avoid the "quick fix." The field of sport psychology is still paying a heavy price for the "snake oil" salespeople of past years. It's one thing to generalize the effects of certain techniques on meeting a particular objective. But it's quite another to "know the answer" and "sell" the coach on an unproven "formula" for success. We need to be cautious and to make promises to no one. An applied sport psychologist should have a menu of alternative treatments and strategies that are warranted in a given situation. No single approach works for every athlete or in all situations. Be careful about what can be promised in a consultancy.

Do not take public credit for player or team success. Coaches and the athletes they coach must take center stage when it comes to determining who is responsible for their success. If a sport psychologist had a role with that success, this must not become public knowledge. Virtually all athletes and their coaches work hard to perform successfully; it's not in the competitor's best interest to anoint "my sport psychologist" for having a role in the outcome. Any publicity surrounding the "bag of tricks" that sport psychologists bring to the coach or athlete might diminish the public's proper recognition of and respect for that performer. The tangible benefits of observing clients improve their mental disposition or use psychological strategies to enhance performance are the consultant's best reward.

Research" is not a four-letter word. Some practicing sport psychology consultants and coaches are "turned off" by the word research. For the practitioner, it represents an area that is unfamiliar, insecure, and disconnected from providing any benefit to the competitive situation. The thinking is that research is conducted under artificial conditions and has little to do with the realistic conditions of actual sport. Nothing can be further from the truth.

To encourage the use of research by coaches and sport practitioners, researchers and educators need to do two things. First, more studies are needed that are field based, have an applied dimension, and that establish stronger links between theory and practice. Second, useful research findings need to be translated into forms accessible to nonresearchers, such as coaches and athletes, most of whom are not familiar with the scholarly jargon found in most research journals.

Separate the qualifications, skills and training of consultants from psychologists. The title psychologist is legally protected and requires that the professional be licensed by a state board of licensed psychologists—each state may have a similar, but not identical, board identification—to practice psychology in the state of residence and practice. In addition, graduate psychology programs that result in licensure do not include courses in the sport and exercise sciences, so a graduate of such a program probably would not have completed sport psychology-related courses. Thus, licensed psychologists are rarely trained to work in sport settings; they are unlikely to have mastered the professional literature in providing counsel to skilled performers.

The field of sport psychology is evolving in very favorable, exciting directions, with several implications for coaches of sports teams. There is considerable information available about ways to apply "the mental game" into one's preparation for competition. More books, journals, and conference presentations are available from which to obtain and apply considerable information. However, one issue that continues to plague the discipline is disagreement about who "owns" this field of study and practice. Which discipline—psychology? sport science/physical education? exercise science?—has the rightful claim to govern and provide a coherent framework to sport psychology?

Who "Owns" Sport Psychology?

For many years, there has been a serious and contentious issue concerning the academic discipline that governs education, training, and practice of sport psychology. While members of professional sport psychology organizations often share conference programs and co-authorships on articles and books, there is a clear political and philosophical battle for territory and ownership in representing this field nationally and internationally. Coaches need to be aware of these issues so that they can make an informed choice about hiring a consultant with the credentials most consistent with his or her team's needs and required skills and services.

There are two fields of study—or academic disciplines—that have valid claims to maintaining a strong influence on the development of sport psychology. One area is sport and exercise science, also referred to as departments entitled physical education, health and human performance, kinesiology, and human movement. The second discipline is psychology. Neither field is going to "own" or be the sole representative of sport psychology. There is much to be said for the fact that both disciplines bring to the field, and to students, complementary needs and skills. My attempt at examining how each discipline contributes to the growth and development of sport psychology is not intended to polarize the field, but rather to recognize the importance of bringing together *both* disciplines in an effort to provide the optimal quality of education, research, and practice of our field.

In favor of sport and exercise sciences. A perusal of the *Directory of Graduate Programs in Applied Sport Psychology* edited by Dr. Michael Sachs and colleagues (2010) clearly indicates that sport and exercise science is the primary area from which sport psychology programs are offered. It is the rare psychology department that includes a required course or specialization in sport psychology. This is understandable, given the strict requirements placed on psychology departments to have a program approved by the American Psychological Association (APA).

In most states, people with the title psychologist can be licensed only if they graduate with a PhD from an APA-approved program. Course requirements and many— hours—f field supervision – 400 hours in most psychology licensure programs - do not easily allow graduate students to complete additional courses, such as sport psychology. Consequently, it is the graduate students from an exercise and sport science background who register for courses in sport psychology and complete internships and practicum related to human performance psychology (sport, exercise, rehabilitation, dance, corporate, law enforcement/dispatchers, first responders, and so on). It is also students from these departments who train to conduct research in sport psychology when writing their master's theses or doctoral dissertations.

Further testimony to the origins of sport psychology comes from the sport psychology literature, which acknowledges the "father" of sport psychology as Dr. Coleman Griffith, a professor of physical education. The point here is that sport and exercise science/physical education educators and researchers appear to have given birth to the field. Perhaps it is not surprising, then, that AASP has created and maintained the only certification program in applied sport psychology, although Division 47 (Psychology of Exercise, Sport, and Performance) within the American Psychological Association has developed its own set of criteria for recognition as a sport psychologist for individuals whose credentials include the title *licensed psychologist*. It may be contended that the practice of sport psychology warrants a level of sophistication that goes beyond traditional training in psychology. Let's take a balanced look at the position of both camps—psychology and sport science—in determining the type of background, training, education, and skills necessary to provide effective service in this field.

In favor of psychology. The three main strengths of the field of psychology linked to sport psychology include the legal title of psychologist, the status of licensure that allows clinicians/counselors/therapists to receive third-party payments (from the client's health insurance), and, of course, the training in counseling or clinical psychology that provides experience in administering and interpreting psychological tests that are available only to licensed psychologists and conducting various forms of psychotherapy on their athlete-clients.

The student's decision to seek graduate training in sport psychology should be primarily determined by professional aspirations. If the student plans on an academic career, then the sport and exercise sciences are more likely to have courses in sport psychology and, therefore, require a professor to teach and supervise graduate students who wish to conducted research for their thesis or doctoral dissertation in this area. If, however, private practice is the student's goal, then he or she should follow the road for licensure as a psychologist. Paid consultancies in sport psychology without licensure are difficult to find because a licensed psychologist is eligible to collect third-party payments from health insurance.

This means two things. First, the client can be financially supported, perhaps paying only a fraction of the psychologist's fee. Second, licensure means that the psychologist can be covered by the organization's insurance policy, a requirement to guard against a possible lawsuit. Sport psychology consultants who are not licensed psychologists can gain employment if paid out-of-pocket by clients or by organizations for which the consultant is not—repeat, not—engaging in counseling or any form of psychotherapy. The consultant's content is restricted to performance enhancement techniques.

And then there is the small matter of who "owns" the title of sport psychologist. This issue is frustrating for those in academic circles who have spent their entire careers in sport psychology, yet may not legally use the title sport psychologist because the title psychologist is legally protected by state boards of licensed psychologists. Each state has its own set of rules and its own licensure board that arbitrates who may become or remain licensed, so there are exceptions to these criteria, including a master's-degree-level certification program in psychology that will also allow for third-party payments. However, only earning a doctoral degree will allow use of the title "psychologist," including sport psychologist. Some sport science professionals are not concerned about titles because, they say, the title psychologist is threatening for many athletes and coaches. Therefore, it is best to avoid that title, anyway. Alternative titles include mental skills coach, performance coach/consultant, or performance counselor.

To be fair, psychologists make a valuable contribution to sport psychology by their sophisticated published research describing clinical issues among competitive athletes, individuals who often require psychological intervention due to deep-rooted issues that cannot be addressed effectively by applying mental skills (just think of a few professional athletes who are in clear need of a psychologist, according to media reports), and through their support and collaboration with sport and exercise science departments in the education and training of sport psychology graduate students.

On the other hand, however, the field is replete with psychologists who have never taken a course in sport psychology, have not read and mastered the literature, and do not have a sport background (they are nonathletes), yet lay claim to the title of, and market themselves as a, sport psychologist. Is this unethical, or a misrepresentation? It depends who you ask. A person's training and experience often dictate their strengths, skills, and practices. Thus, trained psychologists will rely on their clinical training in representing the field, and sport psychology consultants with a sport science background will rely on mental skills training. What is apparent, however, is that many individuals, primarily academics, in the sport sciences perceive psychologists as intrusive and undertrained in sport psychology, and hence, a threat to the integrity of the field. It is an area of contention that is still being debated by scholars, writers, and practitioners. Who, then, "owns" sport psychology? In a capitalistic, open market society, it is the individual who delivers the most effective, highest quality product and is wanted by others for their service. Most of the advertisements for full-time sport psychology services are recruiting individuals with credentials in counseling and clinical psychology and allows the service provider to work in other settings such as a student academic counseling center. Still, the field continues to emerge and offers athletes and coaches a fresh perspective on obtaining optimal performance.

Appendix A

Athlete's Fitness Training Checklist: Guidelines for Physical Training

Name of Athlete: _____
Date: _____

The purpose of this checklist is to provide guidelines for conducting a proper exercise program to get into top shape by improving and maintaining fitness. This checklist serves two purposes: instruction and monitoring progress. It lists desirable thoughts, emotions, and actions that *should* be present before, during, and after your exercise sessions. If used correctly, this checklist is intended to help you form new habits that accompany your exercise routine. Individual athletes may wish to deviate from listing and performing every item. Delete and replace any items you wish if your conditioning coach approves. *The key issue is to compare current with past scores with higher numbers over time. You want to see improvement (higher numbers; more items used).* Individualize this checklist to meet your own habits and needs. Consider having two lists, one for strength training and one for cardio, or combine.

Clients should rate each item, ranging from 1 (*not at all like me; never*) to 5 (*very much like me/always*). Try to complete this form as often as you wish, but at least weekly.

        1   2   3   4   5
Not at   Very much
all like me   like me

I. Lifestyle habits (exercise preparation)

1. I think about physical training with enthusiasm.

   1   2   3   4   5

2. I feel ready to give my exercise routine 100% effort.

   1   2   3   4   5

3. I will always find the time for physical training.

   1   2   3   4   5

4. I know the benefits of my training regimen.

   1   2   3   4   5

5. I feel more energy as a result of my exercise routine.

   1   2   3   4   5

6. I am happy to receive feedback from others on my exercise technique.

   1   2   3   4   5

7. I am confident in my ability to meet my exercise goals.

   1   2   3   4   5

8. My family/friends/partner support my exercise habit.

   1   2   3   4   5

9. I drink plenty of water during the day.

    1   2   3   4   5

10. To make exercise a habit, I *schedule* my exercise sessions.

    1   2   3   4   5

    Score: _____

           1   2   3   4   5
        Not at   Very much
       all like me   like me

II. Day of exercise

1. I look forward to exercising with great enthusiasm.

      1   2   3   4   5

2. I am mentally committed to my training time.

      1   2   3   4   5

3. I will not have food, coffee or alcohol within one hour before I exercise.

      1   2   3   4   5

4. If I feel sick, I will not exercise.

      1   2   3   4   5

5. I have prepared my exercise gear in advance.

      1   2   3   4   5

6. My transportation to the exercise location is all set.

      1   2   3   4   5

7. I have organized my day to accommodate my training session.

      1   2   3   4   5

        Score: _____

III. Pre-workout activity (at exercise location)

1. I arrived at the exercise venue on time/with enthusiasm.

   1   2   3   4   5

2. I have an exercise plan before starting.

   1   2   3   4   5

3. I remember my exercise goals and plan to meet them.

   1   2   3   4   5

4. As I prepare to exercise, I feel energetic.

   1   2   3   4   5

5. I planned to have several water breaks before, during, and immediately after the exercise routine.

   1   2   3   4   5

6. I complete my exercise session as planned.

   1   2   3   4   5

7. I used positive self-talk before exercising ("I can do it," "I'm ready," "Stay with it!").

   1   2   3   4   5

   Score: _____

IV. During my exercise session

1. I enjoy my exercise session and give 100%.

   1   2   3   4   5

2. I begin my session with mental imagery or psyching up.

   1   2   3   4   5

3. I jog lightly to slowly increase my heart rate.

   1   2   3   4   5

4. I stretch lightly *after* I complete light aerobic exercise.

   1   2   3   4   5

5. Most of my stretching occurs *after* my workout.

   1   2   3   4   5

6. I used positive self-talk while exercising.

   1   2   3   4   5

7. I complete all exercises as planned.

   1   2   3   4   5

8. I complete as many repetitions as possible.

   1   2   3   4   5

9. I avoid negative thoughts while exercising.

   1   2   3   4   5

10. My exercise performance has improved; I am more fit.

    1   2   3   4   5

11. I view each exercise bout as a challenge, not as a threat to fail.

    1   2   3   4   5

12. During my workout I avoid focusing my attention on internal sensations (e.g., fatigue, sweating, and discomfort).

    1   2   3   4   5

13. I try to reach my performance goals at all workouts.

    1   2   3   4   5

14. If I feel tired, I rest briefly but then keep going.

    1   2   3   4   5

15. I keep sipping water during my routine.

    1   2   3   4   5

    Score: _____

IV. After the exercise session

1. I feel good after my exercise session.

    1   2   3   4   5

2. I feel that my performance has improved.

    1   2   3   4   5

3. I have recorded my exercise data.

    1   2   3   4   5

4. I am open to advice and feedback on my performance.

    1   2   3   4   5

5. I feel a sense of accomplishment.

    1   2   3   4   5

6. I reached my target heart rate (220 – age × 75%).

    1   2   3   4   5

7. I replaced my bodily fluids with water.

    1   2   3   4   5

8. I plan to maintain my exercise program.

    1   2   3   4   5

    Score: _____

    GRAND TOTAL: _____

Appendix B

Summary of Mental Skills for Competitive Sport (in alphabetical order)

Anticipation The performer uses past experience to increase speed of decision making and reactions to environmental stimuli

Association Focusing attention on muscles and other bodily processes, such as a weight lifter who focuses on the muscle group during exertion

Attentional focusing (internal) Focusing on one's thoughts, emotions, and reactions to environmental stimuli

Attentional focusing (external) Focusing on actions and reactions to environmental stimuli in dealing with immediate task demands

Automation Performing skills "on automatic," that is, with little or no thinking, after performance has been initiated

Boxing Placing one's thoughts in a mental "box" before competition so they do not upset or distract the athlete

Chunking Learning and storing information or sub-skills as chunks or units. It reduces a series of movements or team strategies to a single unit of information; reduces information load

Coping (approach) Athlete confronts the source of stress—acute (sudden) or chronic (long term)—and attempts to use thoughts, emotions or actions to reduce stress intensity

Coping (avoidance) Athletes attempt to reduce sudden or ongoing stress intensity by mentally reducing its importance, walking away and moving to the next task at hand, or using humor or labeling ("umpire made a dumb mistake" or "made an error in judgment")

Cueing Focusing on sights or sounds of the sport environment during performance execution to reduce information overload and to improve movement speed and accuracy

Discounting A stress-reducing technique consisting of consciously reducing the importance of or ignoring a person's verbal communication that is otherwise interpreted as stressful. An example is how to react to the "trash talk" of an opponent

Dissociation Ignoring bodily sensations (e.g., fatigue, pain, heart rate)—separating mind from body—during performance and, instead, focusing one's attention on external stimuli—more pleasant visual and auditory stimuli

Distraction Focusing the opponent's attention on a meaningless or harmless stimulus during performance execution and, instead, focusing on the intended task toward reaching the performance goal

Filtering A learning strategy in which the athlete consciously excludes selected stimuli or information while attending to other information to enter the information-processing system

Imagery (also see visualization) Creating a mental representation of the intended performance task under the accurate external conditions (e.g., opponents, spectators, perceived tension and anxiety). Use imagery while alone and relaxed; replicating real-world sport competitive conditions

Labeling The athlete's use of a word, such as "silly," "foolish," "nasty," or insecure" that has a stress-reducing effect. The label puts the person's actions in perspective and adds humor to describing the unpleasant person

Mental practice Consists of the mere replication of the physical (intended) task, but excludes real-world conditions inherent in imagery

Mindfulness A low arousal mental state achieved by focusing one's awareness on the present moment, while calmly acknowledging and accepting one's feelings, thoughts, and bodily sensations

Organizing Selectively filtering out irrelevant, distracting input that slows decision making and anticipation, while taking in important and meaningful input

Planning Thinking about one's actions prior to its execution, start to finish. Also see "Plan B"

Plan B This strategy addresses the question, "What if the original plan goes wrong?"

Pre-cueing Visually scanning or listening for a stimulus before a play or event is executed, which allows the athlete to anticipate a forthcoming action

Psyching up Consciously raising emotional intensity, verbally ("Let's beat this team") or physically by performing an action that raises the athlete's arousal level

Psychological distancing Usually done in response to an uncontrollable stressful situation, the athlete feels emotionally detached from the source or cause of an unpleasant (stressful) event

Relaxation (progressive; muscular) A state of very low mental and physical arousal achieved by reducing heart rate, muscle tension, or blood pressure. Several techniques are available to meet the relaxation goal

Self-monitoring Athlete attempts to observe and regulate one's thoughts to remain positive, upbeat, and optimistic

Self-monitoring (positive) Observing and regulating one's positive thoughts and emotions, while maintaining (monitoring) optimal arousal and effort. Favored to maintain confidence and use of performance feedback

Self-monitoring (negative) Observing and regulating one's negative thoughts and emotions while maintaining (monitoring) optimal arousal and effort. Favorable for error detection and correction

Self-talk (positive) Covert (internal) self-statements that result in favorable feelings and emotions and reduce the likelihood of unpleasant mood states or distracting thoughts

Self-talk (negative) Covert (internal) self-statements that are self-critical and result in unpleasant thoughts and a negative mood. In some instances, however, negative self-talk increases the athlete's arousal and assertiveness, which can benefit performance

Thought stopping Athlete, using self-talk, tells him- or herself to "STOP!" when repeating negative, distracting thoughts and statements

Appendix C

The inventory that follows consists of a few items on an anxiety inventory that coaches (or athletes) may use to identify an athlete's pre-competition anxiety level. The following set of items reflect what is called "state anxiety," that is, how the athlete feels *now*, before the competition, *not* how the athlete usually feels in sports events, what is called *trait* sport anxiety. This is not a personality inventory, but rather a set of questions that measures an athlete's thoughts prior to beginning a competition. These items have been adapted from other inventories that measure anxiety in the sport psychology literature.

Pre-Competition Sport Anxiety Scale

Please circle the number that best describes your *current* pre-competition feelings, ranging from **1** (very low) to **5** (very high).

1. I feel uneasy.

    1   2   3   4   5

2. I am worried.

    1   2   2   4   5

3. I think about how I will perform in the competition.

    1   2   3   4   5

4. I feel nervous.

    1   2   3   4   5

5. We are playing against a superior opponent.

    1   2   3   4   5

6. I feel tense.

    1   2   3   4   5

7. I feel impatient for the competition to begin.

    1   2   3   4   5

8. I do not feel confident that my team will win.

    1   2   3   4   5

    Total score: _____

Elite athletes make optimal use of information feedback. They incorporate considerable information from coaches, video, firsthand experience with opponents, and other sources of information at various times prior to, during, and following the competition. Many athletes engage in debriefing and self-evaluation to formalize the feedback process, which sometimes changes their strategies in future competitions.

Appendix D

Team Climate Athlete Assessment

Athletes' perceptions determine team climate (referenced in chapter 8). Please write in the number that best describes your team situation. There is no right or wrong answer.

1 = never occurs, 2 = sometimes occurs, 3 = usually occurs, 4 = almost always occurs, and 5 = always occurs.

___ 1. My coach encourages me to make performance decisions.

___ 2. I can count on the coach to keep the things I say confidential.

___ 3. Members of the coaching staff pitch in to help one another.

___ 4. I have enough time to do the things the coach asks me to learn and perform.

___ 5. I can count on my coach to help me out when I need it.

___ 6. I can count on my coach offering me positive feedback when I play well.

___ 7. The coach encourages me to create and develop ideas that affect the team.

___ 8. I have a role in selecting my physical conditioning procedures, including during the offseason.

___ 9. The coaching staff tend to agree with one another and do not argue with each other.

___ 10. Practice sessions are places to learn and implement new strategies and techniques.

___ 11. My coach is interested in my growth as a player and as a person.

___ 12. Coach feedback is both positive and negative and always informative.

___ 13. The goals the coach feels I can reach are reasonable.

___ 14. The coach is open to alternative, or "different," ways of getting the job done.

___ 15. I am allowed to make decisions about my performance strategy.

___ 16. The coaching staff takes a personal interest in one another.

___ 17. The coach is behind me and believes in my skills 100%.

___ 18. The coach knows my strengths and lets me know it.

___ 19. The coach follows through on his or her commitments and promises to me.

___ 20. The coach is honest with me in statements and actions.

___ 21. The coach recognizes me when I perform well.

___ 22. The coach is approachable—easy to talk to—about personal or team-related problems.

___ 23. The coach understands the players' need to take time away from the sport rather than risk burnout.

___ 24. I don't feel overworked and mentally drained as an athlete.

___ 25. I have a role in setting my own goals, expectations, and performance standards.

___ 26. The coach does not play favorites among team members.

___ 27. The coach encourages me to find new ways to overcome strengths of our opponents.

___ 28. The coach talks to me (or the team) about new approaches to coaching skills.

___ 29. The coach criticizes players (including me) who deserve or need it but does not embarrass a player.

___ 30. The coach helps each player learn from his or her mistakes.

___ 31. I have a lot in common with my teammates and we socialize.

___ 32. When appropriate, the coach uses me as a positive example in front of other team members.

___ 33. I am aware of my role on the team.

___ 34. Practice sessions and drills change during the season to prevent boredom or to learn new strategies.

___ 35. The coach keeps in touch with my parents (in youth sports).

___ 36. The coach is supported by his or her supervisor (athletic director).

Total score: _____

Higher scores represent warmer, more supportive, team climate and better player satisfaction.

References

Anshel, M. H. (March/April, 1986). Bridging the gap through research and a major league baseball coach. *Coaching Review, 9*, 59–63.

Anshel, M. H. (1987). Ten Commandments for effective communication. In *Fundamentals of coaching and understanding sport*. Ottawa, Ontario: Coaching Association of Canada.

Anshel, M. H. (1989a). Examination of a college football coach's receptivity to sport psychology Consulting: A three-year case study. *Journal of Applied Research in Coaching and Athletics, 4*, 139–149.

Anshel, M. H. (1989b). The ten commandments of effective communication for referees, judges, and umpires. *Sports Coach, 12*, 32–35.

Anshel, M. H. (1990). Toward validation of the COPE model: Strategies for acute stress inoculation in sport. *International Journal of Sport Psychology, 21*, 24–39.

Anshel, M. H. (2005). Strategies for preventing and managing stress and anxiety in sport. In D. Hackfort, J. L. Duda, & R. Lidor (Eds.), *Handbook of research in applied sport and exercise psychology: International perspectives* (pp. 199–215). Morgantown, WV: Fitness Information Technology.

Anshel, M. H. (2016). *In praise of failure: The value of overcoming mistakes in sports and in life*. Lanham, MD: Rowman & Littlefield.

Anshel, M. H., & Delany, J. (2001). Sources of acute stress, cognitive appraisals, and coping strategies of male and female child athletes. *Journal of Sport Behavior, 24*(4), 329–353.

Anshel, M. H., & Kaissidis, A. (1997). Coping style and situational appraisals as predictors of coping strategies following stressful events in sport as a function of gender and skill level. *British Journal of Psychology, 88*, 263–277.

Anshel, M.H., & Lidor, R. (2012). Talent detection programs in sport: The questionable use of psychological measures. *Journal of Sport Behavior, 35*, 239–266.

Anshel, M. H., & Si, G. (2008). Coping styles following acute stress in sport among elite Chinese athletes: A test of trait and transactional coping theories. *Journal of Sport Behavior, 31*, 3–21.

Anshel, M. H., & Straub, W. F. (1991). Congruence between players' and coaches' perceptions of coaching behaviors. *Applied Research in Coaching and Athletics Annual*, 49–66.

Anshel, M. H. & Sutarso, T. (2007). Relationships between sources of acute stress and athletes' coping style in competitive sport. *Psychology of Sport and Exercise, 8*, 1–24.

Anshel, M. H., Weinberg, R. S., & Jackson, A. (1992). Effect of goal difficulty, and task complexity on intrinsic motivation and motor performance. *Journal of Sport Behavior, 15*, 159–176.

Arent, S. M., & Landers, D. M. (2003). Arousal, anxiety, and performance. A re-examination of the inverted-U hypothesis. *Research Quarterly for Exercise & Sport, 74(4)*, 436–444.

Bandura, A. (1977). Self effacy: Toward a unifying theory of behavior change. *Psychological Review, 84*, 191–215.

Belgrave, F. Z. & Allison, K. W. (2006). *African American psychology: From Africa to America*. Thousand Oaks, CA: SAGE.

Bloom, G. (2002). Coaching demands and responsibilities of expert coaches. In J. M. Silva & D.E. Stevens (Eds.), Psychological foundations of sport (pp. 438–465). San Francisco: Benjamin Cummings.

Boyd-Franklin, N. (2003). *Black families in therapy: Understanding the African American experience* (2nd. Ed.). New York, NY: Guilford.

Bull, S. J., Albinson, J. G., & Shambrook, C. J. (1996). *The mental game plan: Getting psyched for sport*. Eastbourne, UK: Sports Dynamics.

Carron, A. V. (1984). *Motivation: Implications for coaching and teaching*. London, Ontario, Canada: Sports Dynamics.

Carron, A. V., Prapavesis, H., & Grove, J. R. (1994). Group effects and self-handicapping. *Journal of Sport & Exercise Psychology, 16*, 246–257.

Chappell, A. J. (January-February, 1984). Counseling your athletes. *Coaching Review, 34*, 46–48.

Chelladurai, P., & Arnott, M. (1985). Decision styles in coaching: Preferences of basketball players. *Research Quarterly for Exercise and Sport, 56*, 15–24.

Cribben, J. J. (1981). *Leadership: Strategies for organizational effectiveness.* New York: AMACOM.

Deci, E. L. (1975). *Intrinsic motivation.* New York: Plenum.

Diaz, G. J. (2010, June 24). Left or right? Early clues to soccer penalty kicks revealed. *Science Daily.* Retrieved from http://www.sciencedaily.com / releases/2010/06/100624112310.htm

Dosil, J. (Ed.). (2006). *The sport psychologist's handbook: A guide for sport-specific performance enhancement.* Hoboken, NJ: Wiley.

Duda, J. L. (1993). Goals: A social-cognitive approach to the study of achievement motivation in sport. In R. N. Singer, M. Murphy, & L. K. Tennant (Eds.), *Handbook of research in sport psychology* (pp. 421–436). New York: Macmillan.

Engh, F. (1999). *Why Johnny hates sports.* Garden City Park, NY: Avery.

Feinstein, J. (2986). *A season on the brink.* New York: MacMillan.

Fiedler, F. E. (1964). A contingency model of leadership effectiveness. In L. Berkowitz (Ed.), *Advances in experimental social psychology* (vol. 1) (pp. 141–190). New York: Academic Press.

Fitts, P. M. & Posner, M. I. (1967). *Human performance.* Belmont, CA: Brooks/Cole.

Ginott, H. G. (1965). *Between parent and child.* New York: AVON Books.

Ginott, H. G. (1969). *Between parent and teenager.* New York: AVON Books.

Grayson, E. S. (1978). *The elements of short term group counseling.* College Park, MD: American Correctional Association.

Guralnik, D. B. (1984). *Webster's new world dictionary.* New York: Warner Books.

Hanin, Y. L. (1980). A study of anxiety in sports. In W. F. Straub (Ed.), *Sport psychology: An analysis of athlete behavior* (2nd ed., pp. 236–249).

Hanin, Y. L. (2000). Successful and poor performance and emotions. In Y. L. Hanin (Ed.), *Emotions in sport* (pp. 157–187). Champaign, IL: Human Kinetics.

Heil, J. (Ed.). (1993). *Psychology of sport injury*. Champaign, IL: Human Kinetics.

Hoedaya, D., & Anshel, M. H. (2003). Sources of stress and coping strategies among Australian and Indonesian *Australian Journal of Psychology, 55,* 159–165.

Horn, T. S. (1992). Leadership effectiveness in the sport domain. In T. S. Horn (Ed.), *Advances in sport psychology* (pp. 181-200). Champaign, ILL: Human Kinetics.

Jones, G., & Swain, A. (1995). Predispositions to experience debilitative and facilitative anxiety in elite and non-elite performers. *The Sport Psychologist, 9,* 201–211.

Keathley, K., Heimlein, M. J., & Strigley, G. (2013). Youth soccer participation and withdrawal: Gender similarities and differences. *Journal of Sport Behavior, 36,* 171–188.

Kochman, T. (1981). *Black and white: Styles in conflict*. Chicago, IL: University of Chicago Press.

Landers, D. M. (1980). The arousal-performance relationship revisited. Research Quarterly for exercise and sport, 51, 77–90.

Landers, D. M., & Arent, S. M. (2010). Arousal-performance relationships. In J. M. Williams (Ed.), *Applied sport psychology: Personal growth to peak performance* (6th ed.) (pp. 221-246). New York, NY: McGraw-Hill.

Lanning, W. (1982). The privileged few: Special counseling needs of athletes. *Journal of Sport Psychology, 4,* 19–23.

Lenk, H. (1969). Top performance despite internal conflict: An antithesis to a functional proposition. In J.W. Loy & G. S. Kenyon (Eds.), *Sport, culture and society: A reader on the sociology of sport* (pp. 224–235). New York: Macmillan.

Lepper, M. R., Greene, D., & Nesbitt, R. E. (1973). Undermining children's intrinsic interest with extrinsic reward. *Journal of Personality and Social Psychology, 28*(1), 129–137.

Lidor, R. & Henschen, K. P. (Eds.). (2003). *The psychology of team sports*. Morgantown, WVA: Fitness Information Technology.

Magill, R. A. (1990). Motor learning is meaningful for physical educators. *Quest, 42*(2), 126–133.

Magnotta, J. R. (1986). Positive motivational techniques. A key to teaching excellence. Journal of Sport Psychology, 5, 8–20.

Marteniuk, R. G. (1976). *Information in motor skills*. New York: Holt, Rinehart and Winston.

Martin, G., Hrycaiko, D. (1983). Effective behavioral coaching: What's it all about. *Journal of Sport Psychology, 5*, 8–20.

McCreary, M. L., Cunningham, N., Ingram, K. M., & Fife, J. F. (2006). Stress, culture, and race socialization: Making an impact. In P. T. Wong & L. C. J. Wong (Eds.), *Handbook of multicultural perspectives on stress and coping* (pp. 487–513). New York: Springer.

Mechikoff, R. A., & Kozar, B. (1983). *Sport psychology: The coach's perspective*. Springfield, IL: Thomas.

Messner, M. A. (1992). White men misbehaving: feminism, Afrocentrism, and the promise of a critical standpoint. *Journal of Sport & Social Issues, 16*(2), 136–143.

Mitchell, T. R. (1979). Organizational behavior. *Annual Review of Psychology, 30*, 243–281.

Morgan, W. P. (1979). Prediction of performance in athletics. In P. Klavora & J. V. Daniel (Eds.), Coach, athlete, and the sport psychologist (pp. 173–186). Champaign, IL: Human Kinetics.

Murphy, S. (1999). *The cheers and the tears: A healthy alternative to the dark side of youth sports today*. San Francisco, CA: Jossey-Bass.

National Association for Sport and Physical Education (NASPE) in alliance with the American Heart Association, (2010). *Shape of the Nation Report*. Reston, VA.

Orlick, T. (1986). *Psyching for sport: Mental training for athletes*. Champaign, IL: Human Kinetics.

Passchier, J., Raksadjaya, B., Sijmons, R., Goudswaard, P., Dekker, deVries, P. H. and Orlebeke, J. F. (1991). Physiological response to achievement stress in students with high achievement motivation and fear of failure: Are the reasons similar in Amsterdam and Bandung? In N. Bleichrodt and P. J. D. Drenth (Eds.), Contemporary issues in cross-cultural psychology: *Selected papers from a regional conference of the International Association for cross-cultural psychology* (pp. 297–306). Amsterdam: Swets and Zeitlinger.

Puente-Diaz, R., & Anshel, M. H. (2005). Sources of acute stress, cognitive appraisal, and coping strategies among highly skilled Mexican and U.S. competitive tennis players. *Journal of Social Psychology, 145*(4), 429–446.

Ravizza, K., & Hanson, T. (1995). *Heads-up baseball: Playing the game one pitch at a time*. Chicago, IL: Masters Press.

Ronney, K. (2008). *Proud parents' guide to raising athletic, balanced, and coordinated kids*. Nashville, TN: Thomas Nelson.

Ryan, R. M., & Deci, E. L. (2007). Active human nature: Self-determination theory and the promotion and maintenance of sport, exercise, and health. In M. S. Hagger & N. L. D. Chatzisarantis (Eds.), Intrinsic motivation and self-determination in exercise and sport (p. 1–20). Champaign, IL: Human Kinetics.

Sachs, M. L., Burke, K. L., & Schweighardt, S. L. (Eds.), *Directory of graduate programs in applied sport psychology* (10th ed.). Madison, WI: Association of Applied Sport Psychology.

Sage, G. H. (1980). *Humanistic psychology and coaching*. In W. F. Straub (Ed.), *Sport psychology: An analysis of athlete behavior* (2nd ed., pp. 215–228). Ithaca, New York: Mouvement.

Scherzer, C. B., & Williams, J. M. (2008). Bringing sport psychology into the athletic training room. *Athletic Therapy Today, 13*, 15–17.

Schroeder, P. J. (2010). Changing team culture: The perspective s of ten successful head coaches. *Journal of Sport Behavior, 33*(1), 63–88.

Seefeldt, V. (Ed.). (1987). *Handbook for youth sports coaching*. Reston, VA: American Alliance for Health, Physical Education, Recreation, and Dance.

Singer, R. N., & Anshel, M. H. (2006). *An overview of interventions in sport*. In J. Dosil (Ed.), The sport psychologist's handbook (pp. 89–117). New York: John Wiley & Sons.

Smith, R. E. (2017). A positive approach to coaching effectiveness and performance enhancement. In J. M. Williams (Ed.), *Applied sport psychology: Personal growth to peak performance* (7th ed.) (pp. 42–58). New York, NY: McGraw-Hill.

Smith, R. E., & Smoll, F. L. (2002). *Way to go, coach! A scientifically-proven approach to coaching effectiveness* (2nd ed.). Portaloa Valley, CA: Warde.

Sullivan, P. A. (1993). Communication skills training for interactive sports. *The Sport Psychologist, 7*, 79–91.

Triandis, H. C. (1994). Culture and social behavior. In W. J. Looner and R. S. Malpass (Eds.), *Psychology and culture* (pp. 169–173. Boston: Allyn and Bacon.

Vecsey, G. (2002, March 24). Second year coach teaches Hoosiers how to win. *New York Times*, sec. 8, pp. H3.

White, Joseph. (August 23, 2010). *Tennessean*. Haynesworth objects to role with Redskins (p. 3C)

White, R. W. (1959). Motivation reconsidered: The concept of competence. *Psychological*

Review, 66, 297–331.

Will, G. F. (1990). *Men at work*. New York: Macmillan.

Williams, J. M. & Scherzer, C. B. (2013). Injury risk and rehabilitation: Psychological considerations. In J. M. Williams & V. Krane (Eds.), *Applied sport psychology: Personal growth to peak performance* (7th ed.) (pp. 462–489. New York, NY: McGraw Hill.

Wooden, J. R. (1988). *They call me coach*. Chicago, IL: Contemporary Books.

Yukelson, D. P. (2010). Communicating effectively. In J. M. Williams (Ed.). Applied sport psychology. Personal growth to peak performance (6th ed., pp. 149–165). New York: McGraw-Hill.

About the Author

Dr. Mark H. Anshel, Ph.D., is professor emeritus at Middle Tennessee State University (Murfreesboro, TN). His degrees are from Illinois State University, McGill University (Montreal), and Florida State University in the combined areas of psychology of sport and motor performance. He has an extensive publication record of over 140 journal articles, 22 book chapters, and 10 books. His published books include *Sport Psychology: From Theory to Practice* (2012) (5th ed.), *In Praise of Failure: The Value of Overcoming Mistakes in Sports and in Life* (2016), and *Applied Health Fitness Psychology* (2014). In 2009, Dr. Anshel was awarded the Distinguished Research Scholar Award from Middle Tennessee State University. In addition to his publications, Dr. Anshel has consulted with dozens of sports coaches and hundreds of athletes at all levels of sport competition as a consulting sport psychologist and has worked with other areas of performance enhancement, including individuals in law enforcement, corporate/business, fitness and exercise, sports injury rehabilitation, and the performing arts.